GOOD HOUSEKEEPING

COMPLETE BOOK OF
VEGETARIAN
COOKERY

Good Housekeeping

Complete book of

Vegetarian Cookery

Janet Smith

EBURY PRESS
LONDON

Published in 1992 by Ebury Press
an imprint of The Random Century Group
Random Century House
20 Vauxhall Bridge Road
London SW1V 2SA

The recipe for *Wild Mushroom Strudel* on page 78 is
reproduced courtesy of Roselyne Masselin of *La Cuisine
Imaginaire Cookery School*.

Catalogue record for this book is available from the British
Library.

ISBN 0 09 175364 3

Special Photography: James Murphy
Editor: Helen Southall
Design: Patrick McLeavey
Stylist: Róisín Nield
Food Stylists: Janet Smith, Emma-Lee Gow
Set Painter: Annabel Playfair
Illustrations: Hilary Downing

Typeset by Textype Typesetters, Cambridge

Printed and bound in Great Britain by Butler & Tanner Ltd,
Frome and London

ONTENTS

INTRODUCTION

A meatless diet is no longer regarded as bizarre or cranky. Vegetarian eating has taken on new vitality and dimensions and in the early 1990s attracts at least 3.7 per cent of the British population; that's over 3 million people.

There are as many different types of vegetarian as there are reasons for being one. The term vegetarian covers a wide range of diets but the one thing they all have in common is that they are meat and fish free. Vegans are very strict vegetarians; they won't eat any animal product whatsoever, including gelatine and, in some cases, honey. Look for vegan recipes marked with the V symbol in the index (see page 222). Less strict vegetarians eat eggs, cheese, butter and milk. Some eat cheese, butter and milk but will not eat eggs. Others prefer a wholefood diet. This book has something for everyone. All the recipes have been thoroughly tried and tested in the Good Housekeeping kitchens, where they were enjoyed by vegetarians as well as by confirmed meat-eaters.

BALANCING A VEGETARIAN DIET

Many people make the mistake of assuming that a vegetarian diet is automatically healthier than a carnivore's. This isn't always the case – there are good and bad vegetarian diets. It is not enough simply to stop eating meat; the nutrients that would normally be obtained from meat must be replaced. It's quite common for vegetarians to rely too heavily on dairy products like cheese and eggs which are high in saturated fats and calories. Such a limited diet is not only unhealthy but will eventually become boring and tedious.

As with any diet, variety is important. If a wide range of foods is eaten, a vegetarian diet is no more likely to be lacking nutritionally than any other diet. However, it is useful to have a basic understanding of nutrition and the importance of certain foods – even if it's only to convince meat-eaters that a vegetarian diet is healthy! So here's our brief guide, pinpointing the important areas.

PROTEIN
Contrary to popular belief, there are lots of good vegetable sources of protein, such as beans, grains, nuts, tofu, Quorn and texturised vegetable protein as well as eggs, cheese, milk and yogurt.

Protein is made up of smaller units called amino acids. They form about 75 per cent of the body's solid mass and are needed in every cell, so they are very important. The body can manufacture some amino acids itself, but others, known as the 'essential amino acids', must come from food. Animal protein contains almost all of these and is therefore known as 'complete' protein.

With the exception of soya products, vegetable proteins are lacking or low in one or more amino acid. However, by eating certain foods together at the same meal any deficiency is overcome. This isn't as complicated as it sounds and usually happens automatically when menu planning. For example, cereals should be eaten with dairy products, pulses or nuts (muesli with yogurt or milk, chilli beans with rice, nut roast made with breadcrumbs, peanut butter on toast). Pulses and nuts should be eaten with cereals or dairy products (dal with raita, nut burgers with a cream-based sauce).

VITAMINS
Vitamins are vital for proper body functioning. They can be divided into two categories – fat soluble and water soluble. As

the name suggests, the fat soluble vitamins A, D, E and K are found mostly in foods which contain fat. They are stored in the body by the liver.

The water soluble vitamins C and B complex, dissolve in water and cannot be stored, so a regular supply is important.

A varied diet should supply all the vitamins our bodies need. Vegetarians and vegans should be careful to ensure that their intake of vitamins B_{12} and D is sufficient, although a deficiency of either is unlikely.

Vitamin B_{12}

Vitamin B_{12} is essential for the formation of healthy red blood cells; a deficiency causes a form of anaemia. As it is found only in animal foods (with the exception of uncertain amounts in seaweed and fermented soya products) it is the vitamin most likely to be lacking in a vegetarian or vegan diet. Vegetarians who eat milk, eggs and cheese will get sufficient from these, but vegans should be careful to include some fortified foods in their diet. Yeast extracts, some brands of breakfast cereals, soya milk and other products marketed for vegans (such as vegetable spreads and pâtés) are all good sources. Get into the habit of reading labels to identify fortified brands.

Vitamin D

Vitamin D is needed for the growth and formation of healthy teeth and bones. Most of the body's supply comes from the action of sunlight on the skin. The elderly or house-bound, whose exposure to sunlight is limited, and the young, whose bones grow at a much faster rate, could consider taking a supplement. Consult a doctor before doing so and do not exceed the stated dose. Good vegetarian sources of this vitamin are eggs and butter. Some margarines, milk powders and yogurts are fortified; check the labels.

Make the Most of Vitamins

– For maximum vitamin retention, buy fruit and vegetables in peak condition, preferably from a shop with a fast turnover. Eat them as soon as possible. Tough, old vegetables have a lower vitamin content than fresh.

– Store vegetables in a cool, dark place; light is destructive to vitamins, especially the vitamins B and C. Don't leave bottles of milk on the doorstep; Vitamin B_2 (riboflavin) is destroyed when exposed to ultra-violet light.

– Steam or boil vegetables until just tender using the minimum amount of water.

– Don't add soda to cooking water. Once the vegetables are cooked and drained, use the water for stocks, gravies and soups.

– Don't prepare vegetables hours in advance and leave them soaking in water. Leave the skins on whenever you can.

– Eat plenty of raw vegetables and fruit.

– Vitamin losses continue after cooking, particularly when warm foods are left waiting around, so eat soon after cooking.

MINERALS

Minerals cannot be manufactured by the body and must be obtained from food. At present, 15 minerals have been identified as being essential to health and others are still under investigation. The majority of people obtain enough minerals provided a good variety of foods is eaten. Iron, calcium and zinc are the three minerals most often discussed in relation to a vegetarian diet.

Iron

Iron is used to make the haemoglobin in red blood cells. Haemoglobin carries oxygen to every cell in the body and a shortage leads to anaemia. Iron deficiency is fairly common in Britain, particularly in women of child-bearing age, and teenage girls on weight-reducing diets. Vegetarians are susceptible to anaemia because meat is the best food source of iron, and because the body can absorb iron from meat more efficiently than it can from vegetarian foods.

Iron is found in many vegetarian and vegan foods, including leafy green vegetables, cereals, pulses, nuts, eggs and dried fruits (especially apricots). The absorption of iron is greatly increased if vitamin C-rich foods are eaten at the same meal. It is decreased by the presence of tannin, which is found in large amounts in tea – so don't drink tea at meal times!

Calcium

Calcium is essential for the growth and development of bones, teeth and tissues. It is also needed for muscle contraction, nerve functioning, the action of several enzymes and for the normal clotting of blood. Because it is usually associated primarily with milk, eggs, yogurt and cheese, vegans are considered to be at risk of deficiency. However, this is not a problem because calcium is also found in white or brown bread and flour, green vegetables, nuts, sesame seeds, dried fruits and tap water in hard-water areas.

Zinc

Zinc is a trace mineral. Among other things, it's important for the functioning of enzymes and minerals. Recently it has received lots of attention in relation to a vegetarian diet. It has been suggested that zinc from plant sources is not readily absorbed by the body. However, there are so many other factors which affect zinc absorption and requirements, including age, sex and hormonal balance, that it is highly unlikely that vegetarianism would be the cause of a deficiency. As long as a variety of food is included in the diet, a deficiency will be avoided. Good vegetarian sources are sesame seeds, cheese, nuts, pulses and grains.

VEGETARIAN BABIES AND CHILDREN

Breast milk or infant formula contains all the vitamins and minerals a newborn baby needs for the first 4–6 months of life. Although breast milk is preferable for a number of reasons, commercial infant formula will provide complete nutrition. Babies should continue to drink breast or formula milk until they are 1 year old, but they can have 'doorstep' milk on cereals and in cooked dishes from about 6 months. For vegan babies, special soya-based formulas are available; ordinary soya milk is not suitable since it is nutritionally inadequate.

Weaning should start between four and six months (although some larger, hungrier babies may be ready at 3 months – consult your health visitor or midwife). Start with baby rice (check the packets for unsweetened brands) mixed with breast milk or formula, then try puréed and sieved fruits and vegetables. Don't be discouraged if your baby refuses the new food; try again the next day. Introduce one new food at a time and wait three or four days before introducing another new food in case of an allergic reaction. Avoid wheat-based cereals until six months because gluten (a constituent of wheat grains) can cause an allergic reaction. Similarly, children under one year shouldn't be given egg white. It's used in the manufacture of some childhood vaccines so it's unwise to risk triggering off an allergy.

Try to give your child healthy food right from the start. Avoid making food very sweet (there's no need to add sugar to breakfast cereals) or very salty (don't add salt to vegetable cooking water). When buying baby foods, look for varieties without added sugar, salt and chemical additives.

From the age of one, your child should be eating (or at least offered) three small meals a day, along with a mid-morning and a mid-afternoon snack (which could be something as simple as a glass of milk and a plain biscuit).

From the age of two, your child can eat much the same as the rest of the family and should be encouraged to eat a wide variety of foods. Avoid nuts unless they are ground into nut butter because there is danger of choking. Following recent scares about Salmonella food poisoning, the Department of Health issued guidelines advising that children should not be given soft cooked eggs. So make sure that poached eggs are cooked until the yolk is set, and avoid giving children soft scrambled eggs and runny omelettes.

FEEDING A VEGETARIAN TEENAGER

Currently, the biggest growth of new vegetarians is in the 12 to 20 age group. For some families a non-meat-eater in their midst can cause problems at meal times. It's important to view this as a positive move for the family as a whole rather than as a problem. There's no doubt that the consumption of too much animal protein is unhealthy, so it's a good idea to use the opportunity to introduce more meat-free meals to all members of the household. Making meals based on rice, potatoes and pasta is a good way to start. It's easy to cook simple nutritious vegetarian meals using these as a base combined with well flavoured ingredients such as garlic, tomato, spices, herbs and fresh vegetables. Creamy risottos, pilaffs, vegetable gratins and stuffed baked potatoes are delicious and would usually be made without meat anyway. For particularly steadfast carnivorous members of the family, serve these with grilled meat or fish or sliced cold meat, as a last resort or until the appeal of vegetarianism sinks in!

Pizzas are surprisingly quick and easy to make. Piled high with vegetables and cheese, and served with a large mixed salad, they make a splendid supper. A chunky soup made from a mixture of vegetables served with hot garlic bread and followed by cheese and fruit makes a satisfying meal.

Meat substitutes such as Quorn and soya products like soya mince are useful additions to the new vegetarian cook's repertoire. Use them to make meat-free versions of traditional family favourites such as Shepherd's Pie, Lasagne, Spaghetti Bolognese, Kebabs and Curry.

Adolescents need a nutrient-rich diet with lots of calories (girls about 2,300, boys about 2,800 per day). A varied vegetarian diet will easily provide this. Teenage girls may need to take an iron supplement. Encourage them to eat vitamin C and iron-rich foods together (see page 8). Vegan adolescents should eat cereals and yeast extracts fortified with vitamin B_{12} (see page 7).

THE VEGETARIAN STORECUPBOARD

Certain foods are particularly significant in a vegetarian diet, either because they contribute large amounts of a particular nutrient or because they require some explanation.

PULSES
The term pulse covers all the various beans, peas and lentils which have been preserved by drying. Pulses are an important source of protein, carbohydrate and fibre in a vegetarian diet. Most also contain significant amounts of iron, potassium, calcium, and some B vitamins. Soya beans are unique in that they contain complete protein (see page 6) as well

as more calcium and iron than other pulses.

Store pulses in airtight containers in a cool, dark place. They keep well, but after about six months their skins begin to toughen and they take increasingly longer to cook, so buy them from a supplier with a fast turnover of stock.

Before cooking, all beans (with the exception of lentils and split peas) should be soaked overnight in a large bowlful of cold water. In the morning, drain them, bring to the boil in fresh water and boil rapidly for 10 minutes (to destroy the toxins present in some beans – although it is not strictly necessary for all beans it does them no harm and saves the problem of remembering which requires fast boiling), then simmer until the beans are tender (see chart below). Add salt about 15 minutes before the end of the cooking time; salt added at the beginning of cooking tends to toughen the skins. The flavour can be subtly enhanced by the addition of a couple of bay leaves, or cloves of garlic or a peeled onion studded with a few cloves to the cooking water.

To save time, there is a quick-soak method that works just as well. Put the beans into a saucepan, cover with cold water and bring to the boil. Boil rapidly for 10 minutes, then remove from the heat. Cover the pan and leave the beans to soak in the same water for 3 hours. Drain and cook in fresh water for the usual time (see chart).

Although canned beans often have sugar and salt added, they're a good quick alternative to cooking your own. It's a good idea to empty them from the can straight into a colander or sieve and rinse them under cold running water before use. They tend to be quite soft, so add them to chilli, casseroles, stews and curries towards the end of the cooking time.

TYPE	APPEARANCE	COOKING TIME AFTER SOAKING	PRESSURE COOKING TIME★
Aduki beans	Round, red, very small	30–60 minutes	12 minutes
Black beans	Kidney-shaped, black, shiny	1½ hours	20 minutes
Black-eye beans	Small, kidney-shaped, pale cream with black spot or 'eye'	1½ hours	12 minutes
Butter beans	Large, flattish, kidney-shaped, pale cream	1½ hours	17 minutes
Cannellini beans	White, like long haricots	1 hour	25 minutes
Chick-peas	Round with pointed top, ivory	1½–2 hours	20 minutes
Flageolet beans	Kidney-shaped, pale green	1 hour	15 minutes
Haricot beans	Kidney-shaped, pale cream	1–1½ hours	20 minutes
Lentils	Small and red or green or larger and greenish-brown, round, flattish	1 hour	15 minutes
Mung beans	Round, green, very small	40 minutes	12 minutes
Red kidney beans	Kidney-shaped, crimson red	1–1½ hours	20 minutes
Rose cocoa or borlotti beans	Long, pink with dark red flecks	1 hour	17 minutes
Soya beans	Small, round, ivory	3–4 hours	30 minutes
Split peas	Small, green or yellow, round	45–60 minutes	15 minutes

The cooking times given above are approximate and depend on the age of the beans and the soaking time. ★High (15 lb) pressure

A 425 g (15 oz) can of beans, drained, is roughly equivalent to 225 g (8 oz) cooked beans, or 125 g (4 oz) dried (uncooked) beans. The weight of dried pulses approximately doubles during cooking, so if a recipe calls for 225 g (8 oz) cooked beans you will need 125 g (4 oz) to start with. Drained, cooked pulses will keep for several days in a covered container in the fridge. Alternatively, freeze them in usable quantities. Thaw overnight and use as freshly cooked beans.

To Cook Pulses in a Pressure Cooker

To cut down on lengthy cooking times, pulses can be pressure cooked (see chart for times). Overnight soaking is not necessary – just cover with boiling water and leave to soak for 1 hour. Drain, then transfer to the pressure cooker with 600 ml (1 pint) water for every 225 g (8 oz) beans (weighed after soaking). The cooker must not be more than one-third full.

Bring to the boil, then remove any skum that's risen to the surface. Lower the heat so that the beans are simmering gently, then put the lid on the pan. Bring up to pressure and cook for the time given. Reduce the pressure slowly. Season with salt while warm.

Do not cook mixtures of different types of pulses in the pressure cooker at the same time. This is potentially dangerous as overcooked beans can rise up in the pan and block the safety valves and air vents.

SPROUTING BEANS AND SEEDS

Although they can be grown from any type of bean, the best-known are usually grown from mung beans or alfalfa seeds. They are excellent in salads and stir-fries.

To grow them yourself at home, soak the beans or seeds in water overnight (start with about 45 ml/3 tbsp). Drain, then transfer to a large clean jam jar. Cover with a piece of muslin secured with an elastic band. Keep in a warm place (choose a dark place if you want pale sprouts; a light one for green sprouts) for about 4–7 days until the sprouts are about 7.5 cm (3 inches) long. During this time the beans must be rinsed each morning and evening. Simply fill the jar with warm water (through the muslin), swirl the water around in the jar, then pour it out. Before serving, rinse again and drain thoroughly.

TOFU

Also known as soya bean curd, tofu is made from a paste of soya beans which has been pressed into blocks. It is often disregarded by vegetarians and meat-eaters because it's considered to be tasteless. In fact it is virtually tasteless but this can be an advantage – it can be marinated in flavours of your choice, both sweet and savoury, which it readily absorbs. It really is worth experimenting with since it is an excellent source of vegetable protein and it contains no fat.

Silken tofu is soft and creamy and is useful for dressings, cheesecakes, sauces and dips. It adds bulk and texture and greatly increases the nutritional value of these foods, taking on the flavourings of the other ingredients. Firm tofu has been pressed for longer and can be cut into chunks for frying, grilling and inclusion in stews and curries, or it can be grated or chopped and made into burgers and roasts. You can also buy a smoked variety.

Store tofu in the refrigerator. Once the packet is opened, the block of tofu must be kept in a bowl of cold water in the fridge. It will remain fresh for a week if the water is changed daily.

TVP (Texturised Vegetable Protein)

TVP forms the bulk of most veggie burger and veggie mince and banger mixes. It's made from soya flour which is extruded under pressure, then cut into chunks or small pieces to resemble mince. Unlike tofu, it has a slightly chewy, meat-like texture which makes it unappetising to some vegans and vegetarians (although for the same reason it may appeal to some new vegetarians who miss the texture of meat). It is worth keeping a packet for emergencies because it's quite versatile, keeps well, and, like tofu, is an excellent source of low-fat protein.

QUORN

Quorn is a relatively new product; a myco-protein derived from a distant relative of the mushroom. It's very low in fat and calories, yet high in fibre and protein. Although it's unsuitable for vegans, because it contains egg albumen, it's a good source of complete protein for vegetarians. It has a chicken-like texture which, like the texture of TVP, does put some vegetarians off, but its food value is so good that it is worth experimenting with. Its bland flavour means that it benefits from being marinated before cooking. It's also very quick to cook.

Quorn is usually sold in the chilled cabinet in 200–300 g (8–12 oz) packets. This is enough to serve four people. Quorn will keep in the refrigerator for 3 days and can be frozen for up to 3 months. Once thawed, keep it in the refrigerator and use within 24 hours. It can also be used straight from the freezer in very moist dishes; otherwise, thaw it overnight in the refrigerator.

MARGARINE

Choose your brand of margarine carefully. Some manufacturers add fish oils and whey (which contains animal rennet) to boost the vitamin content. Pure vegetable margarines are available from health food shops and supermarkets, as are hard vegetable fats and vegetarian suet. Check the labels on low-fat spreads – some contain gelatine.

CHEESE

Many cheeses are not completely vegetarian. They contain rennet, an enzyme of animal origin added to clot the milk.

Some vegetarians have no objections to this; others prefer to eat cheese that is completely vegetarian. Vegetarian cheeses produced using vegetarian rennet are becoming more widely available. Vegetarian Cheddar is sold in most supermarkets and delicatessens as well as Cheshire cheese, Double Gloucester, Stilton, Mozzarella, goats' cheese and Pencarreg (a delicious Brie-like

organic cheese). Check labels as new varieties are coming into the shops all the time.

Soft cheeses, such as cottage and curd cheese, ricotta, Quark, low and full fat cream cheese and Roulé, are usually manufactured without rennet, but check the labels.

WHITE OR WHOLEMEAL?

There's no doubt that wholemeal flour, rice, bread and pasta are fibre rich. In a varied vegetarian diet based on fruit, vegetables and pulses, wholemeal foods of this kind are less significant in terms of fibre intake, than they might be in a meat-eater's diet.

We found that many people disliked the heavier, denser texture of wholemeal products and preferred pastries, pies, pasta and cakes made with white flour or a mixture of white and wholemeal flours. Nutty brown rice and wholemeal bread make delicious accompaniments to hearty winter casseroles and stews, while a spicy vegetable korma is complemented by fragrant basmati rice. This is not a wholefood book; we prefer to use white or wholemeal products where appropriate. So, we've left the choice up to you. Throughout the book, where the recipes state flour in the ingredients, wholemeal or white flour can be used. Likewise, white or brown rice or breadcrumbs, or wholewheat pasta, are suitable.

GELATINE

Gelatine is produced commercially from boiled beef bones so most vegetarians prefer not to use it. Alternative gelling agents include agar-agar and a product called Gelozone. Agar-agar is a tasteless white powder derived from seaweed. Unlike gelatine, which dissolves at a much lower temperature, agar-agar will only dissolve when it is boiled. It is available mainly from health food shops.

Gelozone contains carrageenan, guar gum and carob gum. Like agar-agar, it should be heated until dissolved. Both products can be used in sweet and savoury dishes.

—One—

TARTERS

Here is a collection of tasty, mouth-watering recipes to get the taste buds tingling ready for the main event. Before choosing a starter, it's vital that you consider the other components of the meal. If you're planning on serving a heavy main course, a casserole or gratin perhaps, then the starter should be light and refreshing, while something more substantial will happily precede a light main course. The style and tone of the meal, and the event as a whole, are important, too. If it's to be a formal affair, perhaps for a special occasion, then an impressive first course is probably called for. Something that looks pretty on the plate, such as Filo Purses with Stir-Fried Vegetables (page 25) or Spinach Parcels with Tomato Coulis (page 20), is ideal.

Start a casual, relaxed meal with something informal, perhaps something that's eaten with the fingers to get everyone in a party mood. Tomato Bruschetta (page 16) fits the bill, as does a dip with canapés. Guacamole and Hummus are here, but it's simple to whip up your own concoctions based on fromage frais, soured cream, thick yogurt, mayonnaise or silken tofu whizzed in the blender. Flavour one of these (or use a mixture of two) with crumbled blue cheese, whole grain mustard, chopped fresh herbs, garlic, tahini or a purée of fruits or vegetables.

If the main course is elaborate, requiring lots of last-minute attention, a cold starter that can be prepared in advance makes life easier. Hot starters which are cooked and served immediately can present problems if the main course is hot as well.

Soup makes a deliciously satisfying starter that needn't be reserved only for winter. See the recipes on pages 29–41.

 CREAMY HUMMUS

The addition of Greek yogurt makes this hummus deliciously creamy, and keeps the calories lower than if made conventionally with lots of oil. Tahini is a thick, creamy, paste, made from ground sesame seeds and sesame oil, which has long been popular in the Middle East. Light and dark varieties are available; the dark version is made from unhusked sesame seeds and has a much stronger, bitter flavour. For this recipe, it is preferable to use one of the lighter blends, but if you already have a jar of dark tahini in your cupboard, reduce the quantity to about 30 ml (2 tbsp). Serve the hummus with Sesame and Cumin Bread Sticks (page 150).

400 g (14 oz) can of chick-peas, drained and rinsed	salt and pepper
1 garlic clove, skinned and crushed	**To serve**
75 ml (3 fl oz) light tahini	paprika
15 ml (1 tbsp) olive oil	lemon wedges
45 ml (3 tbsp) lemon juice	black olives
45–60 ml (3–4 level tbsp) Greek yogurt	

1 Put the chick-peas in a food processor or blender with the remaining ingredients and 25 ml (1 fl oz) water. Blend until smooth, then taste and adjust the seasoning if necessary. Spoon the hummus into a serving dish, cover and chill for at least 20 minutes.

2 Sprinkle the hummus with paprika and serve accompanied by lemon wedges, black olives and bread sticks.

SERVES 4

MUSHROOM FRITTERS

These deliciously spicy morsels are best served as soon as they emerge from the hot oil.

1 medium onion, skinned and finely chopped	5 ml (1 level tsp) cumin seeds
175 g (6 oz) chick-pea or gram flour	450 g (1 lb) button or brown-cap mushrooms, wiped and trimmed
2.5 ml (½ level tsp) salt	
1.25 ml (¼ level tsp) baking powder	vegetable oil for deep frying
2.5 ml (½ level tsp) chilli powder	*To garnish*
10 ml (2 level tsp) dried fenugreek	lemon slices
10 ml (2 tsp) lemon juice	chopped fresh coriander

1 Put all the ingredients, except the mushrooms and oil, in a bowl and mix well. Gradually add about 175 ml (6 fl oz) cold water to make a batter the consistency of thick cream. Leave to stand for 10 minutes.
2 Heat the oil in a deep-fat fryer with a basket to 180°C (350°F). Check the temperature by dropping in a cube of bread; if the oil is hot enough, it should sizzle and turn golden brown in no more than 30 seconds.
3 Lower the basket into the hot oil. Drop the mushrooms into the batter and stir to coat. Remove a few at a time and drop them carefully into the oil. Fry for 2–3 minutes or until golden brown. Remove from the oil, drain on absorbent kitchen paper and serve at once, garnished with lemon and coriander.
SERVES 6

MUSHROOM AND CASHEW NUT PÂTÉ

Serve this protein-rich pâté with chunks of warm granary bread, or use it to top baked potatoes.

45 ml (3 tbsp) vegetable oil	2.5 ml (½ level tsp) cayenne pepper
50 g (2 oz) unsalted cashew nuts	2.5 ml (½ level tsp) ground allspice
700 g (1½ lb) medium open-cup mushrooms, chopped	200 g (7 oz) silken tofu
2 garlic cloves, skinned and crushed	30 ml (2 level tbsp) chopped fresh parsley (optional)
5 ml (1 level tsp) dried thyme	salt and pepper

1 Heat the oil in a large, heavy-based frying pan and fry the cashews for 2–3 minutes or until browned on all sides. Remove from the oil with a slotted spoon and leave to cool.
2 Add the mushrooms, garlic, thyme, cayenne and allspice to the pan and cook for about 10 minutes or until the mushrooms are very soft, stirring all the time. Cool slightly.
3 Meanwhile, put the nuts in a food processor and process until very finely chopped. Tip them into a bowl. Put the tofu in the food processor and process until smooth. Add the mushrooms and process until finely chopped. Add the nuts and parsley, if using, and season with salt and pepper and a little extra cayenne and allspice, if liked.
4 Spoon the pâté into a serving dish, cover and chill until ready to serve. Remove from the refrigerator 30 minutes before serving.
SERVES ABOUT 8

OMATO BRUSCHETTA

Bruschetta is Tuscan garlic bread made with dense Italian bread, rich green virgin olive oil and garlic. The success of this dish depends entirely on the ingredients; soggy pre-sliced white bread and bland vegetable oil just will not do!

700 g (1½ lb) very ripe, juicy tomatoes, roughly chopped	*8–10 thick slices of good white bread cut from a day-old loaf*
a pinch of sugar	*a few basil leaves*
salt and pepper	*a few black olives (optional)*
2–3 large garlic cloves, skinned	
15 ml (1 tbsp) virgin olive oil	

1 Put the tomatoes in a bowl, add the sugar and season generously with salt and pepper. Crush one of the garlic cloves and add it to the tomatoes with the olive oil. Cover and leave to stand for 30 minutes–1 hour.
2 Lightly toast the bread on both sides until golden brown. Cut the remaining garlic cloves in half and rub all over both sides of the toast. (The more you rub, the stronger the garlic flavour will be.)
3 Arrange the toast on four individual serving plates. Spoon the tomatoes on top with a little of their juice. Tear the basil leaves into small pieces and sprinkle over the *bruschetta*. Scatter the olives, if using, on top and serve.
SERVES 4

VOCADO WITH RASPBERRY VINEGAR

The sharpness of the raspberries perfectly offsets the rich avocados in this unusual starter.

125 g (4 oz) fresh raspberries	*salt and pepper*
75 ml (5 tbsp) white wine vinegar	*2 firm, ripe avocados*
45 ml (3 tbsp) olive oil	*a small head of radicchio*
90 ml (6 tbsp) polyunsaturated oil	

1 Pick over the raspberries and place half in a small bowl. Reserve the remainder for garnish. Heat the vinegar until beginning to bubble, then pour over the raspberries. Leave to steep for at least 1 hour or overnight.
2 Strain the raspberries, pressing the fruit gently to extract all juices but not the pulp. Whisk the vinegar together with the oils, and season with salt and pepper.
3 Carefully halve and stone each avocado. Peel away the skin, then slice the flesh straight into the dressing. Stir gently until the avocado is completely covered in dressing. Cover tightly and chill in the refrigerator for 2 hours.
4 Meanwhile, separate the radicchio leaves, rinse and drain. Dry on absorbent kitchen paper, then put in a polythene bag and chill in the refrigerator.
5 To serve, place a few radicchio leaves on four individual plates. Spoon on the avocado mixture and garnish with the raspberries.
SERVES 4

SPINACH RICOTTA TERRINE

This terrine is cooked in a *bain-marie*, a French term used to describe a low-sided container which is half-filled with water kept just below boiling point. Delicate, usually egg-based, mixtures are cooked standing in it and the water prevents overcooking. No special container is needed; a roasting tin will do. Serve this terrine with Fresh Pear Dressing (see page 194).

225 g (8 oz) fresh spinach	salt and pepper
15 ml (1 tbsp) olive oil	Fresh Pear Dressing (page 194), to serve
3 spring onions, trimmed and finely chopped	**To garnish**
2 garlic cloves, skinned and crushed	watercress sprigs
350 g (12 oz) ricotta cheese	pear slices
3 free-range eggs	toasted walnut pieces
300 ml (½ pint) double cream	

1 Lightly oil a 1.4 litre (2½ pint) ovenproof terrine. Line the base and sides with non-stick baking parchment and lightly brush with oil.
2 Wash and drain the spinach and chop roughly. Heat the olive oil in a large saucepan. Add the spring onions and garlic, and cook for 2–3 minutes. Add the spinach and continue to cook, stirring, until the spinach has wilted and all the excess liquid has evaporated.
3 Put the spinach mixture in a blender or food processor and add the ricotta cheese, eggs and double cream. Add salt and pepper to taste and blend until smooth.
4 Pour the mixture into the prepared terrine and cover with oiled foil. Stand the terrine in

a roasting tin and pour in enough boiling water to come about halfway up the sides of the terrine. Cook in the oven at 180°C (350°F) mark 4 for 1½–2 hours or until a skewer inserted into the centre of the terrine comes out clean. Remove from the oven and leave to cool in the *bain-marie*.
5 Pour any excess liquid off the terrine, then chill in the refrigerator for at least 2 hours. Turn the terrine out on to a plate, cut into thick slices and serve garnished with sprigs of watercress, pear slices and toasted walnuts. Spoon a little Fresh Pear Dressing around the slices and serve extra dressing separately.
SERVES 6

CAULIFLOWER SOUFFLÉ TARTS

The cauliflower florets, sauce and pastry cases can all be prepared in advance and stored separately in the refrigerator. Just whisk the egg whites at the last minute, fold into the sauce and complete as directed.

225 g (8 oz) self-raising wholemeal flour	45 ml (3 level tbsp) plain white flour
150 g (5 oz) Cheddar cheese, grated	300 ml (½ pint) milk
a pinch of paprika	salt and pepper
175 g (6 oz) vegetable margarine or butter	2 free-range eggs, separated
1 medium cauliflower (about 550 g/1¼ lb trimmed weight)	

1 Mix together the wholemeal flour, 50 g (2 oz) cheese and the paprika. Rub in 125 g (4 oz) of the margarine or butter, then add 60 ml (4 tbsp) water and mix to a soft dough. Leave to stand for about 15 minutes.

2 Turn the pastry on to a lightly floured surface and knead until smooth, then roll out and use to line six 11.5 cm (4½ inch) tartlet tins. Chill in the refrigerator for 30 minutes.

3 Line the pastry cases with foil or grease-proof paper and baking beans and bake blind in the oven at 200°C (400°F) mark 6 for 10–15 minutes or until just set but not browned.

4 Meanwhile, cut the cauliflower into small florets and steam or boil until just tender. Drain well.

5 Melt the remaining margarine or butter in a saucepan, add the plain flour and cook for 1–2 minutes. Remove from the heat, then gradually stir in the milk. Bring to the boil, stirring continuously, and cook until thickened. Season with salt and pepper.

6 When the pastry cases are cooked, remove them from the oven and remove the beans and paper or foil. Reduce the oven temperature to 190°C (375°F) mark 5. Arrange a few cauliflower florets in each cooked pastry case. Place the remaining cauliflower, the sauce, egg yolks and 50 g (2 oz) of the remaining cheese in a food processor, and process until smooth. Pour into a bowl. Lightly whisk the egg whites and fold into the mixture. Spoon over the cauliflower florets and sprinkle with the remaining cheese.

7 Bake the tarts in the oven for about 20 minutes or until well risen and golden brown. Serve immediately.

SERVES 6

AKED TOMATOES with CHEESE and BASIL

If preferred, use any soft, creamy cheese instead of goats' cheese.

6 medium tomatoes	6 thick slices of bread
125 g (4 oz) mozzarella cheese	**To serve**
30 ml (2 level tbsp) finely chopped fresh basil	salad leaves
175 g (6 oz) rindless goats' cheese	Vinaigrette Dressing (page 185)
salt and pepper	

1 Cut a thin slice from the bottom of each tomato and discard. Using a small, sharp knife or a teaspoon, carefully scoop out all the flesh and seeds, keeping the tomato shells whole. Strain the scooped-out tomato pulp and reserve the juices.

2 Coarsely grate or finely chop the mozzarella cheese and mix with the basil, goats' cheese and enough reserved tomato juice to form a thick, creamy mixture. Season, then spoon into the tomato shells.

3 Using a plain, round 9 cm (3½ inch) pastry cutter, stamp out six rounds from the bread slices. (The bread trimmings can be made into breadcrumbs and frozen for use in stuffings.) Toast the rounds on both sides, then place in a single layer in a lightly oiled ovenproof dish. Place a tomato on top of each toasted bread round.

4 Cook the tomatoes, uncovered, in the oven at 180°C (350°F) mark 4 for 20–25 minutes or until the cheese mixture looks melted and golden and the tomatoes are lightly cooked but not too soft. Serve with salad leaves and Vinaigrette.

SERVES 6

Goats' Cheese and Roasted Pepper Salad

For a less substantial dish, omit the goats' cheese and serve the salad with the French bread rubbed with garlic. This would also make the dish into a suitable starter for a vegan meal.

6 large peppers (preferably a mixture of red, green and yellow)	90 ml (6 tbsp) olive oil
	12 thin slices of French bread
3–4 large garlic cloves	6 small rindless goats' cheeses, each weighing about 50 g (2 oz)
5 ml (1 level tsp) Dijon mustard	
5 ml (1 tsp) runny honey	mixed salad leaves
salt and pepper	a few pine nuts, toasted
30 ml (2 tbsp) white wine vinegar or lemon juice	a few chopped fresh herbs (optional)

1 Grill the whole peppers and garlic cloves (still in their skins) under a very hot grill for 10–15 minutes or until soft and blackened all over, turning occasionally. Leave until cool enough to handle.

2 Remove the skin from the garlic and squeeze the soft insides into a jug. Add the mustard, honey and plenty of salt and pepper. Beat together with a fork, mashing the garlic as you beat. Gradually beat in the vinegar or lemon juice followed by the oil. Taste and add more salt and pepper if necessary.

3 Carefully peel the blackened skin from the peppers, halve them and remove the cores and seeds. Cut the flesh into strips and place in a shallow dish. Pour the dressing over the peppers and leave to marinate for at least 1 hour.

4 Just before serving, toast the bread slices on both sides. Halve the cheeses and place one half on each slice of toast. Arrange on a baking tray and bake in the oven at 180°C (350°F) mark 4 for 8–12 minutes or until the cheese is soft and warmed through, but not completely melted.

5 Meanwhile, arrange the salad leaves on six plates, and spoon over the peppers and marinade. Arrange the bread slices and baked cheeses on top and sprinkle with a few toasted pine nuts and fresh herbs, if using. Season with black pepper and serve immediately.
SERVES 6

Spinach Parcels with Tomato Coulis

These parcels are equally delicious served warm or cold. If spinach is not available, you could use a round lettuce instead.

350 g (12 oz) celeriac, peeled and finely diced	a pinch of cayenne pepper
salt and pepper	1 bay leaf
75 g (3 oz) Cheddar cheese, grated	15 ml (1 level tbsp) chopped fresh basil
25 g (1 oz) full-fat soft cheese	5 ml (1 level tsp) sugar
15 ml (1 tbsp) olive oil	15–30 ml (1–2 tbsp) red wine
450 g (1 lb) ripe tomatoes, chopped	150 ml (¼ pint) vegetable stock
15 ml (1 level tbsp) tomato purée	16 medium fresh spinach leaves

1 For the filling, cook the celeriac in boiling salted water for 12–15 minutes or until tender. Drain, mash and beat in the cheeses. Season with salt and pepper and leave to cool.

2 Meanwhile, make the tomato coulis. Heat the olive oil in a saucepan, add the tomatoes, cover and cook until soft. Uncover, bring to the boil and add the tomato purée, cayenne pepper, bay leaf, basil, sugar, red wine and stock. Simmer for 10–15 minutes. Remove the bay leaf, pour the mixture into a food processor and blend until smooth. Sieve, then season and pour into a saucepan.

3 Wash the spinach leaves and steam for 4–6 minutes or until tender. As there will be a lot of filling in each parcel, steam a few extra leaves in case some tear or split. Drain well.

4 Lay two spinach leaves, slightly overlapping, on a board and place one-sixth of the filling on top. Wrap the leaves around to enclose it. Repeat to make six parcels.

5 Steam the parcels gently for about 10 minutes or until heated through. Reheat the coulis and pour a little on to each of six warmed serving plates. Place a spinach parcel on each plate and serve immediately.
SERVES 6

DEEP-FRIED POTATO SKINS

Don't throw the scooped-out potato flesh away; use it to top Lentil Potato Pies (page 171), to make Potato Scones (page 154), or in any other recipe that calls for mashed potato. As these deep-fried skins are rather more-ish we're suggesting that this recipe will only serve 2–3. Serve a few vegetable crudités as well, if liked, to scoop up any excess dip, and to please those who are watching their weight! Make this a starter to precede a low-calorie main course.

8 potatoes, each weighing about 125 g (4 oz)	15 ml (1 tbsp) chilli sauce
30 ml (2 tbsp) vegetable oil	150 ml (¼ pint) soured cream
salt and pepper	30 ml (2 level tbsp) chopped fresh chives
350 g (12 oz) juicy ripe tomatoes, finely chopped	vegetable oil for deep frying
2 spring onions, trimmed and finely chopped	chopped spring onions or chives, to garnish

1 Scrub the potatoes clean and dry them with absorbent kitchen paper. Thread the potatoes on skewers, then brush them with the oil and sprinkle with salt. Place directly on the oven shelf and bake at 200°C (400°F) mark 6 for 45 minutes–1 hour or until the potatoes feel soft when squeezed.

2 Meanwhile, make the dips: mix the tomatoes with the onions and chilli sauce and season with salt and pepper. In a separate bowl, mix the soured cream with the chives and season with salt and pepper. Cover the dips and chill in the refrigerator.

3 When the potatoes are tender, remove them from the oven and cut them in half

lengthways. Scoop out the flesh, leaving a layer of potato about 1 cm (½ inch) thick on the skin. Cut each skin in half lengthways.

4 Heat the oil in a deep-fat fryer to 190°C (375°F). Deep-fry the potato skins, a few at a time, for 30–60 seconds or until crisp. Remove with a slotted spoon and drain upside-down on absorbent kitchen paper.

5 As soon as all the potato skins are fried, sprinkle them with a little salt and serve immediately. Place the bowls of dip in the centre of a large platter and arrange the potato skins around them. Garnish with chives or spring onions.
SERVES 2–3

FRIED COURGETTES WITH ROSEMARY AÏOLI

The quantities given in this recipe will make more aïoli than you need, but it's difficult to make a smaller amount. Leftover aïoli will keep well in a screw-topped jar in the refrigerator for a week. You can serve it with baked potatoes, grilled and fried dishes, and salads. If fresh rosemary is unavailable, omit it and make plain garlic aïoli instead; dried rosemary is not suitable for this recipe.

15 ml (1 level tbsp) very finely chopped fresh rosemary	*freshly ground black pepper*
2–4 garlic cloves, skinned and crushed	*900 g (2 lb) thin courgettes, trimmed*
1.25 ml (¼ level tsp) salt	*plain flour for coating*
2 free-range egg yolks	*oil for deep frying*
30 ml (2 tbsp) lemon juice	*rosemary sprigs, to garnish*
300 ml (½ pint) olive oil	

1 To make the aïoli, put the rosemary, garlic and a little of the salt in a bowl and mash with a fork until a paste is formed. (It won't be perfectly smooth because of the rosemary.) Add the egg yolks, the remaining salt and 5 ml (1 tsp) of the lemon juice, and beat well.
2 Gradually add the olive oil, drop by drop, whisking all the time, until the mixture is thick and smooth. When all of the oil has been added, whisk in the remaining lemon juice. Season with pepper, cover and leave to stand for at least 1 hour to allow the flavours to develop.
3 Just before serving, thinly slice the courgettes. Put some plain flour in a bowl and season with salt and pepper. Add the courgettes and toss until coated.
4 Heat the oil in a deep frying pan or electric deep-fat fryer to 190°C (375°F). Put enough courgette slices into the frying basket to quarter fill it, shaking off excess flour, and lower the basket into the oil. Cook for 3–4 minutes or until golden brown. Drain on crumpled absorbent kitchen paper and keep warm while cooking the remainder.
5 Pile the fried courgettes on to warmed individual serving plates and add a spoonful of rosemary aïoli. Garnish with sprigs of rosemary and serve immediately.
SERVES 4

GUACAMOLE WITH CRUDITÉS

Ripe avocados are essential to guacamole; a ripe avocado always 'gives' slightly when pressed at the pointed end. A hard, under-ripe fruit will ripen in 1–2 days at room temperature if stored in a fruit bowl with ripe fruit, or in about a week in the refrigerator.

1 small onion, skinned and quartered	*10 ml (2 level tsp) ground coriander*
2–3 garlic cloves, skinned	*10 ml (2 level tsp) ground cumin*
2.5 cm (1 inch) piece of fresh root ginger, peeled	*5 ml (1 level tsp) chilli powder*
4 large ripe avocados	*2 ripe tomatoes, seeded and roughly chopped*
finely grated rind and juice of 2 small limes	*salt and pepper*
60 ml (4 level tbsp) chopped fresh coriander	*paprika, to garnish*

1 Put the onion, garlic and ginger in a food processor and process until finely chopped.
2 Halve, stone and peel the avocados, then chop roughly and add to the mixture in the processor with all the remaining ingredients, except the tomato and seasoning. Process until almost smooth, then transfer to a bowl and stir in the tomato. Season with salt and pepper. Cover and chill in the refrigerator for 30 minutes to let the flavours develop. Garnish with paprika and serve with crudités.
Crudités to serve with Guacamole
Serve an assortment of crudités chosen and prepared to appeal to the eye as well as the taste buds. Baby vegetables, such as carrots, baby corn, cherry tomatoes and button mushrooms can be served whole. Traditionally, crudités are cut into neat strips, all about the same size and arranged in tidy rows of colour. You may prefer the wild approach, where vegetables are cleaned and trimmed to a manageable size, retaining their original shape. Arrange these in a more chaotic fashion on plain white china or a bed of crushed ice.

Sliced fresh fruit, such as apples, pears, nectarines, grapes, mangoes, star fruit and fresh dates, as well as dried figs, dates and apricots, all make good crudités.
SERVES 6–8

WARM WINTER VEGETABLE SALAD

Serve with warm herb or garlic bread.

75 ml (5 tbsp) olive oil	15 ml (1 level tbsp) chopped fresh herbs, such as
15 g (½ oz) onion or shallot, skinned and finely chopped	coriander, parsley, chives or thyme
1 garlic clove, skinned and crushed	350 g (12 oz) celeriac or turnips, trimmed and peeled
30 ml (2 tbsp) hazelnut oil	225 g (8 oz) carrots, trimmed and peeled
2 oranges	225 g (8 oz) leeks, trimmed
15 ml (1 tbsp) lemon juice	orange segments, to garnish
5 ml (1 tsp) honey	

1 Heat 30 ml (2 tbsp) of the olive oil in a saucepan and sauté the onion or shallot and garlic for 3–4 minutes or until golden. Remove from the heat and add the remaining olive oil and the hazelnut oil.

2 Thinly pare the rind from one of the oranges and squeeze the juice from both. Add the rind and about 150 ml (¼ pint) orange juice to the onion and garlic with the lemon juice, honey and half the chopped herbs. Cover and leave at room temperature for at least 2 hours.

3 Meanwhile, thinly slice the celeriac or turnips and carrots and cut into thin matchstick strips. Halve the leeks lengthways and cut into similar-sized strips. Blanch the vegetables separately in boiling salted water for about 5 minutes or until just tender. Drain well.

4 Strain the dressing mixture and reheat with the remaining herbs until warm. Arrange the warm vegetable strips in piles on six individual plates. Spoon over the dressing, garnish with orange segments and serve.
SERVES 6

SATAY

This variation of the Indonesian classic is made with Quorn (see page 12). Choose a packet containing large, even-sized chunks. The peanut sauce can be made well in advance and stored in the refrigerator; the Quorn is marinated in advance. It then takes a mere 3–4 minutes' cooking to complete a delicious starter.

450 g (1 lb) Quorn	75 ml (5 tbsp) crunchy peanut butter
vegetable oil for grilling	30 ml (2 tbsp) soy sauce
For the marinade	5 ml (1 level tsp) brown sugar
2 garlic cloves, skinned and crushed	1 garlic clove, skinned and crushed
2.5 cm (1 inch) piece of fresh root ginger, peeled and	5 ml (1 level tsp) chilli powder, or to taste
grated	5 ml (1 level tsp) chopped fresh lemon grass or finely
45 ml (3 tbsp) soy sauce	grated lemon rind
10 ml (2 level tsp) brown sugar	30 ml (2 tbsp) Crisp Fried Onions (see page 115),
For the peanut sauce	crumbled (optional)
50 g (2 oz) creamed coconut, roughly chopped	

1 To make the marinade, mix all the ingredients together with 45 ml (3 tbsp) water in a large shallow dish. Add the Quorn and stir. Cover and leave to marinate in the refrigerator for 2–3 hours or overnight.

2 Meanwhile, to make the peanut sauce, pour 150 ml (¼ pint) boiling water over the coconut and stir until dissolved. Add all the remaining ingredients and mix thoroughly. Cover and leave to stand.

3 Thread the Quorn on to 16 bamboo skewers and brush with a little vegetable oil. Cook under a very hot grill for 3–4 minutes or until lightly browned, turning occasionally. Serve hot with the cold peanut sauce.
SERVES 4–6

FILO PURSES WITH STIR-FRIED VEGETABLES

These light, low-calorie parcels could be made ahead and baked just before serving. If you are making them in advance, brush them generously with melted margarine or butter and keep them well covered to prevent the pastry drying out.

125 g (4 oz) celery, trimmed
125 g (4 oz) carrots, trimmed
75 g (3 oz) spring onions, trimmed
75 g (3 oz) vegetable margarine or butter
2.5 cm (1 inch) piece of fresh root ginger, peeled and chopped

125 g (4 oz) bean sprouts
juice of 1 small lemon
salt and pepper
5 large sheets of filo pastry, each measuring about 45.5 × 30.5 cm (18 × 12 inches)

1 Cut the celery, carrots and spring onions into thin shreds.

2 Heat 25 g (1 oz) of the margarine or butter in a large frying pan. Add the ginger, vegetables and bean sprouts, and stir-fry over a high heat for 3–4 minutes or until beginning to soften. Add the lemon juice and continue to stir-fry briskly until the vegetables are tender and most of the moisture has evaporated. Season and leave to cool.

3 Melt the remaining margarine or butter. Cut the pastry sheets in four to make a total of 20 rectangles. Layer the pieces in six stacks of three, using up the two spare rectangles on any thin or split pastry stacks and brushing each layer with melted margarine or butter.

4 Divide the vegetable mixture between the six stacks and draw the pastry edges up around the filling, pinching the tops together to form little 'money bags'. Place the pastries on a greased baking sheet and brush again with melted margarine or butter.

5 Bake in the oven at 200°C (400°F) mark 6 for about 20 minutes or until well browned and crisp. If necessary, cover the pastries lightly with greaseproof paper to prevent over-browning towards the end. Serve warm.
SERVES 6

AUBERGINE BLINIS

These are tiny, well flavoured pancakes, topped with sautéed vegetables and yogurt, crème fraîche or mayonnaise. If you increase the portion size, this makes a good main course.

1 aubergine, weighing about 450 g (1 lb)
olive oil
125 g (4 oz) plain flour
5 ml (1 level tsp) baking powder
3 free-range eggs
2 garlic cloves, skinned and crushed

salt and freshly ground black pepper
about 125 g (4 oz) baby carrots, trimmed and scraped
125 g (4 oz) large mushrooms, wiped and thickly sliced
3 medium courgettes, thickly sliced
thick Greek yogurt, crème fraîche or flavoured mayonnaise (see page 192), to serve

1 Prick the aubergine all over with a fork and rub the skin with a little olive oil. Bake in the oven at 200°C (400°F) mark 6 for about 30 minutes or until soft when pressed. Cool slightly, then halve and scrape out the flesh.
2 Mash the aubergine flesh with a potato masher, then add the flour, baking powder, eggs and one garlic clove. Mix well to make a fairly stiff batter. Season generously with salt and pepper and set aside.
3 Heat a little olive oil in a large saucepan, add the carrots and remaining garlic and fry over a high heat for 1–2 minutes. Lower the heat and continue to cook while frying the blinis.
4 To fry the blinis, heat a little olive oil in a large, heavy-based frying pan. Drop large tablespoons of batter into the oil and fry for

2–3 minutes or until firm and golden brown underneath. Turn the blinis and fry for a further 2–3 minutes or until the second sides are golden brown. Remove from the pan and keep warm while frying the remaining blinis. There should be enough batter to make about 20 blinis.
5 When all the blinis are cooked, increase the heat under the carrots, add the remaining vegetables and cook for 2–3 minutes or until the mushrooms and courgettes are just tender, shaking the pan continuously.
6 Arrange the blinis on warmed serving plates and top with the vegetables and a spoonful of yogurt, crème fraîche or mayonnaise. Grind black pepper over the top and serve immediately.
SERVES 6

—Two—

Soups and

Stocks

Good stock is essential for flavoursome soups. Unlike meat-based stock, vegetarian stocks are quick and pleasant to make – so there's no excuse for not making your own. Delicate chilled or fine-flavoured soups, and dishes such as risotto, rely heavily on good strong stock to give a rich depth of flavour. However, for some heartier soups, such as Mixed Bean and Vegetable Soup (see page 30), or heavily spiced or curried dishes, it's possible to get away with using a stock cube. Commercially prepared stocks, sold as cubes or tubs of concentrate, have improved dramatically in recent years, so it is well worth experimenting with different brands until you find a flavour that appeals. Vegans should scrutinise labels because some manufacturers add lactose – a milk sugar. For those worried about their salt consumption, low sodium brands are available.

On a practical note, both stocks and soups freeze well. Boil the strained stock vigorously in a large saucepan to reduce the volume, then freeze in ice-cube trays or in usable quantities in freezer bags. This intensely flavoured stock is excellent for flavouring noodles, stuffed vegetables and for making sauces.

Similarly, when making soups for the freezer, add less liquid to reduce the bulk, but remember to replace the missing liquid when reheating. Even with the help of a microwave, stocks and soups seem to take forever to thaw. They're best thawed overnight at cool room temperature; attempts to thaw quickly inevitably result in ruining the texture of chunky soups as it's impossible to resist mashing to try to speed up the process. Don't add cream, yogurt, fromage frais or eggs to soups for the freezer because they have a tendency to curdle when reheated.

Whether you're serving soup as a starter or a meal in itself, warm bread is the obvious but perfect accompaniment. Any of the breads featured in the chapter on page 143 are suitable as long as you choose appropriately. Nan-style bread or poppadums are good with spicy lentil and bean soups, while something lighter and more delicate, like poppy seed-topped white bread rolls or crisp Melba toast, is better with subtly flavoured soups like Vichyssoise (page 30) or Pea and Chervil Soup (page 34). If you haven't got the time or the ingredients to bake a loaf from scratch, commercially produced bread is easily transformed into something special. Garlic bread is the obvious choice but, following the same principle, why not flavour the butter or margarine with finely grated lemon rind and a squeeze of juice; chopped fresh herbs; chopped fresh chillies and a pinch of garam masala; or a little curry paste, pesto sauce or whole grain mustard.

$\mathscr{S}$PICY BEAN AND COURGETTE SOUP

This soup is really quick and easy to make using canned beans. It makes an excellent supper dish served with crusty bread.

30 ml (2 tbsp) olive oil	225 g (8 oz) potato, peeled and diced
1 medium onion, skinned and finely chopped	425 g (15 oz) can red kidney beans, drained and rinsed
2 garlic cloves, skinned and crushed	425 g (15 oz) can flageolet beans, drained and rinsed
10 ml (2 level tsp) ground coriander	1.4 litres (2½ pints) vegetable stock
15 ml (1 level tbsp) paprika	salt and pepper
5 ml (1 level tsp) mild curry powder	
450 g (1 lb) courgettes, halved lengthways and sliced	

1 Heat the oil in a large saucepan, add the onion and garlic and cook for 2 minutes, stirring constantly. Add the spices and cook for 1 minute, stirring. Mix in the courgette and potato, and cook for 1–2 minutes.
2 Add the remaining ingredients and season with salt and pepper. Cover and simmer for 25 minutes or until the potato is tender, stirring occasionally. Taste and adjust the seasoning, if necessary, before serving with crusty bread.
SERVES 4

$\mathscr{A}$NDALUSIAN SUMMER SOUP

Serve this version of gazpacho, the classic chilled tomato soup, at an *al fresco* lunch party, with bowls of finely chopped cucumber, onion and green or red pepper, plus croûtons fried in olive oil (see page 35). Guests should help themselves to the accompaniments, sprinkling them over individual bowls of soup.

60 ml (4 tbsp) olive oil	30 ml (2 tbsp) wine vinegar
1 large onion, skinned and roughly chopped	1 dried red chilli, finely chopped
2 garlic cloves, skinned and roughly chopped	salt and pepper
2 large red peppers, cored, seeded and roughly chopped	60 ml (4 tbsp) mayonnaise
450 g (1 lb) ripe tomatoes, roughly chopped	

1 Heat the oil in a large saucepan, add the onion and garlic and fry gently for 5 minutes or until soft but not coloured.
2 Add the red peppers and fry for a further 5 minutes, stirring constantly, then add the tomatoes and stir to break them up. Add 900 ml (1½ pints) water, the wine vinegar and chilli. Season with salt and pepper.
3 Bring to the boil, then lower the heat, cover and simmer for 45 minutes.
4 Sieve the soup or purée in a blender or food processor. If using a blender or processor, pass the puréed soup through a sieve to remove the tomato skins.
5 Put the mayonnaise in a large bowl and gradually whisk in the soup. Taste and adjust the seasoning, if necessary. Chill in the refrigerator for at least 4 hours before serving with chopped vegetables and croûtons.
SERVES 4–6

*M*IXED BEAN AND VEGETABLE SOUP

Use this basic recipe to make soup from any mixture of vegetables and beans available.
Freshly cooked beans could be used, but we've used cans to make the soup quick to cook.
Cut the vegetables into generous chunks to give the soup a good, hearty texture.

15 ml (1 tbsp) olive oil	*2 bay leaves*
1 medium onion, skinned and roughly chopped	*about 1.1 litres (2 pints) vegetable stock*
450 g (1 lb) mixed root vegetables, including carrots,	*425 g (15 oz) can red kidney beans, drained and rinsed*
* potatoes and parsnips, peeled and roughly chopped*	*425 g (15 oz) can black-eyed beans, drained and rinsed*
450 g (1 lb) mixed vegetables, such as peppers, celery	*2 courgettes, trimmed and sliced*
* and fennel, prepared as necessary and roughly chopped*	*45 ml (3 level tbsp) chopped fresh parsley or coriander*
1 garlic clove, skinned and crushed	*salt and pepper*
10 ml (2 level tsp) mild curry powder	

1 Heat the oil in a large heavy-based saucepan. Add all the vegetables, except the beans and courgettes, and cook over a high heat for 4–5 minutes, stirring all the time. Add the garlic, curry powder and bay leaves and continue cooking for 2–3 minutes.
2 Pour in the stock. (There should be enough to cover the vegetables; if not, add a little more.) Bring to the boil, then reduce the heat, cover and simmer for 20 minutes.

3 Add the beans and cook for a further 10 minutes. Remove the bay leaves. Purée about half the soup in a blender.
4 Return the puréed soup to the saucepan and bring to the boil, then add the courgettes and herbs. Season to taste with salt and pepper and simmer gently for 3–4 minutes or until the courgettes are just tender. Add a little extra stock, if necessary, to thin the soup.
SERVES 6 AS A MAIN COURSE

*V*ICHYSSOISE

Serve this classic chilled soup with Melba toast for an elegant start to a celebration meal.

50 g (2 oz) vegetable margarine or butter	*2 medium potatoes, peeled and thinly sliced*
4 leeks, trimmed and sliced	*salt and pepper*
1 onion, skinned and sliced	*200 ml (7 fl oz) single cream*
1 litre (1¾ pints) vegetable stock	*snipped fresh chives, to garnish*

1 Melt the margarine or butter in a heavy-based saucepan, add the leeks and onion and cook gently for about 10 minutes. Add the stock and potatoes and bring to the boil.
2 Lower the heat, season with salt and pepper and cover. Simmer for about 30 minutes.

3 Sieve the soup or purée in a blender or food processor. Pour into a large serving bowl and stir in the cream. Taste and adjust the seasoning, if necessary. Chill for at least 4 hours before serving sprinkled with chives.
SERVES 4

Mixed Bean and Vegetable Soup

WINTER VEGETABLE SOUP

This is a really substantial soup, best served as a meal in itself, with crusty baguettes, garlic bread or warm granary rolls. Along with the bread, serve a bowl of grated sharp farmhouse Cheddar cheese or a wedge of Stilton, either of which would hold its own against the flavours in the soup.

10 ml (2 tsp) lemon juice	*75 g (3 oz) vegetable margarine or butter*
225 g (8 oz) Jerusalem artichokes	*125 g (4 oz) haricot beans, soaked overnight in cold water*
½ small cabbage, trimmed and washed	*bouquet garni*
450 g (1 lb) carrots, trimmed and peeled	*Brown Onion Stock (see page 41) or water*
225 g (8 oz) turnips, trimmed and peeled	*salt and pepper*
2 onions, skinned, or 2 leeks, trimmed and washed	*chopped fresh parsley, to garnish*
2–3 celery sticks, trimmed	

1 Fill a bowl with cold water and add the lemon juice. Peel the artichokes, slice them, then cut them into strips. Drop them into the acidulated water as you work, to prevent them from discolouring.
2 Shred the cabbage coarsely, discarding all thick or woody stalks. Cut the remaining vegetables into fairly small pieces.
3 Melt the margarine or butter in a large saucepan and add all the vegetables (except the cabbage and beans). Fry for about 10 minutes, stirring, until soft but not coloured.

Drain the beans and add to the vegetables with the bouquet garni and enough stock or water to cover. Add plenty of pepper and bring to the boil, then lower the heat, cover with a lid and simmer for 45 minutes–1 hour.
4 Add the cabbage and season with salt. Cook for a further 20–30 minutes, adding more liquid as required. When all the ingredients are soft, discard the bouquet garni and taste and adjust the seasoning. Serve hot, sprinkled with parsley.
SERVES 4

TUSCAN BEAN SOUP

This thick wholesome soup is a meal in itself. In Italy it comes in a number of guises, but always with cannellini beans and a variety of vegetables, depending on the season. Serve sprinkled with Parmesan cheese, or vegetarian Cheddar cheese, and accompanied by chunks of rustic bread.

350 g (12 oz) cannellini beans, soaked overnight in cold water	*450 g (1 lb) tomatoes, skinned and roughly chopped*
60 ml (4 tbsp) olive oil	*1.4 litres (2½ pints) vegetable stock*
2 large onions, skinned and roughly chopped	*15 ml (1 level tbsp) chopped fresh thyme or sage*
6 celery sticks, trimmed and roughly chopped	*salt and pepper*
2 garlic cloves, skinned and crushed	*freshly grated Parmesan cheese, to serve*

1 Drain the beans and put them in a saucepan. Cover with fresh water, bring to the boil and boil rapidly for 10 minutes. Lower the heat, cover and simmer for about 50 minutes or until the beans are tender. Drain, reserving the cooking liquor.

2 Put half the beans in a blender or food processor. Add 300 ml (½ pint) of the reserved cooking liquor and purée until smooth.

3 Heat the oil in a large saucepan. Add the onions, celery and garlic and cook over a moderate heat for 5–10 minutes or until beginning to brown.

4 Stir in the tomatoes, stock, whole beans and bean purée with the thyme or sage. Season with salt and pepper and bring to the boil. Reduce the heat, cover and simmer for about 40 minutes or until all the ingredients are tender. Serve hot, sprinkled with Parmesan cheese and accompanied by crusty bread.
SERVES 6

$\mathscr{S}$PICED DAL SOUP

Channa dal is a yellow pulse that is often mistaken for the yellow split pea. In fact it is the husked and split black chick-pea. It is a high-protein pulse with a slightly nutty flavour. If you find channa dal difficult to obtain, red lentils can be used instead.

125 g (4 oz) channa dal	30 ml (2 tbsp) vegetable oil or ghee (clarified butter)
5 ml (1 level tsp) cumin seeds	225 g (8 oz) tomatoes, skinned and roughly chopped
10 ml (2 level tsp) coriander seeds	2.5 ml (½ level tsp) ground turmeric
5 ml (1 level tsp) fenugreek seeds	15 ml (1 tbsp) lemon or lime juice
3 dried red chillies	5 ml (1 tsp) black treacle
15 ml (1 level tbsp) shredded coconut	5 ml (1 level tsp) salt

1 Pick over the dal and remove any grit or discoloured pulses. Put into a sieve and wash thoroughly under cold running water, then drain well.

2 Put the dal in a large saucepan, cover with 600 ml (1 pint) water and bring to the boil. Reduce the heat, cover and simmer for at least 1 hour or until tender.

3 Finely grind the cumin, coriander, fenugreek, chillies and coconut in a small electric mill or with a pestle and mortar. Heat the oil or ghee in a heavy-based frying pan, add the spice mixture and fry, stirring, for 1 minute. Remove from the heat and set aside.

4 Purée the dal with any remaining liquid in a blender or food processor and transfer to a large saucepan. Stir in the tomatoes, spice mixture, turmeric, lemon or lime juice, treacle, salt and a further 300 ml (½ pint) water.

5 Bring to the boil, then lower the heat, cover and simmer for about 20 minutes. Taste and adjust the seasoning. Serve hot.
SERVES 4–6

CARROT AND CORIANDER SOUP

Add extra flavour and crunch to this soup by serving it sprinkled generously with delicious home-made croûtons. Simply cut thick slices of bread into small dice and fry in olive oil or butter until golden. Drain on absorbent kitchen paper. Store in an airtight container until needed. Lower-fat croûtons can be made by toasting the bread instead of frying, but they aren't as delicious!

40 g (1½ oz) vegetable margarine or butter	*salt and pepper*
175 g (6 oz) trimmed leeks, washed and sliced	*150 ml (¼ pint) natural yogurt or soured cream*
450 g (1 lb) carrots, trimmed, peeled and sliced	***To garnish***
10 ml (2 level tsp) ground coriander	*fresh coriander leaves*
5 ml (1 level tsp) plain flour	*croûtons (see above)*
1.1 litres (2 pints) vegetable stock	

1 Heat the margarine or butter in a large saucepan. Add the vegetables, cover the pan and cook gently for 5–10 minutes or until the vegetables begin to soften but not colour.
2 Stir in the ground coriander and flour and cook for about 1 minute, then pour in the stock and bring to the boil, stirring all the time. Season with salt and pepper, reduce the heat, cover and simmer for about 20 minutes or until all the ingredients are quite tender.
3 Leave the soup to cool slightly, then purée in a blender or food processor until quite smooth. Return the soup to the pan and stir in the yogurt or cream. Taste and adjust the seasoning, if necessary, and reheat gently, without boiling. Serve garnished with coriander and croûtons.
SERVES 6

SPINACH SOUP

When buying spinach, choose bright green leaves and avoid spinach that is yellow and wilted. Summer spinach is light green and fine textured, while winter spinach is darker and coarser.

450 g (1 lb) fresh spinach, trimmed and washed	*salt and pepper*
900 ml (1½ pints) vegetable stock	*450 ml (¾ pint) buttermilk*
15 ml (1 tbsp) lemon juice	*a few drops of Tabasco*

1 Place the spinach, stock and lemon juice in a large saucepan. Season with salt and pepper and bring to the boil, then reduce the heat and simmer for 10 minutes.
2 Work the spinach through a sieve, or strain off most of the liquid and reserve, then purée the spinach in a blender or food processor until smooth.
3 Reheat the spinach purée gently with the cooking liquid, buttermilk and Tabasco, to taste.
SERVES 4

PEA AND CHERVIL SOUP

Don't throw away empty pea pods – they can be used to make this light summer soup.
We've used fresh chervil to add a subtle aniseed flavour, but any herb will do.

15 ml (1 tbsp) vegetable oil	*1 garlic clove, crushed*
125 g (4 oz) spring onions, trimmed and roughly chopped	*5 ml (1 level tsp) plain flour*
	750 ml (1¼ pints) vegetable stock
225 g (8 oz) empty pea pods or mangetouts, trimmed and roughly chopped	*10 ml (2 level tsp) chopped fresh chervil*
	salt and pepper

1 Heat the oil in a large saucepan and stir in the spring onions, pea pods and garlic. Cook for 2–3 minutes, stirring constantly.

2 Stir in the flour and stock and bring to the boil. Reduce the heat, cover and simmer gently for 25–30 minutes.

3 Cool the mixture slightly, then purée in a blender or food processor until quite smooth. Sieve and return to the pan. Stir in the chopped chervil and season the soup well with salt and pepper. Serve hot.
SERVES 2

Pea and Chervil Soup

SUMMER VEGETABLE SOUP

This summer soup can be served hot with chunks of French bread topped with grated cheese and grilled. Alternatively, try blending it to a smooth purée with a little yogurt and serving it chilled.

30 ml (2 tbsp) vegetable oil	50 g (2 oz) button mushrooms, wiped and thinly sliced
125 g (4 oz) carrots, trimmed, peeled and cut into matchsticks	1.1 litres (2 pints) vegetable stock
½ bunch of spring onions, thinly sliced	60 ml (4 level tbsp) chopped fresh parsley
900 g (2 lb) broad beans, shelled	salt and pepper
225 g (8 oz) tomatoes, skinned, seeded and roughly chopped	

1 Heat the oil in a large saucepan and add the carrots and spring onions. Cook, stirring, for 1–2 minutes or until the vegetables are well browned.
2 Add the remaining vegetables and cook for a further minute. Add the stock and 45 ml (3 level tbsp) parsley. Season with salt and pepper.
3 Bring to the boil, then reduce the heat, cover and simmer for about 40 minutes. Garnish with the remaining parsley.
SERVES 4–6

SPICED LEEK AND POTATO SOUP

Mild curry paste is a useful item to keep in the storecupboard. The spices are already cooked so it can be stirred straight into soups, sauces and dips to add a subtle, spicy flavour without any hint of the raw spice flavour associated with powdered spices.

25 g (1 oz) vegetable margarine or butter	600 ml (1 pint) Brown Onion Stock (see page 41)
225 g (8 oz) trimmed leeks, roughly chopped	salt and pepper
1 medium onion, skinned and roughly chopped	150 ml (¼ pint) single cream
225 g (8 oz) potato, peeled and roughly chopped	chopped fresh coriander, to garnish
7.5 ml (1½ level tsp) mild curry paste	

1 Melt the margarine or butter in a saucepan and sauté the vegetables with the curry paste for 2–3 minutes or until they start to soften and colour. Add the stock and bring to the boil. Reduce the heat, cover and simmer for 45 minutes or until all the vegetables are soft.
2 Purée the mixture in a food processor or blender until smooth. If time allows, push through a nylon sieve for a really smooth result. Season with salt and pepper. Serve hot or cover and chill for 2 hours or, preferably, overnight. Either stir in the cream or swirl it on top of the soup as a garnish with the fresh coriander.
SERVES 3–4

CREAM OF JERUSALEM ARTICHOKE SOUP

When buying Jerusalem artichokes, choose firm tubers with the smoothest surface available as they will be easier to peel. Use them as soon as possible after buying as they quickly lose their lovely creamy colour.

900 g (2 lb) Jerusalem artichokes	25 ml (1½ tbsp) lemon juice
2 slices of lemon	30 ml (2 level tbsp) chopped fresh parsley
25 g (1 oz) vegetable margarine or butter	150 ml (¼ pint) single cream
1 medium onion, skinned and chopped	salt and pepper
450 ml (¾ pint) milk	croûtons (see page 35), to serve

1 Wash the artichokes well and put them in a large saucepan with the lemon slices. Cover with 900 ml (1½ pints) cold water, bring to the boil and cook for about 20 minutes or until tender. Drain off the water, reserving 600 ml (1 pint), and leave the artichokes to cool.
2 Peel the artichokes, then mash them roughly.
3 Melt the margarine or butter in a saucepan, add the onion and cook gently for 5–10 minutes or until soft but not coloured. Stir in the reserved artichoke cooking water, the artichokes and milk. Bring to the boil, stirring, then simmer for 2–3 minutes.
4 Sieve the soup or purée in a blender or food processor. Return to the rinsed-out pan and stir in the lemon juice, parsley, cream and plenty of salt and pepper. Reheat gently and serve hot, sprinkled with croûtons.
SERVES 4

CELERIAC SOUP WITH DILL

Make sure that the soup is well blended to give a smooth texture, and don't forget the final touches just before serving.

25 g (1 oz) vegetable margarine or butter	45 ml (3 tbsp) single cream
225 g (8 oz) celeriac, trimmed, peeled and sliced	lemon juice
1 medium onion, skinned and sliced	10 ml (2 level tsp) chopped fresh dill or a pinch of dried dill weed
750 ml (1¼ pints) vegetable stock	
salt and pepper	

1 Melt the margarine or butter in a saucepan, add the celeriac and onion, and cook gently for 1–2 minutes, stirring constantly. Cover with a piece of damp greaseproof paper pressed down on to the vegetables, and a tight-fitting lid. Cook for about 10 minutes.
2 Remove the greaseproof paper and pour in the stock. Season with salt and pepper and bring to the boil. Reduce the heat, cover and simmer for about 30 minutes or until tender. Cool slightly, then purée in a blender or food processor until very smooth.
3 Return the soup to the pan and reheat, then remove from the heat and stir in the cream, a dash of lemon juice and the dill. Taste and adjust the seasoning, if necessary, before serving in warmed soup bowls.
SERVES 3–4

Minestrone

$\mathcal{B}$ROCCOLI AND STILTON SOUP

Served with chunks of hot crusty bread, this soup makes a delicious, filling supper dish.

25 g (1 oz) vegetable margarine or butter	*45 ml (3 level tbsp) split red lentils*
1 large onion, skinned and chopped	*900 ml (1½ pints) vegetable stock*
225 g (8 oz) broccoli, trimmed and chopped	*50 g (2 oz) Stilton cheese*
a good pinch of cumin seeds	*salt and pepper*

1 Melt the margarine or butter in a large saucepan, add the onion, broccoli and cumin and cook for 5–10 minutes or until beginning to soften.
2 Stir the lentils and stock into the vegetables. Bring to the boil, then reduce the heat, cover and simmer for 20–30 minutes or until the lentils are soft. Leave the soup to cool slightly, then purée in a blender or food processor until smooth.
3 Return the soup to a saucepan and reheat gently. Crumble in the Stilton and season with salt and pepper. Serve hot.
SERVES 4

INESTRONE

The addition of Pesto and Pecorino or Parmesan cheese makes this a typical Genoese minestrone. It's really hearty, comforting food, perfect for a cold winter's evening.

175 g (6 oz) dried cannellini beans, soaked overnight in cold water

60 ml (4 tbsp) olive oil

2 onions, skinned and chopped

3 garlic cloves, skinned and crushed

2 carrots, trimmed, peeled and diced

2 celery sticks, trimmed and diced

397 g (14 oz) can chopped tomatoes

2.3 litres (4 pints) Brown Onion Stock (see page 41) or vegetable stock

350 g (12 oz) floury potatoes (such as King Edward or Maris Piper), peeled and diced

125 g (4 oz) small pasta shapes

125 g (4 oz) shelled fresh or frozen peas

175 g (6 oz) French beans, topped, tailed and sliced

225 g (8 oz) dark green cabbage, tough stalks removed and roughly chopped

75 ml (5 level tbsp) chopped fresh parsley

60 ml (4 tbsp) Pesto (see page 193)

salt and pepper

To serve

Pesto (see page 193)

freshly grated Pecorino or Parmesan cheese

1 Drain the beans, put them in a very large saucepan and cover with fresh water. Bring to the boil and boil rapidly for 10 minutes, then cover and simmer for 1 hour, then drain.

2 Heat the oil in a large saucepan, add the onions and garlic and fry for 5–10 minutes or until golden brown. Add the carrots and celery and cook for 2 minutes.

3 Stir in the beans, tomatoes, stock, potatoes, pasta and fresh peas, if using. Bring to the boil, then reduce the heat, half-cover and simmer for 1 hour.

4 Add the frozen peas, if using, French beans, cabbage, parsley and Pesto. Season with salt and pepper and simmer for 30 minutes or until the vegetables are all tender. Serve immediately in a warmed soup tureen, with the Pesto and cheese in separate bowls for guests to stir into their soup.

SERVES 6–8 AS A MAIN COURSE

CED TOMATO AND BASIL SOUP

A refreshing chilled soup, best made when tomatoes are at their cheapest and most flavoursome. The pungency of fresh basil adds a delicious flavour.

450 g (1 lb) tomatoes, chopped

1 small onion, skinned and chopped

15 ml (1 level tbsp) tomato purée

15 ml (1 level tbsp) chopped fresh basil

600 ml (1 pint) Brown Onion Stock (see page 41)

salt and pepper

1 Put the tomatoes, onion, tomato purée and basil in a blender or food processor and purée until smooth. Pass through a sieve into a saucepan, then stir in the stock and heat gently to remove froth. Season with salt and pepper.

2 Remove from the heat and leave to cool, then chill in the refrigerator for at least 2 hours or overnight.

SERVES 4

PARSNIP AND APPLE SOUP

The velvety texture of a creamy soup is always welcoming, and the unmistakable flavour of parsnips, blended with a hint of tart cooking apple, is very warming.

25 g (1 oz) vegetable margarine or butter	*2 cloves*
700 g (1½ lb) parsnips, trimmed, peeled and roughly chopped	*150 ml (¼ pint) single cream*
1 cooking apple, cored, peeled and roughly chopped	*salt and pepper*
	To garnish
1.1 litres (2 pints) vegetable stock	*fresh sage leaves or parsley*
4 fresh sage leaves or 2.5 ml (½ level tsp) dried sage	*croûtons (see page 35)*

1 Melt the margarine or butter in a large saucepan, add the parsnips and apple, cover and cook gently for 10 minutes, stirring occasionally.

2 Pour in the stock, and add the sage and cloves. Bring to the boil, cover, then simmer for 30 minutes or until the parsnip is very soft.

3 Remove the sage leaves and cloves, leave the soup to cool slightly, then purée in a blender or food processor.

4 Return the soup to the saucepan, add the cream and reheat gently. Season with salt and pepper. Serve hot, garnished with the sage or parsley and croûtons.

SERVES 6

GINGERED DAL SOUP

Garlic and Spring Onion Sauce is a commercially prepared sauce, sold in bottles. You can usually find it in the supermarket alongside the soy and chilli sauces.

90 ml (6 level tbsp) instant coconut milk powder or 75 g (3 oz) creamed coconut	*1.7 litres (3 pints) vegetable stock or water*
30 ml (2 tbsp) olive oil	*45 ml (3 tbsp) Garlic and Spring Onion Sauce*
2 large garlic cloves, skinned and crushed	*45 ml (3 tbsp) chopped fresh coriander*
	salt and pepper
2.5 cm (1 inch) piece of fresh root ginger, peeled and chopped	***To garnish***
	natural yogurt
400 g (14 oz) split red lentils	*chopped fresh coriander*

1 Pour 300 ml (½ pint) boiling water over the coconut and stir until dissolved.

2 Heat the oil in a large saucepan, add the garlic and ginger and fry for 3 minutes or until soft and golden brown. Add all the remaining ingredients, including the coconut milk. Bring to the boil, cover and simmer for 15–20 minutes or until the lentils are very tender. Season to taste with salt and pepper.

3 Cool slightly, then purée, in batches, in a food processor. Return to the saucepan and reheat gently. Taste and adjust the seasoning if necessary. Serve hot, topped with a swirl of yogurt and plenty of chopped fresh coriander.

SERVES 6

CHESTNUT AND ROASTED GARLIC SOUP

Dried chestnuts are available from good health food shops or Italian and continental delicatessens. This soup can also be made with two 425 g (15 oz) cans peeled whole chestnuts in water, drained, but the flavour will not be as good.

225 g (8 oz) dried chestnuts, soaked overnight in cold water	*a pinch of freshly grated nutmeg*
4 large garlic cloves, unskinned	*salt and pepper*
900 ml (1½ pints) Brown Onion Stock (see below)	*120 ml (8 tbsp) Greek yogurt*
45 ml (3 tbsp) dry sherry	*5 ml (1 level tsp) curry paste*
	fresh coriander leaves, to garnish

1 Drain the chestnuts and put them in a saucepan. Cover with cold water, bring to the boil and simmer for 20–30 minutes or until tender, then drain.

2 Put the garlic and chestnuts on a baking tray and roast in the oven at 200°C (400°F) mark 6 for 20 minutes or until the garlic is soft to the touch and the chestnuts are lightly browned. Cool slightly, then pop the garlic cloves out of their skins.

3 Put the garlic, chestnuts and stock in batches in a blender or food processor and process until smooth. Pour into a saucepan, add the sherry and season with nutmeg, salt and pepper. Bring to the boil, then reduce the heat and simmer for 10–15 minutes.

4 Mix the yogurt with the curry paste. Serve the soup in warmed bowls, topped with yogurt and garnished with coriander leaves.
SERVES 8

BROWN ONION STOCK

Caramelising the onions before adding the other ingredients produces a stock with a strong, slightly sweet flavour and a good brown colour.

30 ml (2 tbsp) vegetable oil	*a few sage leaves, thyme stalks and parsley stalks or 10 ml (2 level tsp) dried mixed herbs*
2 large onions, skinned and roughly chopped	
2 garlic cloves, skinned and halved	*2 bay leaves*
2 celery sticks, washed and chopped	*5 ml (1 level tsp) yeast extract (optional)*
2 carrots, washed and chopped	*salt*

1 Heat the oil in a large, heavy-based saucepan. Add the onions and cook, stirring all the time, for about 10 minutes or until they turn a dark golden brown. Be careful not to let the onions burn. Add the remaining vegetables, herbs and yeast extract, if using. Cook over a high heat for 4–5 minutes or until the vegetables are lightly browned.

2 Add 1.1 litres (2 pints) water to the pan and bring to the boil. Season with salt, lower the heat and simmer gently for 30 minutes. Strain through a fine sieve into a jug or bowl. The stock is now ready to use, or it can be returned to a clean saucepan and boiled rapidly to reduce the quantity and intensify the flavour. Cool and store in the refrigerator for 2–3 days or freeze for later use.
MAKES ABOUT 900 ML (1½ PINTS)

EGETABLE STOCK

If using onion skins for colour, remove them after 30 minutes or the stock will be bitter.

30 ml (2 tbsp) vegetable oil	vegetable trimmings, such as celery tops, cabbage leaves,
1 medium onion, skinned and finely chopped	Brussels sprouts leaves, mushroom peelings, tomato
1 medium carrot, washed and diced	skins and potato peelings
50 g (2 oz) turnip, washed and diced	onion skins (optional)
50 g (2 oz) parsnip, washed and diced	bouquet garni
4 celery sticks, washed and roughly chopped	6 whole black peppercorns

1 Heat the oil in a large saucepan, add the onion and fry gently for about 5 minutes or until soft and lightly coloured.
2 Add the other vegetables to the pan with any vegetable trimmings, outer leaves or peelings available. If a dark brown coloured stock is required, add onion skins.
3 Cover the vegetables with 1.7 litres (3 pints) cold water and add the bouquet garni and peppercorns. Bring to the boil.
4 Half cover the pan and simmer the stock for 1½ hours, skimming occasionally with a slotted spoon.
5 Strain the stock into a bowl and leave to cool. Cover and chill in the refrigerator. This stock will only keep for 1–2 days, after which time it will begin to go sour.
MAKES ABOUT 1.1 LITRES (2 PINTS)

USHROOM STOCK

Dried mushrooms are expensive but they have a really strong flavour. Use this special stock for risottos, soups and stir-fries.

15 ml (1 tbsp) vegetable oil	10 g (¼ oz) packet dried porcini (cep) mushrooms
125 g (4 oz) open-cup mushrooms, roughly chopped	a few fresh herb sprigs, such as thyme, rosemary and
1 onion, skinned and roughly chopped	parsley
2 carrots, washed and roughly chopped	salt and pepper
½ head of fennel, roughly chopped	

1 Heat the oil in a large saucepan. Add the mushrooms, onion, carrots and fennel and fry for 5 minutes or until softened. Add the dried mushrooms, the herbs and 1.7 litres (3 pints) water. Bring to the boil and simmer for 45–50 minutes.
2 Strain the stock through a fine sieve into a jug or bowl and season with salt and pepper. The stock is now ready to use, or it can be returned to a clean saucepan and boiled rapidly to reduce the quantity and intensify the flavour. Cool and store in the refrigerator for 2–3 days or freeze for later use.
MAKES ABOUT 1.4 LITRES (2½ PINTS)

—THREE—

ALADS

The days when a salad consisted of tired lettuce leaves, a sliced tomato and a limp piece of cucumber are over – or at least they should be. Market stalls, greengrocers and supermarkets now positively abound with brilliant displays of fruits and vegetables.

To start with, cast your eye over the varieties of lettuces now on offer. New, interesting, well flavoured leaves are appearing all the time, from the ubiquitous Cos and Iceberg, to exotica like the frilly leaved frisée or curly endive, or the russet brown Feuille de Chêne (Oak Leaf). Other interesting varieties worth looking out for are batavia, Lollo Rosso (Red Lollo) and Quattro Stagioni (Four Seasons) and the bitter, dark red radicchio.

Lamb's lettuce, a delicate green leaf which is not a true lettuce, but a weed native to Europe, is now cultivated mainly in France and makes a delicious addition to any salad bowl. Rocket (arugula), with its distinctive, peppery taste, is not a lettuce but a salad herb. It's experiencing a revival and makes a spectacular salad dressed simply with olive oil.

Whichever variety you choose, the leaves should be firm and crisp with no signs of browning or insect damage. To prepare, pull off and discard any damaged outer leaves and wash the lettuce thoroughly in plenty of cold water. Drain thoroughly and dry in a clean tea-towel or salad shaker. Transfer the clean leaves to polythene bags and store in the salad drawer in the refrigerator.

Not all salads are based on lettuce. Experiment with your own favourite combinations of vegetables, fruits, nuts, seeds, pulses and pasta, tossed with one of the dressings on pages 181–194 to create your own masterpieces. If it's a salad based on robust ingredients like root vegetables, pulses, rice, pasta, dried fruit, seeds, nuts and grains, add the dressing when everything is freshly cooked and still warm. Leave to cool, stirring occasionally, so that the flavours have time to be absorbed and mellow. Delicate leaf- and herb-based salads tend to flop if dressed too soon, so get everything ready and toss together at the last minute.

Finally, if you get the opportunity, take advantage of the ever-growing range of edible flowers that appears in the shops in the summer. A few scattered on top of leafy salads make an eye-catching display.

$\mathcal{H}$OT SPICED CHICK-PEA SALAD

Serve this hot salad with wholemeal bread for a light lunch or with baked potatoes or a rice dish as a main meal.

15 ml (1 tbsp) vegetable oil	two 425 g (15 oz) cans cooked chick-peas, drained
1 medium onion, skinned and chopped	15 ml (1 tbsp) lemon juice
10 ml (2 level tsp) ground turmeric	60 ml (4 level tbsp) chopped fresh coriander
15 ml (1 level tbsp) cumin seeds	salt and pepper
450 g (1 lb) tomatoes, roughly chopped	fresh coriander leaves, to garnish

1 Heat the oil in a saucepan, add the onion and cook for 5–10 minutes or until golden brown, stirring constantly.
2 Add the turmeric and cumin seeds and cook, stirring, for 1–2 minutes. Add the

remaining ingredients. Cook for 1–2 minutes, stirring frequently.
3 Taste and adjust the seasoning, if necessary, before serving garnished with fresh coriander.
SERVES 4

BABY VEGETABLE AND PASTA SALAD

This salad is meant to be served lukewarm rather than hot or cold. However, if you would like to make it in advance and serve it cold, cool the vegetables and pasta completely and refrigerate until required. Let them come to room temperature before spooning them on top of the salad leaves.

350 g (12 oz) dried pasta shapes, such as ruotini, penne, conchiglie or fusilli	*60 ml (4 tbsp) olive oil*
salt and pepper	*45 ml (3 tbsp) home-made or bought Pesto (see page 193)*
750 g (1½ lb) mixed baby vegetables, such as courgettes, patty pan squash, asparagus tips, sugar snap peas and leeks	*125 g (4 oz) black olives*
	125 g (4 oz) cherry tomatoes
	a handful of mixed salad leaves
	a few chopped fresh herbs (optional)

1 Cook the pasta in boiling salted water for 5–10 minutes or until tender.
2 Meanwhile, prepare the vegetables, leaving them whole wherever possible. Any larger, slower cooking vegetables, such as patty pan squash, should be halved or quartered. Steam the prepared vegetables until just tender.
3 Whisk together the olive oil and Pesto.

Drain the pasta and put it in a large bowl with the Pesto mixture, the steamed vegetables and the olives and tomatoes. Toss well together. Put the salad leaves in the bottom of a large serving bowl and spoon over the pasta mixture. Sprinkle with herbs, if using, and serve immediately.
SERVES 6

GREEK SALAD

Feta, a Greek cheese, is available in supermarkets as well as Greek and Middle Eastern shops. Traditionally, feta is made from sheep's milk, but nowadays it is often made from cow's milk or a mixture of the two. It is milky white in colour, with a crumbly texture and salty taste.

700 g (1½ lb) beefsteak tomatoes	**For the dressing**
1 large cucumber	*135 ml (9 tbsp) olive oil*
2 medium red onions, skinned and thinly sliced	*45 ml (3 tbsp) lemon juice*
125 g (4 oz) black olives, stoned	*45 ml (3 level tbsp) chopped fresh coriander*
225 g (8 oz) feta cheese	*a good pinch of sugar*
	salt and pepper

1 Cut the tomatoes into bite-sized chunks, discarding the cores. Cut the cucumber into bite-sized chunks.
2 Whisk the dressing ingredients together in a jug or shake together in a screw-topped jar (go easy on the salt because of the saltiness of olives and feta cheese).

3 Put the tomatoes, cucumber and onions in a large bowl, add the olives and toss the ingredients together with your hands. Pour over the dressing and toss gently to mix, then crumble over the feta cheese. Serve as soon as possible.
SERVES 4–6

Tomato and Red Onion Salad

700 g (1½ lb) mixed tomatoes, halved	20 ml (4 tsp) balsamic vinegar
1 large red onion, skinned and finely chopped	salt and pepper
60 ml (4 tbsp) olive oil	

1 Combine the tomatoes and onion.
2 Whisk together the remaining ingredients and season with salt and pepper. Pour over the tomatoes, toss well and leave to marinate for at least 20 minutes before serving.
SERVES 6

Orange and Garlic Salad

Make the most of ready-prepared bags of salad with this delicious dressing.

2 garlic cloves, skinned and crushed	salt and pepper
60 ml (4 tbsp) olive oil	a selection of mixed lettuce leaves, such as oak leaf, frisée and lollo rosso
15 ml (1 tbsp) red wine vinegar	
finely grated rind and juice of 1 small orange	

1 Put the garlic in a small bowl and mix to a paste with 5 ml (1 tsp) olive oil. Whisk in the vinegar, remaining olive oil, orange rind and 45 ml (3 tbsp) orange juice. Season to taste.

2 Pour the dressing over the mixed salad leaves, toss well and serve immediately.
SERVES 4

Tomato and Artichoke Salad

400 g (14 oz) can artichoke hearts, drained and halved	45 ml (3 tbsp) olive oil
450 g (1 lb) ripe tomatoes, quartered	30 ml (2 level tbsp) fromage frais
1 large garlic clove, skinned and crushed	salt and pepper
20 ml (4 tsp) lemon juice	1 small onion, skinned and roughly chopped

1 Arrange the artichoke hearts and tomatoes in a serving dish.
2 Whisk together the garlic, lemon juice, oil and fromage frais. Season with salt and pepper and stir in the roughly chopped onion.
3 Spoon the dressing over the vegetables, cover and chill for about 30 minutes.
SERVES 4

Tomato and Red Onion Salad *top*, Orange and Garlic Salad *bottom*

HERB OMELETTE SALAD

If available, use the classic *fines herbes* mixture of parsley, tarragon, chives and chervil to flavour the omelettes. See pages 56–57 for more information about omelette-making.

4 free-range eggs, beaten	1 large green pepper, cored, seeded and cut into strips
30 ml (2 tbsp) chopped fresh herbs (see above)	1 small head of fennel, trimmed and thinly sliced
salt and pepper	1 bunch of spring onions, trimmed and cut into strips
vegetable margarine or butter	½ cucumber, cut into thin strips
1 large red pepper, cored, seeded and cut into strips	1 quantity Vinaigrette Dressing (see page 185)

1 Beat the eggs with the herbs and 30 ml (2 tbsp) water. Season with salt and pepper. Heat a knob of margarine or butter in an omelette pan and use the eggs to make two thin, lightly set omelettes. Turn out on to a sheet of greaseproof paper, roll up and leave to cool slightly. Toss the remaining ingredients together.

2 Thinly slice the omelette and toss over the salad. Serve immediately.

SERVES 4

BULGAR WHEAT SALAD

This salad is excellent as part of a buffet and is simple to double up to serve larger numbers.

225 g (8 oz) bulgar wheat	30 ml (2 level tbsp) chopped fresh mint
½ cucumber	30 ml (2 level tbsp) chopped fresh parsley
salt and pepper	60 ml (4 tbsp) olive oil
½ green pepper, cored, seeded and diced	45 ml (3 tbsp) lemon juice
½ red pepper, cored, seeded and diced	1 garlic clove, skinned and crushed
1 bunch of spring onions, trimmed and chopped	450 g (1 lb) tomatoes, sliced
125 g (4 oz) feta cheese, diced	125 g (4 oz) hazelnuts, toasted and skinned

1 Soak the bulgar wheat in 300 ml (½ pint) boiling water for about 30 minutes or until the water has been absorbed, stirring occasionally.

2 Meanwhile, roughly chop the cucumber, sprinkle with salt and leave for 15 minutes. Rinse, drain and dry. Blanch the peppers in boiling water for 1 minute, then drain.

3 If necessary, drain the bulgar wheat. Mix with all the other ingredients, except the tomatoes and hazelnuts. Season with salt and pepper, cover and refrigerate until required.

4 Serve on a bed of sliced tomatoes topped with the hazelnuts.

SERVES 6

SPICED CAULIFLOWER SALAD

In this recipe, the cauliflower is stirred into the dressing while it is still warm to gain maximum flavour from the spices.

1 bunch of spring onions, trimmed	30 ml (2 level tbsp) mango chutney
90 ml (6 tbsp) vegetable oil	45 ml (3 tbsp) white wine vinegar
10 ml (2 level tsp) ground coriander	45 ml (3 tbsp) single cream
5 ml (1 level tsp) ground cumin	60 ml (4 level tbsp) chopped fresh parsley
5 ml (1 level tsp) ground turmeric	salt and pepper
50 g (2 oz) unsalted cashew nuts	1 medium cauliflower

1 Cut the spring onions into 1 cm (½ inch) lengths. Heat the oil in a small frying pan. Add the spices, onions and nuts and cook, stirring, for 2–3 minutes, then tip into a large bowl.

2 Roughly chop the mango chutney and stir it into the bowl with the vinegar, cream and 45 ml (3 level tbsp) chopped parsley. Season with salt and pepper.

3 Divide the cauliflower into small florets and cook in boiling salted water for 2–3 minutes only. Drain and, while still warm, stir into the dressing. Leave to marinate for several hours, turning occasionally. Taste and adjust the seasoning, if necessary.

4 To serve, spoon the salad into a glass bowl and garnish with the remaining chopped parsley.

SERVES 6

RAW VEGETABLES WITH GARLIC DRESSING

This vividly coloured salad is excellent served with grilled and fried dishes (see pages 111–118), or as a starter served with warm lemon bread. Make lemon bread like garlic bread but omit the garlic and flavour the butter with grated lemon rind and a few chopped fresh herbs.

175 g (6 oz) carrots, trimmed and peeled	30 ml (2 tbsp) wine vinegar
175 g (6 oz) courgettes, trimmed	2.5 ml (½ level tsp) sugar
175 g (6 oz) celeriac, trimmed	2.5 ml (½ level tsp) mustard powder
15 ml (1 tbsp) lemon juice	1 garlic clove, skinned and crushed
175 g (6 oz) raw beetroot, trimmed and peeled	salt and pepper
90 ml (6 tbsp) olive or vegetable oil	chopped fresh parsley, to garnish

1 Grate the carrots and courgettes into a bowl.

2 Peel and grate the celeriac, toss immediately in the lemon juice and add to the carrot and courgette mixture. Lastly, grate the beetroot and add to the mixture.

3 Put the oil, vinegar, sugar, mustard and garlic in a screw-topped jar and season with salt and pepper. Shake the jar until the dressing is thoroughly combined.

4 Pour the dressing over the vegetables and toss lightly just to coat. Serve immediately, garnished with chopped parsley.

SERVES 4

GRILLED VEGETABLE SALAD

This cold vegetable dish is good as part of a summer barbecue or buffet.
The vegetables and dressing can be prepared separately well in advance and mixed just before
serving. The blanching water makes an excellent base for vegetable stock (see page 42).

1 red pepper	
1 green pepper	
350 g (12 oz) courgettes, trimmed	
about 6 whole garlic cloves	
1 bunch of asparagus, trimmed	
olive oil for brushing	
a few cherry tomatoes	
chopped fresh herbs, such as basil, marjoram, parsley and chives	

For the dressing

10 ml (2 tsp) balsamic or garlic vinegar
5 ml (1 tsp) runny honey
5 ml (1 level tsp) Dijon mustard
75 ml (5 tbsp) olive oil
salt and pepper

1 Halve the peppers and remove the seeds and cores. Cut each half into four. Thickly slice the courgettes on the diagonal. Remove the loose, papery outer skins from the garlic cloves, but leave the inner skins attached.

2 Pour enough water to come to a depth of about 5 cm (2 inches) into a saucepan, and bring to the boil. When the water is boiling fast, add the peppers and the garlic. Bring back to the boil and boil for 1 minute.

Remove the peppers with a slotted spoon (leaving the garlic in the water), refresh under cold running water and leave to drain. Repeat this process with the courgettes, using the same water. Remove the garlic from the pan and drain.

3 Steam the asparagus until just tender (see page 53). Drain, arrange on a serving plate and leave to cool. Brush the blanched peppers, courgettes and garlic with a little olive oil and cook under a hot grill until the vegetables are flecked with brown. Turn the vegetables over, brush with more oil and cook the second side. Leave to cool, then arrange on the serving plate with the asparagus. Halve the tomatoes and scatter over the vegetables.

4 To make the dressing, put the vinegar, honey and mustard in a small bowl, and whisk together with a fork until well blended. Gradually whisk in the olive oil to make a very thick dressing. Season with salt and pepper.

5 Just before serving, drizzle the dressing over the vegetables and sprinkle with herbs.

SERVES 3 AS A MAIN COURSE OR 4–6 AS AN ACCOMPANIMENT

WILD RICE AND THYME SALAD

If fresh broad beans are out of season, use frozen instead, or replace them with any cooked beans of your choice.

150 g (5 oz) French beans, topped, tailed and halved	*50 g (2 oz) chanterelles, trompets des morts or small button mushrooms, roughly sliced*
salt and pepper	
150 g (5 oz) shelled broad beans	*30 ml (2 level tbsp) chopped fresh thyme*
50 g (2 oz) wild rice	*25 ml (1 fl oz) walnut oil*
175 g (6 oz) long-grain white rice	*30 ml (2 tbsp) white wine vinegar*
50 ml (2 fl oz) vegetable oil	*15 ml (1 level tbsp) Dijon mustard*

1 Cook the French beans in boiling salted water for 10–12 minutes or until they are just tender. Drain, refresh under cold running water and set aside to cool completely. Cook the broad beans in boiling salted water for 5–7 minutes. Drain and refresh under cold running water, slipping off their outer skins if wished, and set aside to cool completely.

2 Cook the wild rice in a large pan of boiling salted water for 25 minutes, then add the long-grain white rice. Boil together for a further 10 minutes or until both are just tender. Drain and refresh under cold running water. Stir together the French beans, broad beans and rice in a large mixing bowl.

3 Heat the vegetable oil in a small frying pan and fry the mushrooms with the thyme for 2–3 minutes, stirring constantly. Remove from the heat and stir in the walnut oil, vinegar and mustard. Season with salt and pepper, spoon into the rice mixture and stir well. Taste and adjust the seasoning, if necessary. Cool, cover and leave to stand for at least 30 minutes before serving.

SERVES 6–8

$\mathscr{S}$WEET ONION SALAD

To make sure button onions stay whole when cooked, simply trim the root end when peeling – don't remove it completely. This salad is delicious with baked potatoes and nut burgers.

450 g (1 lb) button onions	1 bay leaf
150 ml (¼ pint) red wine	30 ml (2 level tbsp) soft light brown sugar
75 ml (3 fl oz) olive oil	salt and pepper
45 ml (3 level tbsp) tomato purée	

1 Put the button onions in a large bowl and pour over enough boiling water to cover. Leave to soak for 3–4 minutes, then drain and peel.
2 Put the onions in a saucepan with all the remaining ingredients. Season with salt and pepper, cover and simmer for 20 minutes or until the onions are tender but still retain their shape. Stir occasionally to prevent the sugar burning on to the pan.
3 Spoon the contents of the pan into a bowl, cool, cover and chill in the refrigerator for 10–15 minutes before serving, or keep for up to 2 days.
SERVES 3–4

$\mathscr{S}$PINACH AND CORN SALAD

If fresh baby sweetcorn is not available, look for the precooked canned variety. Alternatively, toss sliced, boiled new potatoes into the salad instead.

350 g (12 oz) fresh young spinach, washed and dried	10 ml (2 level tsp) Dijon mustard
175 g (6 oz) fresh baby sweetcorn	5 ml (1 level tsp) caster sugar
salt and pepper	125 g (4 oz) alfalfa sprouts or sprouted beans of your
50 ml (2 fl oz) olive oil	choice
1 garlic clove, skinned and crushed	1 head of chicory, shredded
15 ml (1 tbsp) white wine vinegar	

1 Remove any coarse stalks from the spinach. Halve the sweetcorn cobs lengthways and cook in boiling salted water for about 10 minutes or until just tender. Drain and refresh under cold running water.
2 Whisk together the olive oil, garlic, vinegar, mustard and sugar. Season with salt and pepper.
3 Mix the spinach, sweetcorn, alfalfa sprouts and chicory in a salad bowl. Pour over the dressing, toss well and serve immediately.
SERVES 6–8

PEASANT SALAD

This hearty, colourful salad makes a meal in itself. The best way to steam asparagus is to stand it, tied in a bundle, tips upwards, in about 5 cm (2 inches) of simmering salted water in a saucepan. Cover the tips with a tent of foil and cook for 5–8 minutes (depending on the thickness of the asparagus). The stems cook in the simmering water, while the delicate tips are gently steamed.

700 g (1½ lb) potatoes	1 yellow pepper, cored, seeded and chopped
salt	chopped fresh parsley
3 free-range eggs	2 courgettes, trimmed and very thinly sliced
450 g (1 lb) asparagus (or 1 large bundle), trimmed	50 g (2 oz) green or black olives
1 avocado	45 ml (3 tbsp) capers
2 small red onions, skinned, halved and thinly sliced	45 ml (3 tbsp) mayonnaise
1 red pepper, cored, seeded and chopped	1 quantity Mustard and Parsley Dressing (see page 185)

1 Cook the potatoes in boiling salted water for about 15 minutes or until tender. Cook the eggs in boiling water for about 10 minutes or until hard-boiled. Drain, cover with cold water and leave to cool.

2 Steam the asparagus (see above).

3 Drain the potatoes. Leave to cool slightly, then peel off the skins, if preferred. Cut the potatoes into large chunks. Cut off the asparagus tips and reserve. Chop the stems into 2.5 cm (1 inch) pieces. Shell the eggs and cut into wedges. Peel and stone the avocado, and cut the flesh into chunks.

4 Mix all the ingredients together in a serving bowl. Whisk the mayonnaise into the dressing and pour over the salad. Toss together and serve immediately.

SERVES 8

ZATZIKI

Different versions of this Greek dish are found in countries stretching from the Near East to India. The Turkish version is known as *cacik* and the Indian version is known as *raita*. It can be served as a salad, a sauce or a dip, depending on the proportion of yogurt to solid ingredients used.

¼ cucumber	30 ml (2 tbsp) chopped fresh mint or 2.5 ml (½ tsp)
about 300 ml (½ pint) Greek or other natural yogurt	concentrated mint sauce
1 garlic clove, skinned and crushed (optional)	salt and pepper
1 spring onion, trimmed and finely chopped (optional)	paprika

1 If making a salad, halve the cucumber lengthways, then slice thinly into crescents. If making a sauce or a dip, finely chop the cucumber.
2 Mix the cucumber with the remaining ingredients and season with salt, pepper and paprika.
VARIATIONS
Omit the garlic and spring onion. Substitute fruit for the cucumber, such as one sliced banana or one finely chopped dessert apple. If liked, add one seeded and very finely chopped fresh green chilli. Substitute chopped fresh coriander for the mint.

Raita is usually a much simpler mixture made with less cucumber and without garlic or spring onion. Serve as a cooling accompaniment to curries and fried dishes.
MAKES ABOUT 300 ML (½ PINT)

USTARDY POTATO SALAD

French smooth-skinned potato varieties, such as La Ratte, Cornichon or Belle de Fontenay, make excellent potato salads. Alternatively, the Pink Fir Apple, an old English variety that has recently been relaunched on to the supermarket shelves, is delicious and well worth looking out for.

700 g (1½ lb) very small potatoes, thoroughly washed	75 ml (5 tbsp) mayonnaise
salt and pepper	30 ml (2 level tbsp) whole grain mustard
225 ml (8 fl oz) fromage frais	10 ml (2 level tsp) Dijon mustard

1 Cook the potatoes in boiling salted water for about 10 minutes or until tender. Meanwhile, mix together the remaining ingredients and season to taste with salt and pepper.
2 When the potatoes are cooked, drain them well and add them to the mayonnaise mixture, mixing well so the potatoes are completely covered. Leave to cool before serving.
SERVES 4

—FOUR—

OMELETTES, SOUFFLÉS AND
PANCAKES

The perfect omelette, soufflé or pancake is much easier to make than culinary myth would have us believe. In reality, once a few basic principles are grasped, no special skill is required for any of them.

An essential for both pancake- and omelette-making is a good heavy-based pan. Ideally, it should be kept solely for pancake- or omelette-making and should never be washed or scrubbed, just carefully wiped out with kitchen paper after use. It is also a good idea to store the pan wrapped, either in its original box or in kitchen paper, to prevent the surface becoming scratched. When buying a pan, choose one with a base that measures about 20.5–23 cm (8–9 inches) across, with or without a non-stick coating. The added advantage of a non-stick coating is that less fat is needed, making it the best choice if you're watching your weight.

A new pan should be 'seasoned' before it is used for cooking. If available, follow the manufacturer's instructions; otherwise fill the pan with oil and heat it gently until hot. Repeat the process once or twice to seal the surface of the pan. Pour out the oil and the pan is ready for action. When cooking an omelette or pancake, heat the empty pan first so that the mixture begins to cook as soon as it is added to the pan; slow cooking makes them tough.

For soufflé-making, a deep, straight-sided soufflé dish with a perfectly smooth inside gives the most spectacular result. Grease it thoroughly to help the mixture glide up the sides. The basic soufflé mixture, or panada, is simply a very thick sauce mixture usually made with flour, butter or margarine and milk. The egg yolks are always separated from the white and beaten into the panada, then the egg whites are whisked and folded in. The sauce must be cooled sufficiently first, or the yolks will scramble. Ideally, for the greatest volume, whisk the egg whites in a metal bowl; copper is best, but stainless steel is also good. Ensure that the whisk and bowl are spotlessly clean; if there is even a trace of grease lurking in the bowl the whites won't whisk to volume. When folding together the panada and whisked whites, a large metal spoon or a plastic spatula is best.

Finally, a word about eggs. Following recent scares involving the salmonella virus, it is prudent to treat eggs carefully. Free-range eggs are best. Buying from a farm shop or other reputable supplier with a fast turnover ensures that the eggs really are free-range and that they are fresh. Always check the date marked on the packet, store the eggs in the refrigerator (preferably in the egg box) and use within 2 weeks of purchase. To test an egg for freshness, put it in a bowl of water. If it floats it is bad; a fresh egg will sink. Bring eggs to room temperature just before using; eggs that are too cold are difficult to whisk to sufficient volume.

MELETTE

An omelette must be served immediately so have a warmed plate ready along with an
accompanying salad and warmed baguettes.

2–3 free-range eggs per person	*15 ml (1 tbsp) milk or water per person*
salt and pepper	*vegetable margarine or butter for frying*

1 Whisk the eggs just enough to break them
down; don't make them frothy as overbeating
spoils the texture of the finished omelette.
Season with salt and pepper and add the milk
or water.

2 Place an omelette or non-stick frying pan
over a gentle heat and, when it is hot, add a
generous knob of vegetable margarine or
butter and heat until it is foaming but not
brown.

3 Add the beaten eggs. Stir gently with a fork
or wooden spatula, drawing the mixture from
the sides to the centre as it sets and letting the
liquid egg in the centre run to the sides.
When the eggs have set, stop stirring and
cook for another minute until the omelette is
golden brown underneath and still creamy on
top. Don't overcook or the omelette will be
tough.

4 If making a filled omelette, add the filling
at this point. Tilt the pan away from you
slightly and use a palette knife to fold over a
third of the omelette to the centre, then fold
over the opposite third. Slide the omelette
out on to a warmed plate, letting it flip over
so that the folded sides are underneath. Serve
at once.

OMELETTE FILLINGS
Fines herbes Add 15 ml (1 level tbsp) finely
chopped fresh chervil, chives and tarragon or
a large pinch of mixed dried herbs to the
beaten egg mixture before cooking.
Cheese Grate 40 g (1½ oz) cheese. Put half
of it in the centre of the omelette before

folding. Sprinkle the rest over the finished
omelette.
Tomato Skin and chop 1–2 tomatoes and
fry in a little butter or vegetable margarine in
a saucepan for 5 minutes or until soft and
pulpy. Put in the centre of the omelette
before folding.
Mushroom Thickly slice about 50 g (2 oz)
mushrooms and cook in vegetable margarine
or butter until soft. Put in the centre of the
omelette before folding. (When available,
wild mushrooms make a delicious filling.)
Curried Vegetable Roughly chop leftover
vegetables, such as potato, green beans, broad
beans or parsnips. Fry in oil with about 2.5 ml
(½ level tsp) curry powder and a little garlic
until heated through.
Lovage and Blue Cheese Add 10 ml
(2 level tsp) finely chopped fresh lovage to the
beaten egg mixture. Cut 25–50 g (1–2 oz)
Blue Cheshire, Blue Stilton, or Blue
Wensleydale cheese into thin slices and scatter
over the omelette before folding.
Goats' Cheese Soften about 25 g (1 oz)
mild goats' cheese and blend with a little
fromage frais. Season with salt and pepper and
put in the centre of the omelette before
folding.
Soy Sauce For this Indonesian omelette,
omit the salt and flavour the eggs with
5–10 ml (1–2 tsp) soy sauce. Serve with
Peanut Sauce (see page 24).

A spoonful or two of Ratatouille (page 96),
Pesto (page 193) or steamed spinach seasoned
with nutmeg all make good omelette fillings.

$\mathscr{S}$PINACH AND MUSHROOM OMELETTE

Serve with warm crusty bread to mop up the delicious creamy mushroom sauce.

225 g (8 oz) frozen chopped spinach, thawed and thoroughly drained	40 g (1½ oz) vegetable margarine or butter
4 free-range eggs	125 g (4 oz) button mushrooms, sliced
1.25 ml (¼ level tsp) grated nutmeg	10 ml (2 level tsp) whole grain mustard
salt and pepper	150 ml (¼ pint) soured cream

1 Pureé the spinach in a blender with the eggs, nutmeg and salt and pepper to taste.
2 Melt half the margarine or butter in a frying pan, add the mushrooms and mustard and cook for about 5 minutes or until soft. Add the soured cream, season with salt and pepper and bring to the boil. Reduce the heat and simmer very gently.

3 Heat the remaining margarine or butter in a large non-stick frying pan. When foaming, add the spinach mixture. Cook until the base sets, then cook the top under a hot grill.
4 Spoon the mushrooms on one half of the omelette and flip over the other half to enclose the mixture. Serve immediately.
SERVES 2

$\mathscr{T}$ORTILLA ESPAGNOLE

A Spanish tortilla, or omelette, should be much thicker than an ordinary omelette. Use a good heavy-based non-stick frying pan about 25.5 cm (10 inches) in diameter to get the right depth with this number of eggs.

about 60 ml (4 tbsp) olive oil	2 medium onions, skinned and sliced
450 g (1 lb) waxy potatoes (such as Maris Bard or Wilja), peeled and diced	6 large free-range eggs
	salt and pepper

1 Heat half the oil in a heavy-based, non-stick frying pan. Add the potatoes and onions and cook over a high heat for 1–2 minutes, stirring all the time, so that the potatoes are coated with oil and sealed on all sides.
2 Reduce the heat and cook for 5–10 minutes or until the potatoes are soft. Loosen any sediment at the bottom of the pan with a wooden spatula. Add a little extra oil, if necessary, and heat for a minute until very hot. Beat the eggs with a fork and season with

salt and pepper. Stir into the hot oil.
3 Cook over a high heat for 1–2 minutes, then reduce the heat and cook until the eggs are just set. Loosen the tortilla from the sides of the pan, then turn it out on to a serving plate.
4 Heat the remaining oil in the pan, then add the tortilla, browned side up, and cook for a further 1–2 minutes. Serve warm or cold, cut in wedges.
SERVES 4

Spinach and Mushroom Omelette

CARROT AND BUTTER BEAN SOUFFLÉS

Canned chick-peas could be used in place of the butter beans. If you prefer to use home-cooked beans, make sure that you cook them until really soft or they will spoil the texture of the soufflés.

450 g (1 lb) carrots, trimmed, peeled and thinly sliced	75 g (3 oz) Gruyère or Gouda cheese, grated
salt and pepper	3 free-range eggs, separated
30 ml (2 tbsp) vegetable oil	30 ml (2 level tbsp) chopped fresh coriander
15 ml (1 level tbsp) plain wholemeal flour	10 ml (2 level tsp) medium oatmeal or fresh brown
425 g (15 oz) can butter beans, drained and rinsed	breadcrumbs

1 Cook the carrots in boiling salted water for 10–12 minutes or until well softened. Drain well, reserving 150 ml (¼ pint) of the cooking water.

2 Heat the oil in a saucepan. Add the flour and cook, stirring, for 1 minute. Remove from the heat and gradually add the reserved water. Bring to the boil, stirring, then reduce the heat and simmer for 2 minutes.

3 Put the carrots, sauce, butter beans, cheese and egg yolks in a food processor. Process until well mixed and almost smooth. Season

with salt and pepper. Turn into a bowl and fold in the coriander. Whisk the egg whites until stiff and fold carefully into the mixture.

4 Spoon into four 450 ml (¾ pint) capacity well-greased, deep, individual, ovenproof dishes. Sprinkle with the oatmeal or breadcrumbs.

5 Bake in the oven at 200°C (400°F) mark 6 for 20–25 minutes or until golden brown and just firm to the touch. Serve immediately.
SERVES 4

CHEESE SOUFFLÉ

Use a proper straight-sided soufflé dish to get the best rise. Run your finger around the edge of the mixture before it goes into the oven to achieve the classic 'hat' effect.

15 ml (1 level tbsp) freshly grated Parmesan cheese	10 ml (2 level tsp) Dijon mustard
200 ml (7 fl oz) milk	salt and pepper
slices of onion and carrot, 1 bay leaf and 6 black	cayenne pepper
peppercorns, for flavouring	4 free-range eggs, separated
25 g (1 oz) vegetable margarine or butter	75 g (3 oz) mature Cheddar cheese, finely grated
30 ml (2 level tbsp) plain flour	1 free-range egg white

1 Grease a 1.3 litre (2¼ pint) soufflé dish. Sprinkle the Parmesan into the dish and tilt the dish, knocking the sides gently until they are evenly coated with cheese.

2 Put the milk in a saucepan with the flavouring ingredients. Bring slowly to the boil, then remove from the heat, cover and

leave to infuse for 30 minutes. Strain off and reserve the milk.

3 Melt the margarine or butter in a saucepan and stir in the flour and mustard. Season with salt, pepper and cayenne, and cook gently for 1 minute, stirring. Remove from the heat and gradually stir in the milk. Bring to the boil slowly and continue to cook, stirring, until the sauce thickens. Cool a little.

4 Beat the egg yolks into the cooled sauce one at a time. Sprinkle the Cheddar cheese over the sauce, reserving 15 ml (1 level tbsp). (At this stage, the mixture can be left to stand for several hours if necessary.)

5 Stir in the cheese until evenly blended. Using a hand or electric mixer, whisk all the egg whites until they stand in stiff peaks.

6 Mix one large spoonful of egg white into the sauce to lighten its texture. Gently pour the sauce over the remaining egg whites and carefully fold the ingredients together. Do not overmix; fold lightly, using a metal spoon, until the egg whites are just incorporated.

7 Pour the soufflé mixture gently into the prepared dish. The mixture should come

about three-quarters of the way up the side of the dish. Sprinkle with the reserved cheese.

8 Stand the soufflé on a baking sheet and cook in the oven at 180°C (350°F) mark 4 for about 30 minutes. When cooked, the soufflé should be golden brown on the top, well risen and just firm to the touch, with a hint of softness in the centre.

SERVES 4

VARIATIONS

Don't use too great a weight of filling or the soufflé will be heavy. Omit the cheese and add one of the following:

Blue Cheese Use a blue cheese, such as Stilton or Wensleydale.

Mushroom 125 g (4 oz) mushrooms, chopped and cooked in margarine or butter.

$\mathscr{S}$PINACH AND GRUYÈRE SOUFFLÉ

Gruyère or Emmenthal gives a good cheesy flavour but, of course, any other cheese can be used instead.

450 g (1 lb) fresh spinach, cooked or 225 g (8 oz) frozen leaf spinach, thawed	*salt and pepper*
50 g (2 oz) vegetable margarine or butter	*3 free-range eggs, separated*
45 ml (3 level tbsp) plain flour	*125 g (4 oz) Gruyère or Emmenthal cheese, grated*
200 ml (7 fl oz) milk	*1 free-range egg white*

1 Grease a 1.3 litre (2¼ pint) soufflé dish. Put the spinach in a sieve and press to remove all moisture. Chop finely.

2 Melt the margarine or butter in a saucepan, add the spinach and cook for a few minutes to drive off any remaining liquid.

3 Add the flour and cook gently for 1 minute, stirring. Remove the pan from the heat and gradually stir in the milk. Season with salt and pepper and bring to the boil slowly. Reduce the heat and continue to cook, stirring, until thickened. Cool slightly,

then beat in the egg yolks, one at a time, and 75 g (3 oz) grated cheese.

4 Whisk all four egg whites together until stiff, then fold into the mixture. Spoon into the prepared soufflé dish and sprinkle with the remaining cheese.

5 Stand the dish on a baking sheet and bake in the oven at 190°C (375°F) mark 5 for about 30 minutes or until well risen and just set. Serve immediately.

SERVES 3–4

$\mathcal{B}$ASIC PANCAKES

Pancake batter should be left to stand for about 20 minutes to allow the starch granules to swell; the resulting pancake will be lighter. Use this basic recipe and the variations to create your own sweet or savoury pancake dishes. Almost any mixture of cooked vegetables, pulses and nuts, moistened with one of the sauces in the chapter on page 181 can be used as a pancake filling.

125 g (4 oz) plain flour (all white or half wholemeal and half white)	1 free-range egg
	about 300 ml (½ pint) milk
pinch of salt	vegetable oil

1 Sift the flour and salt into a bowl. Make a well in the centre.

2 Break the egg into the well and add a little of the milk. Mix the liquid ingredients with a wooden spoon, then gradually beat in the flour until smooth.

3 Add 15 ml (1 tbsp) oil and the remaining milk to obtain the consistency of thin cream.

4 Alternatively, the batter can be made by placing all the ingredients in a blender and blending for a few seconds until smooth.

5 Cover the batter and leave to stand in the refrigerator for about 20 minutes.

6 Heat a pancake pan until hot, then brush with the minimum of oil and wipe off any excess. Add a little extra milk to the batter if it has thickened. Pour a small amount of batter into the pan and swirl it around until it is evenly and thinly spread over the bottom of the pan. Cook over a moderate to high heat for about 1 minute or until the edges are curling away from the pan and the underside is golden. Flip the pancake over using a palette knife and cook the second side.

7 Turn the pancake out on to a sheet of greaseproof paper (or non-stick baking

parchment if the pancakes are to be frozen). Loosely fold a clean tea towel over the top.

8 Repeat until all the pancake batter has been used, lightly oiling the pan between pancakes.
MAKES ABOUT 8 PANCAKES

VARIATIONS
Buckwheat Pancakes Prepare as above, replacing half the flour with buckwheat flour. Don't sift the flour.

Spiced Chick-pea Pancakes Prepare as above, replacing the flour with 125 g (4 oz) chick-pea (gram) flour. Toast 10 ml (2 level tsp) cumin seeds under the grill, then grind to a powder. Add to the flour with 1.25 ml (¼ level tsp) ground turmeric. Replace 150 ml (¼ pint) of the milk with water. Use a little more batter each time to make slightly thicker pancakes. Use more oil if necessary.

Sweet Pancakes Use the same basic mixture to make sweet pancakes. Serve sprinkled with sugar and lemon juice or drizzled with honey or maple syrup. Sweet pancakes can be filled with apple purée, bananas or soft fruits, such as strawberries or raspberries, mixed with cream, yogurt or fromage frais.

PANCAKE HINTS

1 To freeze pancakes, cool, then pack interleaved with non-stick baking parchment and freeze for up to 3 months. Thaw overnight at cool room temperature. Reheat wrapped in foil.

2 Pancakes can be wrapped and stored in the refrigerator for several days.

3 To warm pancakes, wrap small stacks in foil. Heat at 190°C (375°F) mark 5 for about 15 minutes.

4 Tortillas (see page 66) are a good vegan alternative to pancakes. They can be used in any of the following recipes.

Spinach–Filled Basic Pancakes

CRESPELLE

Crespelle, sometimes called *crespellini*, are Italian-style pancakes. They are similar to cannelloni in appearance but are made from a pancake batter rather than a pasta dough. Fillings can be as varied as those for cannelloni, so there is no reason to stick to this combination of cheese and spinach, which comes from Florence.

450 g (1 lb) washed fresh spinach, cooked, or 225 g (8 oz) frozen leaf spinach, thawed	*65 g (2½ oz) freshly grated Parmesan cheese*
50 g (2 oz) vegetable margarine or butter	*600 ml (1 pint) Béchamel Sauce (see page 189)*
1 small onion, skinned and finely chopped	*salt and pepper*
	8 Basic Pancakes (see page 62)

1 Drain the spinach well and chop finely.
2 Melt the margarine or butter in a saucepan, add the onion and fry gently for 5 minutes or until soft but not coloured. Stir in the spinach and cook for a further 2 minutes. Remove from the heat and stir in 50 g (2 oz) Parmesan cheese and 90 ml (6 tbsp) béchamel sauce. Season with salt and pepper.
3 Spread an equal amount of the filling on each pancake, leaving a border around the edge. Roll up the pancakes loosely.
4 Arrange the pancakes in a single layer in a buttered ovenproof dish, then pour over the remaining béchamel sauce and sprinkle with the remaining Parmesan cheese.
5 Bake in the oven at 220°C (425°F) mark 7 for 15–20 minutes or until golden brown.
SERVES 4

RATATOUILLE PANCAKES

Buckwheat pancakes, with their distinctive nutty flavour, make the most suitable partners for a ratatouille filling. If buckwheat flour is unavailable, pancakes made with half plain and half wholemeal flour would be the next best thing. Serve with a crisp salad.

½ quantity Ratatouille (see page 96)

8 Buckwheat Pancakes (see page 62)

about 50 g (2 oz) freshly grated Parmesan or Cheddar
   cheese

chopped fresh parsley

1 Divide the ratatouille between the pancakes. Fold to enclose the filling, then arrange in a single layer, seam-side down, in a lightly greased gratin dish.
2 Cover with foil and bake in the oven at 200°C (400°F) mark 6 for 20–25 minutes or until the pancakes are heated through. Sprinkle with the cheese and parsley and serve immediately.
SERVES 4–6

SPICY VEGETABLE PANCAKES

This filling can be made in advance, cooled and stored in the refrigerator ready for reheating when required. If you forget to warm the pancakes, fill them with the vegetable mixture, arrange them in a greased ovenproof dish, cover with foil and bake in the oven at 200°C (400°F) mark 6 for 20–25 minutes.

30 ml (2 level tbsp) grated creamed coconut

30 ml (2 tbsp) vegetable oil

225 g (8 oz) onion, skinned and sliced

1 garlic clove, skinned and crushed

10 ml (2 level tsp) ground coriander

2.5 ml (½ level tsp) chilli powder

1.25 ml (¼ level tsp) ground turmeric

350 g (12 oz) small cauliflower florets

225 g (8 oz) potato, peeled and finely diced

350 g (12 oz) tomatoes, skinned, seeded and roughly
   chopped

1 green pepper, cored, seeded and roughly chopped

30 ml (2 tbsp) lemon juice

salt and pepper

about 8 Spiced Chick-pea Pancakes (see page 62),
   warmed

1 Dissolve the coconut in 200 ml (7 fl oz) hot water.
2 Heat the oil in a large frying pan. Add the onion and garlic with all the spices and cook, stirring, for 2–3 minutes or until the onions are just beginning to soften.
3 Add the cauliflower and the potato, cover and cook gently for 7–8 minutes or until just beginning to soften. Stir in the tomato and green pepper with the coconut water.
4 Cover and simmer gently for about 25 minutes or until the vegetables are tender and the liquid is reduced. Stir in the lemon juice and season with salt and pepper.
5 Divide the filling among the warm pancakes and serve immediately.
SERVES 4–6

SOUFFLÉED BROCCOLI PANCAKES

The crispness of these baked pancakes complements the soft soufflé filling. Each pancake is fairly substantial so serve only with a simple salad.

60 ml (4 tbsp) milk
1 slice each of onion and carrot for flavouring
4 black peppercorns
1 bay leaf
225 g (8 oz) broccoli florets
salt and pepper
50 g (2 oz) vegetable margarine or butter

40 g (1½ oz) plain flour
3 free-range eggs, separated
large pinch of grated nutmeg
50 g (2 oz) mature Cheddar cheese, grated
about 6 Buckwheat Pancakes (see page 62)
30 ml (2 level tbsp) grated Parmesan cheese

1 Put the milk in a small saucepan with the onion and carrot slices, peppercorns and bay leaf. Bring just to the boil, remove from the heat, cover and leave to infuse for about 15 minutes. Strain and discard the flavourings.
2 Cook the broccoli in boiling salted water for 7–8 minutes or until tender, then drain.
3 Melt the margarine or butter in a saucepan, add the flour and cook for 1–2 minutes. Remove from the heat and gradually stir in the flavoured milk. Bring to the boil, stirring all the time; the mixture will be very thick. Allow to cool a little, then beat in the egg yolks.
4 Put the broccoli and sauce in a food processor or blender and blend until smooth. Transfer to a bowl, stir in the nutmeg and

Cheddar cheese and season with salt and pepper.
5 Whisk the egg whites until stiff, but not dry. Stir 30 ml (2 level tbsp) of the egg white into the broccoli mixture to lighten it, then carefully fold in the remainder.
6 Spoon a generous amount of the broccoli mixture down the middle of each pancake. Fold the two sides loosely over the top, then arrange the pancakes side by side in a shallow ovenproof dish. Sprinkle the Parmesan cheese over the top.
7 Bake in the oven immediately, uncovered, at 200°C (400°F) mark 6 for 15–20 minutes or until the soufflé mixture has risen and set and the pancakes are crisp.
SERVES 3–4

ENCHILADAS

If you find the tortillas have cooled too much and become stiff and dry after frying, then immerse each one in the sauce to make it pliable before filling. To make vegan enchiladas, omit the cheese and add an extra can of beans to the filling. Sprinkle the top with a few breadcrumbs.

150 g (5 oz) plain wholemeal flour
150 g (5 oz) plain white flour
salt and pepper
50 g (2 oz) white vegetable fat
vegetable oil for frying
1–2 garlic cloves, skinned and crushed
1–2 fresh green chillies, chopped

1 green pepper, cored, seeded and chopped
450 (1 lb) cooked red kidney beans or two 425 g (15 oz) cans red kidney beans, drained and rinsed
45 ml (3 tbsp) chopped fresh coriander
1½ quantities Tomato Sauce (see page 190)
a few drops of Tabasco
225 g (8 oz) Cheddar cheese, grated

1 To make the tortillas, sift the flours and 7.5 ml (1½ level tsp) salt into a bowl, adding any bran left in the sieve. Rub in the white vegetable fat. Gradually stir in about 150 ml (¼ pint) warm water, or enough to make a pliable dough.

2 Turn the dough on to a lightly floured surface and knead for a few minutes, then divide it into eight equal pieces. Roll out each piece into a 23 cm (9 inch) circle, keeping the remaining pieces of dough covered with a damp cloth.

3 Heat a large, heavy-based frying pan and brush lightly with oil. Cook the tortillas, one at a time, for 1–2 minutes on each side or until lightly flecked with brown and slightly puffed up. When all the tortillas are cooked, stack them between greaseproof paper.

4 To make the filling, heat about 30 ml (2 tbsp) oil in the frying pan and fry the garlic, chillies and green pepper for about 10 minutes or until the pepper is very soft. Meanwhile, mash the beans with 150 ml (¼ pint) water, using a potato masher. Add them to the pan and keep frying and mashing until the mixture is very soft and mushy. Stir in the coriander and season with salt and pepper.

5 Heat the tomato sauce and flavour with Tabasco. Divide the fried bean mixture equally between the tortillas. Sprinkle with half the cheese, then roll up to enclose the filling. Arrange, seam-side down, in a gratin dish. Pour the sauce over the top and sprinkle with the remaining cheese. Bake in the oven at 200°C (400°F) mark 6 for 20–25 minutes or until piping hot.

SERVES 4–6

—FIVE—

PASTRIES, PIES AND FLANS

The art of making good pastry lies in light, careful handling and accurate measuring. For most pastries, plain white or plain wholemeal flour is best; self-raising gives an uneven, crumbly texture.

A good range of ready-made pastries is now available in the shops. Puff and flaky pastry are available frozen or in the chilled cabinet and produce such a good result without the time and effort involved in making them at home, that we have used the shop-bought kind in the following recipes. Likewise, commercially-produced filo pastry is now so widely available, that home-made strudel pastry is a rarity. Vegans should read the labels on the packets carefully when buying ready-made pastry to check the ingredients are suitable.

We recommend that most flans and some pies should be baked blind before the filling is added. This ensures that the pastry is cooked through and remains crisp. Make the pastry and line the flan tin or dish following the recipe, then, if you have time, chill the pastry in the refrigerator for about 30 minutes. This 'rests' the pastry and helps to prevent it shrinking when cooked. This is particularly important if you have over-stretched the pastry when lining the tin. Once chilled, prick the pastry base with a fork and line with a large piece of foil or greaseproof paper. Fill with ceramic 'baking beans' or dried pulses (retain some purely for this purpose). Bake in the oven at 200°C (400°F) mark 6 for 10–15 minutes or until the pastry is firm to the touch. Remove the beans and paper and bake for a further 5–10 minutes or until the base is firm and lightly coloured. Pastry cases which need complete baking should be returned to the oven for a further 15 minutes or until firm and golden brown.

For small pastry cases, it should be sufficient to prick well with a fork before baking. Pastry cases which have been baked blind will keep for several days in an airtight tin, and freeze well.

PROVENÇALE PASTRY

This well flavoured, crisp pastry is best for tarts and quiches. Vegans should omit the egg and increase the oil to 75 ml (5 tbsp) and the water to about 45–60 ml (3–4 tbsp).

225 g (8 oz) plain white flour	*60 ml (4 tbsp) olive oil*
large pinch of salt	*tepid water*
1 free-range egg, beaten	

1 Put the flour and salt in a bowl. Make a well in the centre and add the egg, olive oil and 30–45 ml (2–3 tbsp) tepid water. Mix vigorously with a fork or your fingers until the pastry forms a dough.
2 Knead the dough lightly, then form into a ball, cover with a damp tea towel and leave to rest for 30 minutes before rolling out. Use and bake as directed in individual recipes.

VARIATIONS
Olive Pastry Follow the recipe and method for Provençale Pastry, but stir in 50 g (2 oz) finely chopped black or green olives before adding the liquid.
Cumin Pastry Follow the recipe and method for Provençale Pastry, but fry 5 ml (1 level tsp) crushed cumin seeds in the oil for 2–3 minutes. Cool before adding to the flour.

SHORTCRUST PASTRY

For shortcrust pastry, the proportion of flour to fat is two to one. Therefore, for a recipe using quantities of shortcrust pastry other than 225 g (8 oz), simply use half the quantity of fat to the flour weight specified. This basic pastry is suitable for most pies and flans. To make a sweet pastry, add a little caster sugar to taste.

225 g (8 oz) plain white flour	*125 g (4 oz) vegetable margarine or butter, chilled and diced*
pinch of salt	*chilled water*

1 Put the flour and salt in a bowl. Using both hands, rub the margarine or butter lightly into the flour until the mixture resembles fine breadcrumbs.

2 Gradually add 45–60 ml (3–4 tbsp) water, sprinkling it evenly over the surface. (Uneven addition may cause blistering when the pastry is cooked.) Stir with a round-bladed knife until the mixture begins to stick together in large lumps.

3 With one hand, collect the dough together to form a ball. Knead lightly for a few seconds to give a firm, smooth dough. Do not overhandle the dough.

4 To roll out, sprinkle a little flour on a work surface and the rolling pin (not on the pastry) and roll out the dough evenly in one direction only, turning it occasionally. The usual thickness is 0.3 cm (⅛ inch). Do not pull or stretch the pastry.

5 The pastry can be baked straight away, but it is better if allowed to 'rest' for about 30 minutes in the tin or dish, covered with greaseproof paper or foil, in the refrigerator.

6 Bake at 200–220°C (400–425°F) mark 6–7, except where otherwise specified, until lightly browned (see individual recipes).

VARIATIONS

Wholemeal Pastry (1) Follow the recipe and method for Shortcrust Pastry but use plain wholemeal flour instead of white. You will need to add a little extra water because wholemeal flour is usually more absorbent.

Wholemeal Pastry (2) Follow the recipe and method for Shortcrust Pastry, but replace half the flour with plain wholemeal flour.

Nut Pastry Follow the recipe and method for Shortcrust Pastry using white or wholemeal flour, or half and half, but stir in 40 g (1½ oz) very finely chopped walnuts, peanuts, cashew nuts, hazelnuts or almonds before adding the water. When using salted nuts, do not add salt to the flour.

Cheese Pastry Follow the recipe and method for Shortcrust Pastry using white or wholemeal flour, or half and half, but stir in 125 g (4 oz) finely grated Cheddar or other hard cheese, or 45 ml (3 level tbsp) freshly grated Parmesan cheese, and a pinch of mustard powder before adding the water.

Sesame Pastry Follow the recipe and method for Shortcrust Pastry using white or wholemeal flour, or half and half, but stir in 40 g (1½ oz) toasted sesame seeds before adding the water.

Poppy Seed Pastry Follow the recipe and method for Shortcrust Pastry using white or wholemeal flour, or half and half but stir in 15 g (½ oz) poppy seeds before adding the water.

Herb Pastry Follow the recipe and method for Shortcrust Pastry using white or wholemeal flour, or half and half, but stir in 45 ml (3 level tbsp) chopped fresh mixed herbs before adding the water.

Tarte Provençale

This delicious tart combines all the classic flavours of Provence – aubergine, green pepper, tomato, garlic, olives, marjoram and basil.

1 quantity Provençale Pastry (see page 68)	*1 small garlic clove, skinned and crushed*
30 ml (2 level tbsp) Dijon mustard	*175 g (6 oz) mature Cheddar cheese, grated*
275 g (10 oz) aubergines, very thinly sliced	*salt and pepper*
1 small green pepper, halved, cored and seeded	*2 large tomatoes*
olive oil for brushing	*a few black olives*
3 free-range egg yolks	*a few chopped fresh herbs, such as parsley, marjoram and*
350 ml (12 fl oz) double cream	*basil*

1 Roll out the pastry on a lightly floured surface and use to line a greased shallow 28 cm (11 inch) round loose-bottomed, fluted flan tin. Spread the mustard over the pastry case, cover and chill while preparing the filling.

2 Spread the aubergines in a single layer on an oiled baking sheet. Lay the green pepper halves, cut side down, on a chopping board and cut into very fine slices. Sprinkle over the aubergine and brush with a little olive oil. Bake in the oven at 200°C (400°F) mark 6 for 20 minutes or until the vegetables are slightly softened and tinged with brown.

3 Beat together the egg yolks, cream, garlic and cheese, and season with salt and pepper.

Slice the tomatoes thickly and, using a sharp knife, remove and discard the seeds from each slice.

4 Arrange the tomato slices in a single layer in the pastry case. Top with the aubergine and pepper slices and sprinkle with the olives. Carefully pour the custard mixture over the vegetables so that it just comes to the top of the pastry case. Stand the tart on a baking sheet and bake in the oven at 200°C (400°F) mark 6 for 30 minutes. Sprinkle with the herbs, then continue cooking for 15–20 minutes or until the custard has set. Serve warm or cold.

SERVES 6–8

Rich Leek Tart

This is a really rich, moist, filling tart packed with leeks, cream and cheese. It is everything that a savoury tart should be.

Shortcrust Pastry made with 225 g (8 oz) flour (see page 69)	*225 g (8 oz) Gruyère cheese, grated*
	3 free-range eggs, beaten
50 g (2 oz) vegetable margarine or butter	*salt and pepper*
1.1 kg (2½ lb) leeks, trimmed, washed and thinly sliced	*freshly grated nutmeg*
300 ml (½ pint) soured or double cream	

1 Roll out the pastry and use to line an oiled 23 cm (9 inch) spring-release cake tin or a

very deep flan tin. Cover and chill while making the filling.

2 To make the filling, melt the margarine or butter in a large heavy-based saucepan. Add the leeks and cook over a high heat for 2–3 minutes or until the leeks start to soften, stirring all the time. Cover the pan with a lid, lower the heat and cook for about 30 minutes or until the leeks are very soft. Shake the pan from time to time, but resist lifting the lid or you will lose the steam and the leeks will stick to the pan.

3 Add the cream, most of the cheese and the eggs, and season with salt, pepper and nutmeg. Pour into the prepared pastry case and sprinkle with the remaining cheese.

4 Stand the tart on a baking sheet and bake in the oven at 220°C (425°F) mark 7 for 15 minutes, then reduce the temperature to 190°C (375°F) mark 5 and cook for a further 35–40 minutes or until the filling is set and golden brown. Serve warm or cold.

SERVES 8

ᏚWEET PEPPER AND BASIL FLAN

Grilling the peppers makes the skins easy to remove. It also makes them more digestible.

Shortcrust Pastry made with 175 g (6 oz) flour (see page 69)
2 large red peppers (about 350 g/12 oz total weight)
a few strands of saffron
150 g (5 oz) full-fat soft cheese with garlic and herbs

2 free-range eggs
30 ml (2 level tbsp) chopped fresh basil
15 ml (1 level tbsp) chopped fresh parsley
salt and pepper

1 Roll out the pastry on a lightly floured surface. Place a 20.5 cm (8 inch) plain flan ring on a flat baking sheet and line with the pastry. Cover and chill for 10–15 minutes. Line the pastry with foil or greaseproof paper weighed down with baking beans and bake blind in the oven at 200°C (400°F) mark 6 for 20 minutes or until just cooked through. Remove the beans and paper or foil.

2 Meanwhile, place the peppers under a hot grill and cook for 10–15 minutes, turning frequently, until the skins are charred and black. Cool slightly, then peel off the skins.

Halve the peppers and remove the seeds. Cut into 5 cm (2 inch) pieces.

3 Grind the saffron with a pestle and mortar or in a small heavy bowl with the end of a rolling pin. Whisk together the cheese, eggs, herbs and saffron. Stir in the peppers and season with salt and pepper.

4 Spoon the pepper mixture into the prepared flan case. Bake in the oven at 180°C (350°F) mark 4 for 25–30 minutes or until just set. Brown under a hot grill for 1–2 minutes, if wished. Serve warm.

SERVES 4

GREEN TOMATO AND BASIL FLAN

Try this before your tomatoes ripen. Herb or Poppy Seed Pastry would be best.

Shortcrust Pastry made with 225 g (8 oz) flour (see page 69)	*225 g (8 oz) mature Cheddar cheese, grated*
15 ml (1 tbsp) vegetable oil	*5 ml (1 level tsp) caster sugar*
1 large onion, skinned and chopped	*45 ml (3 level tbsp) chopped fresh basil*
450 g (1 lb) firm green tomatoes, thinly sliced	*225 g (8 oz) mayonnaise*
	salt and pepper

1 On a lightly floured surface, thinly roll out the pastry and use to line the base and sides of a deep 23 cm (9 inch) round, loose-bottomed, fluted flan tin. Chill for 30 minutes.
2 Line the pastry case with foil or greaseproof paper weighed down with baking beans and bake blind at 180°C (350°F) mark 4 for 20–25 minutes or until dry and golden.
3 Meanwhile, heat the oil in a frying pan, add the onion and cook for 3–4 minutes, stirring. Add the tomatoes and cook for a further 3–4 minutes or until beginning to soften.
4 Transfer to a bowl and stir in all the remaining ingredients. Spoon into the flan case and bake at 180°C (350°F) mark 4 for 30–35 minutes or until lightly set and golden brown on top. Serve warm.
SERVES 6–8

AVOCADO PIE

The nutty, garlicky crust for this pie can be made in advance and frozen or stored in an airtight container for up to 2 days. However, the filling will discolour if left for too long, so make it no more than 2 hours before you intend to serve it.

225 g (8 oz) wholemeal breadcrumbs	*15 ml (1 tbsp) tahini (see page 14)*
75 g (3 oz) cashew nuts, almonds or hazelnuts, chopped	*½ cucumber, finely chopped*
large pinch of dried thyme	*2 spring onions, trimmed and finely chopped*
1 garlic clove, skinned and crushed	*2 firm tomatoes, chopped*
125 g (4 oz) vegetable margarine or butter, melted	*5 ml (1 level tsp) caster sugar*
salt and pepper	*Tabasco or chilli sauce, to taste*
2 large ripe avocados	*a few black olives*
15 ml (1 tbsp) raspberry vinegar or lime juice	*chopped fresh coriander, chives, parsley or mint*

1 To make the crust, mix together the breadcrumbs, nuts, thyme, garlic and margarine or butter. Season with salt and pepper. Press over the bottom and sides of a 23 cm (9 inch) flan dish or loose-bottomed flan tin. Bake in the oven at 200°C (400°F) mark 6 for 25–30 minutes or until golden brown and firm to the touch. Leave to cool.
2 To make the filling, halve, stone and peel the avocados and mash the flesh. Mix with all the remaining ingredients, except the olives and herbs. Spoon into the flan case and sprinkle the olives and herbs on top of the pie. Serve within 2 hours or the pie filling will discolour.
SERVES 6

TARTE AU CHÈVRE ET MENTHE

This delicately flavoured, creamy tart is delicious served for lunch with a salad, or in thinner slices as a starter, garnished with extra mint leaves.

Hazelnut Pastry made with 175 g (6 oz) flour (see page 69)	*2 free-range eggs*
175 g (6 oz) mild fresh creamy goats' cheese (chèvre)	*salt and freshly ground black pepper*
300 g (10 oz) fromage frais	*a small handful of fresh mint leaves*

1 Roll out the pastry on a lightly floured surface and use to line a greased 23 cm (9 inch) shallow, loose-bottomed, fluted flan tin. Cover and chill while making the filling.

2 To make the filling, beat the cheese until smooth. Gradually beat in the fromage frais, followed by the eggs. Season with salt and pepper.

3 Line the pastry case with foil or greaseproof paper weighed down with baking beans and bake blind in the oven at 200°C (400°F) mark 6

for 10–15 minutes, then remove the paper and beans and bake for a further 5 minutes until the pastry base is cooked through.

4 Stir the filling, then pour it into the pastry case. Sprinkle with the mint leaves and grind a little black pepper over the top. Bake in the oven at 200°C (400°F) mark 6 for about 15 minutes or until firm to the touch. Cook under a hot grill for 2–3 minutes until browned. Serve warm or cold.

SERVES 6

CATALAN PIE

When the recipes in this book were tested, this was one of the most popular. Based on a traditional Spanish pie, it is packed with flavour and texture. We liked it best served with a crisp mixed leaf salad. Before rolling out the pastry, check the size of your baking sheet. If the measurements given in the recipe are too large, make a shorter, squarer pie that will fit on your baking sheet.

175 g (6 oz) strong white flour, plus extra for sprinkling	2 large garlic cloves, skinned and crushed
50 g (2 oz) cornmeal (maize meal), plus extra for sprinkling	15 ml (1 level tbsp) mild chilli powder
	450 g (1 lb) ripe tomatoes, roughly chopped
15 ml (1 level tbsp) sugar	225 g (8 oz) courgettes, trimmed and roughly chopped
salt and pepper	3 hard-boiled free-range eggs, shelled and chopped
5 ml (1 level tsp) fast-action dried yeast	25 g (1 oz) sultanas or raisins
30 ml (2 tbsp) olive oil, plus extra for brushing	30 ml (2 tbsp) capers
350 g (12 oz) onions, skinned and roughly chopped	25 g (1 oz) pine nuts

1 Put the flour, cornmeal, sugar, 5 ml (1 level tsp) salt and the yeast in a bowl. Mix together, then make a well in the centre and add 150 ml (¼ pint) warm water. Stir together to make a dough, adding a little extra liquid if necessary.

2 Turn the dough on to a lightly floured surface and knead for 5–10 minutes or until smooth and elastic. Cover and leave to rise in a warm place for about 35 minutes or until doubled in size.

3 Meanwhile, heat the 30 ml (2 tbsp) olive oil in a heavy-based saucepan with a lid. Add the onions, garlic and chilli powder and cook over a high heat for 5 minutes, stirring all the time. Cover the pan, reduce the heat and cook for 15–20 minutes or until the onions are soft. Add the tomatoes and courgettes and cook for 5 minutes, stirring occasionally. If the mixture is very wet, cook over a high heat for a little longer to evaporate excess moisture. Add the eggs, sultanas or raisins, capers and pine nuts, season with salt and pepper, and leave to cool.

4 Turn the dough out on to a lightly floured surface and knead for 1–2 minutes. Divide it in half and roll one half into a rectangle measuring about 33 × 25.5 cm (13 × 10 inches). Transfer the dough to an oiled baking sheet and cover with the filling, spreading it almost to the edges.

5 Roll out the remaining dough to the same size and place on top of the filling. Twist the edges together to seal. Brush the pie with olive oil, cover loosely with a clean tea towel and leave in a warm place until slightly risen.

6 Mark small indentations all over the pie with the end of a chopstick or your little finger. Sprinkle with cornmeal and bake in the oven at 230°C (450°F) mark 8 for about 20 minutes or until well risen and golden brown. Serve warm or cold.
SERVES 6

VARIATIONS
For a vegan version of this delicious pie, omit the eggs and replace with one of the following: 125 g (4 oz) chopped tofu; 125 g (4 oz) roughly chopped nuts; 125 g (4 oz) cooked and slightly mashed red kidney beans; 125 g (4 oz) cooked black-eyed beans.

ℬEAN AND POTATO PIE

Before rolling out the pastry, check that your baking sheet is large enough. If not, make the pie shorter and squarer to fit. Serve with a mixed salad or steamed fresh vegetables.

450 g (1 lb) floury potatoes (such as King Edward or Maris Piper), peeled and roughly chopped	*150 g (5 oz) full-fat soft cheese with garlic and herbs*
salt and pepper	*225 g (8 oz) cooked black-eyed beans or one 425 g (15 oz) can black-eyed beans, drained and rinsed*
30 ml (2 tbsp) vegetable oil	*freshly grated nutmeg*
1 large onion, skinned and chopped	*two 370 g (13 oz) packets frozen puff pastry, thawed*
450 g (1 lb) leeks, trimmed, washed and sliced	*water, milk or beaten egg, to glaze*
225 g (8 oz) mushrooms, wiped and sliced	*sesame seeds*
125 g (4 oz) fresh spinach, trimmed and washed	

1 Cook the potatoes in boiling, salted water for 10–15 minutes or until tender. Drain well and leave to cool.

2 Meanwhile, heat the oil in a large saucepan, add the onion and leeks and fry for 5–10 minutes or until soft. Add the mushrooms and continue cooking until the mushrooms are soft. Add the spinach and cook for 1 minute or until the spinach is just wilted. Add the full-fat soft cheese, the beans and potatoes and season generously with salt, pepper and nutmeg. Leave to cool.

3 Thinly roll out one packet of pastry on a lightly floured surface to a rectangle measuring about 33 cm (13 inches) long and 25.5 cm (10 inches) wide. Transfer the pastry to a baking sheet.

4 Spoon the filling on to the pastry, leaving a 2.5 cm (1 inch) border around the edges. Roll out the second piece of pastry and use to cover the first. Brush the edges with water, milk or beaten egg and press together to seal. Lightly mark squares on the pastry with the back of a knife. Brush with milk or beaten egg and sprinkle with sesame seeds. Bake in the oven at 200°C (400°F) mark 6 for 30–35 minutes or until well risen and golden brown.
SERVES 6

𝒱EGETABLE STRUDEL

Savoury strudels are delicious. Vary the filling to make use of seasonal vegetables, or add a few cooked beans or nuts. Serve with steamed vegetables and one of the sauces on pages 181–194.

150 g (5 oz) vegetable margarine or butter	*15 ml (1 tbsp) lemon juice*
30 ml (2 tbsp) olive oil	*300 ml (½ pint) fromage frais*
450 g (1 lb) waxy potatoes (such as Maris Bard or Wilja), peeled and diced	*ground mixed spice*
450 g (1 lb) parsnips, trimmed, peeled and diced	*salt and pepper*
225 g (8 oz) leeks, trimmed, washed and sliced	*mild paprika*
1 small bunch of spring onions, trimmed and chopped	*4 large sheets of filo pastry, each measuring 45.5 × 30.5 cm (18 × 12 inches)*
450 g (1 lb) spring greens	*75 g (3 oz) ground almonds*
1 garlic clove, skinned and crushed	*a few poppy seeds*

Vegetable Strudel

1 Melt 50 g (2 oz) of the margarine or butter with half the olive oil in a large saucepan. Add the potatoes, parsnips, leeks and spring onions and fry for 4–5 minutes, stirring all the time. Add 100 ml (4 fl oz) water, reduce the heat, cover and cook gently for 10–15 minutes. Leave to cool.

2 Meanwhile, remove the tough stalks from the spring greens and discard. Finely shred the leaves. Heat 25 g (1 oz) of the remaining margarine or butter with the remaining olive oil in a large frying pan, add the greens and garlic and stir-fry for 2–3 minutes or until softened. Do not overcook. Stir in the lemon juice and leave to cool.

3 Stir the fromage frais into the potato and leek mixture and season with a little mixed spice, salt, pepper and paprika.

4 Melt the remaining margarine or butter. Lay one sheet of filo pastry on a clean work surface and brush lightly with melted fat. Take a second sheet of pastry and place it so that it overlaps the first sheet to make a 45.5 cm (18 inch) square. Brush lightly with melted fat. Repeat with the remaining filo pastry to make a double thickness. Sprinkle the ground almonds evenly over the pastry.

5 Spoon half the potato mixture over the bottom quarter of the pastry, leaving a border around the edge. Top with the spring green mixture and the remaining potato.

6 Carefully fold the sides over the filling, then, starting from the filled end, roll the strudel up like a Swiss roll. Carefully transfer to a baking sheet, seam-side down. Brush with melted fat, sprinkle with poppy seeds and bake in the oven at 200°C (400°F) mark 6 for 20–25 minutes or until golden brown. Leave to stand for 5 minutes before serving.
SERVES 6

ROQUEFORT FEUILLETÉ

Roquefort is a little town in the northern hills of Languedoc and it is there, in the limestone caves, that this famous cheese gains its special flavour. Made from sheep's milk, it has a creamy texture and strong, salty taste.

25 g (1 oz) vegetable margarine or butter
2 medium onions, skinned and sliced
60 ml (4 tbsp) single cream
15 ml (1 level tbsp) chopped fresh rosemary

freshly ground black pepper
175 g (6 oz) Roquefort cheese, crumbled
225 g (8 oz) frozen puff pastry, thawed
1 free-range egg, beaten

1 Melt the margarine or butter in a frying pan, add the onion and cook for 5–10 minutes or until it softens and begins to brown. Drain on absorbent kitchen paper and cool.
2 Whisk together the cream and rosemary, and season with pepper. Add the cheese.
3 Divide the pastry in half and roll out each piece thinly to an oblong about 30.5 × 20.5 cm (12 × 8 inches). Place one on a baking sheet.
4 Spread the onion down the centre of the pastry, leaving a clear border around the edge. Spoon over the cheese mixture. Brush the edges with beaten egg, then top with the second piece of pastry, sealing well. Trim and knock up the edges. Glaze the feuilleté with the remaining egg and decorate with strips made from pastry trimmings. Make a few holes in the top to allow steam to escape.
5 Bake in the oven at 220°C (425°F) mark 7 for 15 minutes or until well browned. Reduce the heat to 180°C (350°F) mark 4, cover the feuilleté loosely with foil and bake for a further 10 minutes. Cool slightly before serving.
SERVES 6

WILD MUSHROOM STRUDEL

This savoury strudel relies on the use of wild mushrooms. Shiitake mushrooms are available fresh from some supermarkets, or you can order them from your greengrocer. Alternatively, replace them with fresh oyster mushrooms. If fresh wild mushrooms are not available, soak a small packet of dried *porcini* (cep) mushrooms for 30 minutes in warm water, strain and substitute for 50 g (2 oz) of the total weight of mushrooms required.

225 g (8 oz) long-grain brown rice
salt and pepper
450 g (1 lb) mixed mushrooms, such as shiitake, morel, flat and field
65 g (2½ oz) vegetable margarine or butter
450 g (1 lb) leeks, trimmed, washed and finely chopped
65 g (2½ oz) walnut pieces, finely chopped

10 ml (2 level tsp) chopped fresh oregano
20 ml (4 tsp) soy sauce
5 ml (1 level tsp) yeast extract
4 sheets of filo pastry, each measuring about 45.5 × 30.5 cm (18 × 12 inches)
sesame seeds
Brandy and Celery Sauce (see page 194), to serve

Wild Mushroom Strudel

1 Cook the rice in boiling salted water for about 20 minutes or until tender. Drain and cool. Finely chop the shiitake and morel mushrooms; roughly chop the flat and field mushrooms.

2 Melt 25 g (1 oz) of the margarine or butter in a large frying pan. Add the leeks and fry for 1–2 minutes. Stir in the mushrooms and continue cooking for about 8 minutes or until quite tender and all excess moisture has been driven off. Mix in the walnuts, oregano, soy sauce, yeast extract and rice. Season with salt and pepper, turn out into a bowl and leave to cool.

3 Melt the remaining margarine or butter. Layer up three sheets of pastry, brushing each sheet with melted margarine or butter. Cut in half crossways. You can leave the pastry whole here and make one long strudel, but we found shorter strudels were easier to roll up.

4 Spoon the filling over the two stacks of sheets, leaving a narrow border around the edge of each. Fold in the sides and roll up the strudels. Transfer to a lightly greased baking sheet and brush with melted margarine or butter. Crumple the remaining pastry decoratively on top, brush with the remaining margarine or butter and sprinkle with sesame seeds.

5 Bake at 220°C (425°F) mark 7 for 25–30 minutes or until the pastry is crisp and golden. Serve accompanied by Brandy and Celery Sauce (see page 194).
SERVES 8

$\mathcal{T}$OMATO AND LENTIL PIE

This pie is light and moist in texture with a crumbly cheese crust. Serve hot, cold or just warm with baked potatoes cooked in the oven at the same time as the pie.

175 g (6 oz) vegetable margarine or butter	5 ml (1 level tsp) dried basil
125 g (4 oz) leeks, trimmed, washed and finely chopped	15 ml (1 tbsp) lemon juice
175 g (6 oz) split red lentils	2 free-range eggs
1 garlic clove, skinned and crushed	salt and pepper
about 500 ml (18 fl oz) vegetable stock	225 g (8 oz) plain white flour
2 tomatoes, skinned and chopped	50 g (2 oz) mature Cheddar cheese, finely grated

1 Melt 50 g (2 oz) of the margarine or butter in a saucepan, add the leeks and cook for about 10 minutes or until golden. Add the lentils and garlic and stir for 1–2 minutes to cover the lentils in fat. Add the stock, bring to the boil, then reduce the heat, half cover with a lid and simmer for about 20 minutes or until the lentils are soft, stirring occasionally. (There should be little free liquid, so stir over a high heat to drive off any excess.) Cool slightly.

2 Remove the pan from the heat and add the tomatoes, basil, lemon juice and 1 egg. Season with salt and pepper and leave to cool.

3 Meanwhile, make the pastry. Place the flour in a bowl and, using a fork, 'cut' in the remaining margarine or butter until the mixture resembles breadcrumbs. Stir in the cheese and add half the second egg, beaten, and about 45 ml (3 tbsp) cold water to form a soft dough.

4 Cover the pastry and chill for 15 minutes, then roll out two-thirds on a lightly floured surface and use to line a 20.5 cm (8 inch) flan dish. Spoon in the cooled lentil mixture and level the surface. Roll out the remaining pastry and use to cover the pie, sealing the edges well. Brush with the remaining egg.

5 Bake in the oven at 200°C (400°F) mark 6 for 40 minutes or until golden brown.

SERVES 4–6

$\mathcal{S}$PANAKOPITTES

Serve these small triangular pastries with Tzatziki, Hummus and olives to make a delicious Greek-style starter. They're also good for packed lunches or as part of a buffet (see the picture on pages 100–101).

30 ml (2 tbsp) olive oil	75 g (3 oz) feta cheese, crumbled
1 small onion, skinned and chopped	1 egg, beaten
1 garlic clove, skinned and crushed	pepper
227 g (8 oz) packet frozen chopped spinach, thawed and squeezed dry	175 g (6 oz) filo pastry
	125 g (4 oz) vegetable margarine or butter, melted

1 Heat the oil in a saucepan, add the onion and garlic and fry gently for 5 minutes or until soft. Remove the pan from the heat and stir in the spinach, cheese and egg. Season with pepper.

2 Cut the filo pastry sheets widthways into

5 cm (2 inch) strips. Cover with a slightly damp tea towel.

3 Brush one strip of the pastry with melted margarine or butter and place 5 ml (1 tsp) of the spinach mixture at the end of the strip.

4 Fold one corner of the strip diagonally over the filling, so the short edge lies on top of the long edge and forms a right angle.

5 Continue folding the pastry at right angles until you reach the end of the strip, forming a

neat triangular package. Repeat with the remaining strips and filling to make about 50 triangles.

6 Place the packages, seam side down, in a large roasting tin, and brush with melted margarine or butter. Bake in the oven at 220°C (425°F) mark 7 for 15 minutes or until golden brown. Serve hot.
MAKES ABOUT 50

SPICY VEGETABLE PIE

Serve with steamed broccoli and green beans.

4 carrots, trimmed, peeled and thinly sliced	125 g (4 oz) Cheddar cheese, grated
4 leeks, washed, trimmed and thickly sliced	1.25 ml (¼ level tsp) ground mace
6 courgettes, washed, trimmed and thinly sliced	45 ml (3 level tbsp) chopped fresh coriander or parsley
salt and pepper	Wholemeal Pastry made with 125 g (4 oz) flour
125 g (4 oz) vegetable margarine or butter	(see page 69)
1 onion, skinned and sliced	beaten egg, to glaze
10 ml (2 level tsp) ground cumin	freshly grated Parmesan cheese
50 g (2 oz) plain wholemeal flour	pinch of cayenne pepper or paprika (optional)
450 ml (¾ pint) milk, plus 30 ml (2 tbsp)	

1 Blanch the carrots, leeks and courgettes in boiling salted water for 1 minute only. Drain.

2 Melt 40 g (1½ oz) margarine or butter in a heavy-based frying pan, add the onion and cumin and fry gently for 5 minutes or until soft. Add the carrots, leeks and courgettes and fry for a further 5 minutes, stirring to coat in the onion mixture. Remove from the heat.

3 Melt the remaining margarine or butter in a separate pan, sprinkle in the flour and cook for 1–2 minutes or until lightly coloured, stirring constantly. Remove from the heat and gradually whisk in 450 ml (¾ pint) milk. Return to the heat and simmer for 5 minutes or until thick and smooth, stirring constantly.

4 Stir in the Cheddar cheese and mace, and season with salt and pepper. Fold into the vegetables with the chopped coriander or parsley and 30 ml (2 tbsp) milk, then turn into a 900 ml (1½ pint) ovenproof pie dish. Leave

for 2 hours or until the pie filling is cold.

5 Meanwhile, make the pastry following the recipe on page 69. Cover and chill.

6 Remove the pastry from the refrigerator and roll it out on a lightly floured surface to a round or oval about 5 cm (2 inches) larger than the pie dish. Cut a strip from the outside edge of the pastry. Moisten the rim of the pie dish with water and place the pastry strip on the rim.

7 Use the remaining pastry as a lid. Moisten the strip of dough, then place the lid on top and press to seal. Trim, knock up and flute the edge. Decorate the top with pastry trimmings. Brush the pastry with beaten egg and sprinkle with Parmesan and cayenne or paprika, if using. Bake in the oven at 190°C (375°F) mark 5 for 20–25 minutes or until the pastry is cooked. Serve hot.
SERVES 4

CHESTNUT PÂTÉ PLAIT

A rich, well flavoured filling enclosed by a plait of light, buttery brioche. If serving for a special occasion, such as Christmas, go to town on the decoration and make leaves and berries.

450 g (1 lb) strong plain flour	225 g (8 oz) open-cup mushrooms, wiped and finely chopped
10 ml (2 level tsp) fast-action dried yeast	100 ml (4 fl oz) vegetable stock
10 ml (2 level tsp) salt	15 ml (1 tbsp) hot horseradish relish
1 free-range egg, beaten	30 ml (2 tbsp) mushroom ketchup
125 g (4 oz) vegetable margarine or butter, melted	salt and pepper
30 ml (2 tbsp) vegetable oil	50 g (2 oz) no-need-to-soak stoned prunes
5 ml (1 level tsp) dried thyme	25 g (1 oz) shelled pistachios
2 celery sticks, trimmed and finely chopped	30 ml (2 tbsp) chopped fresh parsley
1 parsnip, trimmed, peeled and finely chopped	beaten free-range egg, to glaze
1 onion, skinned and chopped	
2 garlic cloves, skinned and crushed	
439 g (15.5 oz) can unsweetened chestnuts, drained and rinsed	

1 Mix together the flour, yeast and salt in a bowl. Make a well in the centre, then pour in the egg, melted margarine or butter and about 200 ml (7 fl oz) tepid water, or enough to make a soft, smooth dough. Beat thoroughly until the dough leaves the sides of the bowl clean.

2 Turn the dough on to a lightly floured surface and knead for about 10 minutes or until smooth and elastic. Put the dough in a large bowl, cover with a clean tea towel and leave in a warm place for about 1 hour or until doubled in size.

3 Meanwhile, make the filling. Heat the oil in a large saucepan and fry the thyme, celery, parsnip, onion and garlic for 5–10 minutes or until softened, stirring. Roughly chop half the chestnuts and add to the pan with the mushrooms, stock, horseradish relish and ketchup. Cover the pan and cook for 15 minutes, stirring occasionally. Season generously with salt and pepper. Remove from the heat and leave to cool.

4 Turn the dough on to a lightly floured surface and knead until smooth. Reserve a small piece for decoration and roll the remaining dough to a rectangle measuring 38 × 30.5 cm (15 × 12 inches). Spoon the filling down the centre of the dough, leaving a 7.5 cm (3 inch) border around the edges. Arrange the remaining chestnuts, the prunes and pistachios down the centre of the filling. Sprinkle with the parsley.

5 Cut the dough diagonally into 1 cm (½ inch) strips on either side of the filling. Fold each end over the filling, then plait the pastry over the filling to enclose it completely. Decorate with shapes cut from the reserved dough. Brush with beaten egg and transfer to a baking sheet. Bake in the oven at 200°C (400°F) mark 6 for about 30 minutes or until risen and firm to the touch. Leave to stand for 5 minutes, then remove and transfer to a serving dish. Serve hot with 'Gravy' (page 190).
SERVES ABOUT 6

—Six—

Curries, Casseroles and
Stews

ere are beans, lentils and vegetables combined with spices, flavourings and herbs to make comforting, hearty meals. Influenced by the cuisines of several continents, the dishes in this chapter make cosmopolitan eating. Indian vegetarian food is always popular; a meal composed of several curry dishes, a delicately spiced basmati pilaff, Nan-style Bread (see page 155) served with chutney or raita is a good way to entertain a large group of people.

Chilled lager or lassi are the appropriate drinks to serve. In India, lassi is either sweet or salty. To make the salty version, mix equal quantities of natural yogurt and water in a blender or food processor. Add salt and dry-fried ground cumin or finely chopped fresh mint to taste. Sweet lassi is made in the same way but flavoured with sugar, ground cardamom or a little rosewater. Serve both salty and sweet lassi in tall glasses filled with crushed ice.

If you prefer something less spicy, try Rich Winter Casserole (see page 95), or Root Vegetable and Tahini Stew (see page 88). Serve these with good, old-fashioned accompaniments like dumplings, cobblers and polenta (see page 142). Make dumplings by mixing 125 g (4 oz) self-raising flour with 50 g (2 oz) vegetable suet. Add salt and

chopped fresh mixed herbs to taste and enough water to mix to a smooth dough. Shape into small balls and add to the casserole or stew about 15–20 minutes before the cooking time is complete. Simmer gently on top of the cooker or bake in the oven at 200°C (400°F) mark 6 unless otherwise stated. Don't let the liquid boil vigorously or the dumplings will disintegrate.

To make a cobbler topping, mix 225 g (8 oz) self-raising flour with a pinch of salt and rub in 50 g (2 oz) butter or margarine. Flavour with a few chopped herbs and a little cheese, then mix to a soft dough with milk. Knead together and roll out on a floured surface as if making scones. Cut out shapes and brush with milk. Arrange overlapping around the edge of the casserole, then bake in the oven at 220°C (425°F) mark 7 for 10–15 minutes or until golden brown.

Highly spiced or seasoned curries, casseroles or stews tend to develop a faint 'musty' flavour after any length of time in the freezer. This is particularly true of strong garlic-flavoured dishes, so if you're planning on long-term freezer storage it's wise to add the garlic when reheating. Casseroles thickened with flour may thin down on freezing, so it may be necessary to thicken the sauce again after reheating.

CAULIFLOWER IN CURRY SAUCE

This curry sauce can be used for other vegetables besides cauliflower. Potatoes, peas, okra, mushrooms, carrots and aubergines can all be cooked in the same way as the cauliflower, although the cooking time will vary.

1 large cauliflower	5 ml (1 level tsp) salt
90 ml (6 tbsp) vegetable ghee or oil	5 ml (1 level tsp) ground turmeric
5 ml (1 level tsp) black mustard seeds	3 tomatoes, skinned and finely chopped
5 ml (1 level tsp) cumin seeds	1 small green chilli, seeded and finely chopped
5 cm (2 inch) piece of fresh root ginger, peeled and finely chopped	2.5 ml (½ level tsp) sugar
1 small onion, skinned and finely chopped	30 ml (2 level tbsp) chopped fresh coriander

1 Divide the cauliflower into small florets, discarding the green leaves and tough stalks. Wash the florets well and dry on absorbent kitchen paper.

2 Heat the ghee or oil in a heavy-based saucepan or flameproof casserole. Add the mustard seeds and, when they begin to pop, stir in the cumin seeds, ginger, onion, salt and turmeric. Fry for 2–3 minutes, stirring constantly.

3 Add the cauliflower and mix well to coat with the spice mixture. Stir in the tomatoes, chilli, sugar and half of the coriander. Cover the pan tightly with a lid and cook gently for 15 minutes or until the cauliflower is tender but not mushy.

4 Uncover the pan and boil rapidly for 1–2 minutes to thicken the sauce. Turn into a warmed serving dish and sprinkle with the remaining chopped coriander. Serve immediately.

SERVES 4 AS AN ACCOMPANIMENT

VEGETABLE CURRY

Don't be put off by this list of spices; mixing them youself gives an infinitely better flavour than commercially prepared curry powder. Make coconut milk by mixing one 225 g (8 oz) block of creamed coconut or one 100 g (3.5 oz) packet of instant coconut milk powder with 600 ml (1 pint) boiling water. Serve this curry with plain boiled rice, pickles and Nan-style Bread (see page 155) or Parathas (see page 156).

1 medium onion, skinned and chopped	8 whole cloves
2.5 cm (1 inch) piece of fresh root ginger, peeled	8 green cardamom pods
1–2 garlic cloves, skinned	1 cinnamon stick
2 fresh green chillies, seeded	1.4 kg (3 lb) mixed vegetables, including cauliflower
30 ml (2 tbsp) vegetable ghee or oil	florets, carrots, potato, parsnip, turnip and frozen peas,
10 ml (2 level tsp) ground turmeric	prepared as necessary and cut into large chunks
10 ml (2 level tsp) ground coriander	600 ml (1 pint) coconut milk
10 ml (2 level tsp) ground cumin	salt and pepper
5 ml (1 level tsp) ground fenugreek	

1 Put the onion, ginger, garlic and chillies in a blender or food processor and purée until almost smooth.

2 Heat the ghee or oil in a large, heavy-based saucepan, add the onion mixture and fry for 5 minutes, stirring constantly. Add all the spices and cook over a high heat for 3–4 minutes, stirring all the time.

3 Add the vegetables to the pan and stir to coat in the spice paste. Gradually stir in the coconut milk and 300 ml (½ pint) water. Bring to the boil, then lower the heat, cover and simmer for 45 minutes–1 hour or until the vegetables are just tender (the time depending on the type of vegetables used). Season with salt and pepper. Leave to stand for 5 minutes to let the flavours develop, then serve.

SERVES 4–6 AS A MAIN COURSE

VEGETABLE KORMA

This traditional southern Indian dish is extremely rich because it contains double cream and ground almonds. Serve it with a spinach curry, a rice pilaff and a dal dish.

30 ml (2 tbsp) vegetable ghee or oil	900 g (2 lb) mixed vegetables, including some root vegetables, prepared as necessary and cut into chunks
1 large onion, skinned and chopped	
1–2 garlic cloves, skinned and crushed	10 ml (2 level tsp) ground turmeric
2.5 cm (1 inch) piece of fresh root ginger, peeled and chopped	finely grated rind and juice of ½ lime or lemon
	50 g (2 oz) ground almonds
15 ml (1 tbsp) coriander seeds	200 ml (7 fl oz) double cream
5 ml (1 tsp) whole cloves	salt
10 ml (2 tsp) black peppercorns	50 g (2 oz) flaked almonds, toasted
6 green cadamom pods	45 ml (3 tbsp) chopped fresh coriander (optional)

1 Heat the ghee or oil in a large, heavy-based saucepan. Add the onion, garlic and ginger and fry very gently, stirring frequently, for about 10 minutes or until soft and lightly coloured.

2 Meanwhile, finely grind the whole spices and peppercorns in an electric grinder or using a pestle and mortar. Add to the pan and fry for 2 minutes, stirring all the time. Increase the heat, add the vegetables and turmeric and fry for 1–2 minutes. Add the lime or lemon rind and juice, the almonds and 300 ml (½ pint) water. Cover and simmer gently for 30–40 minutes or until the vegetables are just tender (the time depending on the type of vegetables used).

3 Slowly stir in the cream and a little water if the korma is too dry. Season with salt and cook gently until heated through. Transfer to a warmed serving dish, sprinkle with the almonds and coriander, if using, and serve immediately.

SERVES 4–6 AS A MAIN COURSE

VARIATION
Quorn Korma (serves 3) Follow the above recipe up to adding the water in step 2. Bring to the boil, cover and simmer for about 20 minutes, stirring occasionally. Stir in the cream and 250 g (9 oz) Quorn and complete step 3.

PANEER

Paneer is a fresh, soft cheese frequently used in Indian dishes. It holds its shape well and cooks to a delicious golden brown colour when fried or grilled. It's not widely available commercially, and there is no reasonable substitute, so it is worth making it at home. Use paneer in Indian dishes or chop it and sauté with spices, herbs and vegetables of your choice. It's also good in stir-fries or in a sauce as a pancake filling. For a firm, creamy texture, use Channel Islands milk; full-cream and semi-skimmed give a softer result.

2.3 litres (4 pints) pasteurised Channel Islands, full-cream or semi-skimmed milk	about 75 ml (5 tbsp) strained lemon juice

1 Pour the milk into a large, heavy-based saucepan and bring to a full rolling boil. Remove the pan from the heat and stir in the lemon juice.

2 Return to the heat and heat for about 1 minute until the curds and whey separate. If the curds do not separate after this time, return the pan to the heat and heat for 30 seconds more. If it still hasn't separated, add a little more lemon juice and heat again.

3 Line a colander with a double thickness of muslin. Pour the mixture through the muslin. Gather up the corners of the muslin and squeeze all the liquid out of the curd.

4 Drain off the remaining whey by hanging the muslin bundle from the taps over the sink or from a suitable kitchen cupboard over a bowl. Leave it to drain for about 3 hours or until firm when squeezed. Paneer can be kept successfully in the refrigerator for up to 4 days.

MAKES ABOUT 275 G (10 OZ)

VARIATIONS

Add any flavourings for paneer at the end of step 3.

Roasted Cumin Paneer Heat 5 ml (1 tsp) vegetable oil in a small frying pan. Add 10 ml (2 level tsp) cumin seeds and fry for 1–2 minutes, stirring all the time. Finely crush in a pestle and mortar.

Mixed Herb Paneer Add 30 ml (2 level tbsp) chopped fresh mixed herbs.

Garlic Paneer Add 1 small garlic clove, skinned and crushed.

Garlic and Herb Paneer Add 1 small garlic clove, skinned and crushed, and 30 ml (2 level tbsp) chopped fresh mixed herbs.

$\mathcal{M}$UTTAR PANEER

Serve this dish as a main course, accompanied by Indian bread and a dal dish, such as Dry Moong Dal (see page 88).

275 g (10 oz) Paneer (see page 86)	*5 ml (1 level tsp) garam masala*
vegetable oil for frying	*2.5 ml (½ level tsp) chilli powder*
2 medium onions, skinned and roughly chopped	*350 g (12 oz) shelled fresh or frozen peas*
2.5 cm (1 inch) piece of fresh root ginger, peeled and roughly chopped	*4 small tomatoes, skinned and finely chopped*
1 garlic clove, skinned and crushed	*100 ml (4 fl oz) vegetable stock*
5 ml (1 level tsp) ground turmeric	*salt*
	30 ml (2 level tbsp) chopped fresh coriander

1 Cut the paneer into small cubes. Heat a little vegetable oil in a deep, heavy-based frying pan until very hot.

2 Add the cubes of paneer to the oil and fry until golden on all sides, turning once. Remove from the oil and drain on absorbent kitchen paper.

3 Pour off all but about 60 ml (4 tbsp) of the oil. Add the onions, ginger and garlic and fry gently, stirring frequently, for 10 minutes. Add the turmeric, garam masala and chilli powder and fry for a further 2 minutes.

4 Add the peas and tomatoes to the pan and stir to combine with the spiced onion mixture. Add the stock, season with salt, then cover tightly and simmer gently for 15 minutes or until the peas are tender.

5 Add the paneer and coriander. Shake the pan gently to mix the cheese with the peas. Simmer for a further 5 minutes before serving.

SERVES 3–4 AS A MAIN COURSE

Root Vegetable and Tahini Stew

This simple, earthy dish makes a satisfying meal on its own. Cut the vegetables into good-sized chunks to make sure the finished stew has plenty of texture.

30 ml (2 tbsp) vegetable oil	450 ml (¾ pint) vegetable stock
225 g (8 oz) carrots, trimmed, peeled and sliced	2 bay leaves
225 g (8 oz) parsnips, trimmed, peeled and sliced	175 g (6 oz) French beans, topped, tailed and halved
225 g (8 oz) old potatoes, peeled and roughly chopped	150 ml (¼ pint) soured cream or fromage frais
2 medium onions, skinned and chopped	45 ml (3 tbsp) sesame seeds, toasted
225 g (8 oz) swede, peeled and roughly chopped	salt and pepper
60 ml (4 tbsp) tahini (see page 14)	

1 Heat the oil in a large heavy-based frying pan or flameproof casserole over a high heat. Add all the vegetables, except the French beans, and fry for 4–5 minutes or until they are just beginning to brown and soften.
2 Stir the tahini into the vegetable stock, then pour over the vegetables. Add the bay leaves. Bring to the boil, then reduce the

heat, cover and simmer for 15 minutes. Add the French beans, re-cover and simmer for a further 20–25 minutes or until all the vegetables are tender.
3 Stir in the soured cream or fromage frais and sesame seeds. Season with salt and pepper and serve immediately.
SERVES 4 AS A MAIN COURSE

Dry Moong Dal

Serve this spicy, dry dal dish as part of an Indian-style meal. It's also delicious flavoured with the finely grated rind of 1–2 lemons and crushed garlic, to taste.

225 g (8 oz) moong dal (mung beans)	1.25 ml (¼ level tsp) ground turmeric
30 ml (2 tbsp) vegetable oil	pinch of cayenne pepper
10 ml (2 level tsp) ground cumin	salt
10 ml (2 level tsp) ground coriander	Crisp Fried Onions (see page 115), to serve

1 Pick over the dal and remove any grit or discoloured pulses. Put into a sieve and wash thoroughly under cold running water. Drain well. Put the dal into a bowl and cover with cold water. Leave to soak for about 4 hours.
2 Drain the dal. Heat the oil in a large saucepan and stir in the cumin, coriander, turmeric and cayenne. Add the drained dal

and stir together. Add 300 ml (½ pint) water and season with salt.
3 Bring to the boil, then reduce the heat, cover and simmer for 25–30 minutes or until the dal is tender and the water absorbed.
4 Turn the dal into a warmed serving dish and sprinkle with the onions. Serve hot.
SERVES 4–6 AS AN ACCOMPANIMENT

$\mathcal{B}$OSTON BAKED BEANS

There are many versions of this classic dark, rich New England dish and they all vary enormously, so much so that haricot beans and black treacle or molasses seem to be the only constants. The chilli sauce and garlic are not particularly traditional and may be omitted if you prefer your beans less spicy. This recipe includes Worcestershire sauce, vegetarian brands of which are quite readily available. Check the label when buying.

450 g (1 lb) dried haricot beans, soaked overnight in cold water	450 ml (¾ pint) lager
2 onions, skinned and chopped	60 ml (4 level tbsp) tomato purée
30 ml (2 level tbsp) Dijon mustard	60 ml (4 tbsp) vegetarian Worcestershire sauce
30 ml (2 level tbsp) dark brown sugar	30 ml (2 tbsp) chilli sauce
75 ml (5 tbsp) black treacle	1 garlic clove, skinned and crushed
450 ml (¾ pint) tomato juice	salt and pepper

1 Drain the beans. Put them in a large flameproof casserole and add enough fresh cold water to cover. Bring to the boil and boil rapidly for 10 minutes, then simmer for 45 minutes. Drain and return to the casserole with the remaining ingredients. Mix thoroughly together, season with salt and pepper, cover with a tightly fitting lid and cook in the oven at 150°C (300°F) mark 2 for 4 hours or until the beans are very tender.

2 Check and stir the beans occasionally during cooking and add a little extra tomato juice or water, if necessary, to prevent them drying out. Taste and adjust the seasoning, if necessary, before serving.

SERVES 6–8 AS A MAIN COURSE

BEAN GOULASH

Use a mixture of beans of your choice for this dish, which is based on the Hungarian classic.

450 g (1 lb) dried beans, such as black-eyed beans, kidney beans or haricot beans, soaked overnight in cold water	60 ml (4 level tbsp) tomato purée
	15 ml (1 level tbsp) mild paprika
	5 ml (1 level tsp) sugar
30 ml (2 tbsp) vegetable oil	30 ml (2 level tbsp) plain flour
450 g (1 lb) onions, skinned and roughly chopped	1 litre (1¾ pints) vegetable stock
450 g (1 lb) waxy potatoes, such as Maris Bard or Wilja, peeled and roughly chopped	300 ml (½ pint) soured cream or Greek yogurt
	30 ml (2 level tbsp) chopped fresh parsley
2.5 ml (½ level tsp) caraway seeds, crushed	salt and pepper

1 Drain the beans and put them in a saucepan. Add enough fresh water to cover, then bring to the boil and boil rapidly for 10 minutes.

2 Meanwhile, heat the oil in a large flameproof casserole and fry the onions and potatoes for about 10 minutes or until golden brown. Add the caraway seeds, tomato purée, paprika and sugar and fry for 1–2 minutes.

Sprinkle in the flour and cook for 1 minute, then gradually add the stock. Bring to the boil, stirring all the time.

3 Drain the beans and add to the casserole. Bring back to the boil, cover and simmer for 1–1½ hours or until the beans are tender. Stir in the cream or yogurt and parsley. Season with salt and pepper and serve.

SERVES 6 AS A MAIN COURSE

RED KIDNEY BEANS WITH GINGER AND CHILLI

With their rich, creamy sauce, these red kidney beans are best served with plain boiled rice.

250 g (9 oz) dried red kidney beans, soaked overnight in cold water, or two 425 g (15 oz) cans red kidney beans, drained and rinsed	2 garlic cloves, skinned and crushed
	2–3 small green chillies, seeded and finely chopped
	150 ml (¼ pint) single cream
30 ml (2 tbsp) vegetable ghee or oil	60 ml (4 level tbsp) tomato purée
2.5 cm (1 inch) piece of fresh root ginger, peeled and finely chopped	salt and pepper

1 Drain the dried beans and place in a large saucepan. Cover with plenty of fresh water, bring to the boil and boil rapidly for 10 minutes. Reduce the heat, cover and simmer for about 1½ hours or until tender, then drain.

2 Heat the ghee or oil in a heavy-based saucepan or flameproof casserole, add the ginger and garlic and fry gently for 2 minutes.

Add the chillies, the cream and tomato purée. Add the cooked or canned kidney beans to the pan. Stir well to mix.

3 Cook over a gentle heat for 3–4 minutes or until thoroughly hot, but without boiling, stirring occasionally. Season with salt and pepper and turn into a warmed serving dish.

SERVES 4 AS A MAIN COURSE

Chick-peas Stewed with Tomatoes *left*, Ajowan Parathas *right (page 156)*

CHICK-PEAS STEWED WITH TOMATO

Serve with boiled basmati rice flavoured with cardamoms and cloves for a really nutrititious supper.

225 g (8 oz) dried chick-peas, soaked overnight, or two 425 g (15 oz) cans chick-peas, drained	*15 ml (1 level tbsp) ground cumin*
4 garlic cloves, skinned and crushed	*15 ml (1 level tbsp) ground coriander*
45 ml (3 tbsp) vegetable ghee or oil	*5 ml (1 level tsp) garam masala*
2 medium onions, skinned and finely chopped	*4 ripe tomatoes, roughly chopped*
2 small green chillies, seeded and finely chopped	*30 ml (2 level tbsp) chopped fresh coriander*
5 ml (1 level tsp) ground turmeric	*15 ml (1 level tbsp) chopped fresh mint*
5 ml (1 level tsp) paprika	*salt and pepper*

1 Drain the dried chick-peas and place in a large saucepan with half of the garlic. Cover with plenty of water, bring to the boil, cover and simmer for 2–3 hours or until tender. Drain.

2 Heat the ghee or oil in a heavy-based saucepan, add the remaining garlic and the onions and fry gently for about 5 minutes. Add the chillies and spices, and fry, stirring, for a further 1–2 minutes.

3 Add the tomatoes, coriander and mint and cook, stirring, for 5–10 minutes or until the tomatoes turn to a purée.

4 Add the cooked or canned chick-peas and stir well. Simmer gently for another 5 minutes or until the chick-peas are heated through. Season with salt and pepper and serve hot.

SERVES 4 AS A MAIN COURSE

$\mathcal{P}$UY LENTILS COOKED WITH BAY

Puy lentils are tiny dark green lentils with a distinctive flavour. They hold their shape very well when cooked. Buy them in good delicatessens and supermarkets or, more cheaply, when holidaying in France. Here they are treated simply to enhance their delicious flavour.

1 medium onion, skinned
about 8 whole cloves
225 g (8 oz) puy lentils
4 bay leaves

2 celery sticks or 1 carrot (optional)
salt and pepper
15 ml (1 tbsp) extra virgin olive oil
a splash of balsamic or red wine vinegar

1 Stick the cloves into the onion. Put this into a large saucepan with the lentils, bay leaves and celery or carrot, if using. Cover with plenty of cold water and bring to the boil. Add plenty of salt. Reduce the heat, cover and simmer gently for about 20–30 minutes or until the lentils are tender.

2 Drain the lentils, reserving the liquid for making stocks, sauces and gravies. Turn the lentils into a serving dish and season with pepper and a little salt if necessary. Toss with the olive oil and vinegar. Serve hot or cold.
SERVES 6–8 AS AN ACCOMPANIMENT

$\mathcal{T}$OFU AND VEGETABLES IN COCONUT SAUCE

This is best with firm pressed tofu (see page 161). It also works well with Paneer (see page 86); cumin-flavoured paneer is particularly good.

75 g (3 oz) creamed coconut, chopped
225 g (8 oz) firm pressed tofu (see page 161)
vegetable oil for deep frying, plus 45 ml (3 tbsp)
6 spring onions, trimmed and finely chopped
2.5 cm (1 inch) piece of fresh root ginger, peeled and finely chopped
1 garlic clove, skinned and crushed
2.5 ml (½ level tsp) ground turmeric
2.5 ml (½ level tsp) chilli powder

30 ml (2 tbsp) soy sauce
4 medium carrots, trimmed, peeled and cut into matchstick strips
225 g (8 oz) cauliflower florets, separated into small sprigs
175 g (6 oz) French beans, topped and tailed
175 g (6 oz) bean sprouts
salt and pepper

1 Put the creamed coconut in a measuring jug. Pour in boiling water up to the 900 ml (1½ pint) mark. Stir until dissolved, then set aside.
2 Drain the tofu and cut into cubes. Pat dry thoroughly with absorbent kitchen paper. Heat the oil to 190°C (375°F) in a wok or deep-fat frier. Deep-fry the cubes of tofu in

the hot oil for 2–3 minutes or until golden brown on all sides, turning them frequently with a slotted spoon. Remove and drain on absorbent kitchen paper.
3 Heat the 45 ml (3 tbsp) oil in a heavy-based saucepan or flameproof casserole. Add the spring onions, ginger and garlic and fry gently for about 5 minutes or until softened.

4 Add the turmeric and chilli powder and stir-fry for 1–2 minutes, then add the coconut milk and soy sauce and bring to the boil, stirring all the time. Add the carrots and cauliflower. Simmer for 10 minutes.

5 Add the French beans and simmer for a further 5 minutes, then add the tofu and bean sprouts and heat through. Season with salt and pepper, then serve immediately.
SERVES 4 AS A MAIN COURSE

VEGETABLE CHILLI

Don't be put off by the length of this recipe. You will have a lot of the ingredients in your storecupboard, anyway, and they do make a difference to the finished flavour. It really is worth making a large batch of chilli since it freezes well or can be kept in the refrigerator for up to 2 days. Serve it with boiled rice, topped with soured cream or thick Greek yogurt, grated cheese and a little extra chopped fresh coriander. Alternatively, use it to top baked potatoes, or to fill shop-bought tacos. Simply warm the tacos in the oven (following the packet instructions), then fill with chilli, shredded lettuce, soured cream or yogurt and top with Guacamole (see page 23) or chopped avocado and grated cheese.

30 ml (2 tbsp) vegetable oil	1 large green pepper, cored, seeded and chopped
2 onions, skinned and chopped	900 g (2 lb) mixed vegetables, including carrots, aubergines, parsnips, potato and celery, prepared as necessary and cut into chunks
2 large garlic cloves, skinned and crushed	
1–2 fresh green chillies, seeded and chopped	
1 bay leaf	two 397 g (14 oz) cans chopped tomatoes
1 cinnamon stick	225 g (8 oz) dried red kidney beans, soaked overnight in cold water, then drained and cooked (see page 10) or two 425 g (15 oz) cans red kidney beans, drained and rinsed
4 cloves	
15 ml (1 level tbsp) mild paprika	
10 ml (2 level tsp) cumin powder	
2.5 ml (½ level tsp) chilli powder, or to taste	pinch of sugar
5 ml (1 level tsp) dried marjoram	5 ml (1 tsp) malt vinegar
30 ml (2 level tbsp) tomato purée	45 ml (3 level tbsp) chopped fresh coriander
225 g (8 oz) button mushrooms, wiped and sliced	salt and pepper

1 Heat the oil in a large saucepan or flameproof casserole. Add the onions, garlic and chillies and fry for 3–4 minutes, stirring continuously. Add the bay leaf, all the spices, the marjoram and the tomato purée, and fry for a further 2 minutes, stirring.
2 Add all the fresh vegetables and stir to coat in the spice mixture. Fry for 1–2 minutes, then add the tomatoes. Increase the heat and bring to the boil, stirring occasionally. Add enough water just to cover the vegetables, half cover the pan or casserole with a lid and simmer for 35–45 minutes.

3 Add the kidney beans with the sugar, vinegar and half the coriander. Add extra chilli powder, if liked, and season with salt and pepper. Bring back to the boil, then lower the heat and simmer for 15 minutes, stirring occasionally. If the chilli looks very wet, leave the lid off during this time. If it is dry, add a little extra water and cover completely.
4 Stir in the remaining coriander, then leave to stand for 5 minutes. Taste and adjust the seasoning, if necessary, before serving.
SERVES ABOUT 8 AS A MAIN COURSE

MIXED LENTIL CASSEROLE

This is a relatively low-calorie main dish. Serve topped with low-fat natural yogurt to keep the calorie content low.

5 ml (1 level tsp) cumin seeds	2 garlic cloves, skinned and crushed
15 ml (1 level tbsp) coriander seeds	25 g (1 oz) piece of fresh root ginger, peeled and grated or finely chopped
5 ml (1 level tsp) mustard seeds	1.25 ml (¼ level tsp) ground turmeric
45 ml (3 tbsp) olive oil	175 g (6 oz) split red lentils, rinsed and drained
350 g (12 oz) onions, skinned and sliced	50 g (2 oz) brown or green lentils, rinsed and drained
450 g (1 lb) carrots, trimmed, peeled and sliced	salt and pepper
350 g (12 oz) trimmed leeks, sliced	60 ml (4 level tbsp) chopped fresh coriander
350 g (12 oz) mooli (white radish), peeled and roughly chopped	
450 g (1 lb) button mushrooms, wiped and halved if large	

1 Crush the cumin, coriander and mustard seeds in a mortar with a pestle or in a strong bowl with the end of a rolling pin.

2 Heat the oil in a very large flameproof casserole. Add the onions, carrots, leeks and mooli, and fry for 2–3 minutes, stirring constantly. Add the mushrooms, garlic, ginger, turmeric and crushed spices, and fry for a further 2–3 minutes, stirring.

3 Stir the lentils into the casserole with 750 ml (1¼ pints) boiling water. Season with salt and pepper and return to the boil. Cover and cook in the oven at 180°C (350°F) mark 4 for about 45 minutes or until the vegetables and lentils are tender. Stir in the fresh coriander and taste and adjust the seasoning, if necessary, before serving.

SERVES 6 AS A MAIN COURSE

ROOT VEGETABLE STEW

This simple combination of root vegetables makes an ideal supper dish served with baked potatoes and salad.

450 g (1 lb) carrots, trimmed and peeled	2 garlic cloves, skinned and crushed
450 g (1 lb) parsnips, trimmed and peeled	350 g (12 oz) button mushrooms, wiped
350 g (12 oz) celeriac	450 ml (¾ pint) vegetable stock
lemon juice	salt and pepper
25 g (1 oz) vegetable margarine or butter	60 ml (4 tbsp) single cream
2 medium onions, skinned and sliced	30 ml (2 level tbsp) chopped fresh parsley

1 Cut the carrots and parsnips into 5 mm (¼ inch) thick slices. Trim the celeriac and chop into large chunks. Drop immediately into cold water lightly acidulated with lemon juice.

2 Melt the margarine or butter in a large flameproof casserole. Add the onions and garlic and fry for 2–3 minutes or until beginning to soften, stirring constantly. Stir in

the carrots, parsnips and mushrooms and fry for a further 4–5 minutes, stirring, then add the stock and season with salt and pepper. Bring to the boil, cover and cook in the oven at 170°C (325°F) mark 3 for 50 minutes or until the vegetables are tender.

3 Meanwhile, remove the celeriac from the acidulated water and cook in boiling salted water for about 35 minutes or until very tender. Drain and purée in a blender or food processor with a little of the casserole juices. Stir the celeriac purée into the casserole, return to the boil, taste and adjust the seasoning, if necessary. Stir in the cream and parsley just before serving.

SERVES 6 AS A MAIN COURSE

$\mathcal{R}$ICH WINTER CASSEROLE

Vary the mixture of beans and vegetables in this casserole according to availability and personal taste. Plump, herby dumplings (see page 84) are an excellent accompaniment.

125 g (4 oz) red kidney beans, soaked overnight in cold water
125 g (4 oz) black-eyed beans, soaked overnight in cold water
50 g (2 oz) vegetable margarine or butter
1 small onion, skinned and chopped
1 garlic clove, skinned and chopped
45 ml (3 level tbsp) plain flour
600 ml (1 pint) Brown Onion Stock (see page 00)

300 ml (½ pint) red wine
175 g (6 oz) button mushrooms, wiped
175 g (6 oz) button onions, skinned
2 celery sticks, trimmed and chopped
3 large carrots, trimmed, peeled and sliced
450 g (1 lb) mixed vegetables of your choice, prepared as necessary and cut into large chunks
bouquet garni
salt and pepper

1 Drain the beans and put them in a saucepan. Add enough fresh water to cover, bring to the boil and boil rapidly for 10 minutes, then drain.

2 Meanwhile, melt the margarine or butter in a flameproof casserole, add the onion and garlic and fry for 5–10 minutes or until softened and slightly tinged with brown. Sprinkle with the flour and cook for 1–2 minutes, stirring all the time. Remove from the heat and gradually stir in the stock and wine. Bring to the boil, stirring all the time.

3 Add the remaining ingredients to the casserole with the drained beans. Cover and cook in the oven at 180°C (350°F) mark 4 for 2–2½ hours or until the beans are tender. Season with salt and pepper and remove the bouquet garni before serving.

SERVES 4 AS A MAIN COURSE

$\mathscr{R}$ATATOUILLE

The addition of lots of chopped fresh herbs is what gives this ratatouille its authentic Provençale flavour. Serve it as a main course with beans, rice, pasta or warm bread, or as an accompaniment to nut roasts, burgers or baked potatoes.

50 ml (2 fl oz) olive oil
2 medium onions, skinned and thinly sliced
1 large garlic clove, skinned and crushed
350 g (12 oz) aubergine, halved or quartered lengthways and thinly sliced
450 g (1 lb) small courgettes, trimmed and thinly sliced
450 g (1 lb) tomatoes, skinned, seeded and roughly chopped

1 green pepper, cored, seeded and roughly chopped
1 red pepper, cored, seeded and roughly chopped
15 ml (1 level tbsp) chopped fresh basil
10 ml (2 level tsp) chopped fresh thyme
30 ml (2 level tbsp) chopped fresh parsley
30 ml (2 level tbsp) tomato purée
pinch of ground or crushed aniseed
salt and pepper

1 Heat the oil in a large saucepan, add the onion and garlic and fry for about 5 minutes or until soft but not brown.
2 Add the aubergine, courgettes, tomatoes, peppers, herbs, tomato purée and aniseed. Season with salt and pepper. Fry for 2–3 minutes, stirring, then cover tightly and simmer for 30–40 minutes or until all the vegetables are just tender. Stir well.
3 If the vegetables produce a great deal of liquid, boil, uncovered, for 5–10 minutes until reduced. Taste and adjust the seasoning, if necessary. Serve hot or cold.
SERVES 4 AS A MAIN COURSE

$\mathscr{A}$UBERGINE WITH SOY SAUCE

This is delicious served with Fragrant Coconut Rice (see page 134).

45 ml (3 tbsp) vegetable oil
1 medium onion, skinned and chopped
2 garlic cloves, skinned and crushed
large pinch of hot chilli powder
550 g (1¼ lb) aubergine, trimmed and roughly chopped

salt and pepper
397 g (14 oz) can chopped tomatoes
30 ml (2 tbsp) dark soy sauce
15 ml (1 level tbsp) dark brown sugar

1 Heat the oil in a saucepan and fry the onion, garlic and chilli powder for 2–3 minutes or until the onion is soft. Add the aubergine and continue cooking for 2–3 minutes, stirring frequently.
2 Add the remaining ingredients, cover and simmer gently for 10–15 minutes or until the aubergine is tender but still retains its shape. Taste and adjust the seasoning, if necessary, before serving hot.
SERVES 2–3 AS A MAIN COURSE

—Seven—

akes and ratins

In this chapter you will find down-to-earth, hearty dishes, such as Gratin Dauphinoise, Tian de Courgettes and Jerusalem Artichoke Gratin – comforting food to be served on cold wintry days with the simplest of accompaniments. Here, too, is Lentil Loaf, Vegetarian Roast, Baked Potatoes and Stuffed Peppers, dishes which have traditionally been the mainstay of vegetarian cuisine.

Most of these creations are based on fresh vegetables. To get the best results, it is essential that you buy good quality produce at the peak of freshness. Leafy vegetables should be bright green with no sign of yellowing or browning. Leaves should be undamaged, not slimy or wilted. Root vegetables should be firm with no discoloured patches or damage to the skin. Tomatoes, peppers, aubergines and courgettes should be firm and heavy with no sign of mould or shrivelling.

All vegetables are best eaten as soon as possible after purchase as far as flavour and vitamin retention are concerned (see page 6). However, root vegetables will keep quite well in a cool, dark place for about a week. More delicate vegetables last longer if stored in the refrigerator.

It's possible to turn almost any mixture of vegetables into a tasty gratin. Simply mix lightly cooked vegetables with a few cooked lentils, beans or grains, season, then add enough tomato, cheese, Béchamel or one of the other sauces on pages 181–194 to moisten. Turn into a gratin dish, sprinkle with an equal mixture of breadcrumbs and grated cheese and bake in the oven at 200°C (400°F) mark 6 until the top is golden and bubbling.

Alternatively, make a savoury crumble topping by rubbing margarine or butter into plain flour until the mixture resembles fine breadcrumbs. A proportion of half fat to flour is about right, as when making shortcrust pastry. Add a few chopped nuts or oats for extra crunch and season with chopped herbs and salt and pepper. Sprinkle on top of the vegetable mixture and bake like a gratin. Incidentally, garlic or flavoured butters make particularly more-ish crumbles.

$\mathcal{N}$UT AND CREAM CHEESE BAKE

Some brands of cream cheese are made without animal rennet; check the labels.

30 ml (2 tbsp) vegetable oil	50 g (2 oz) walnut halves, chopped
450 g (1 lb) onions, skinned and chopped	50 g (2 oz) desiccated coconut
450 g (1 lb) courgettes, trimmed and sliced	30 ml (2 level tbsp) tomato purée
175 g (6 oz) mushrooms, wiped and sliced	a few drops of Tabasco
175 g (6 oz) wholemeal breadcrumbs	2.5 ml (½ level tsp) each of dried rosemary, sage and marjoram
350 g (12 oz) full-fat soft cheese	salt and pepper
50 g (2 oz) unsalted cashew nuts, chopped	

1 Heat the oil in a large frying pan, add the onions and courgettes and fry for 5–10 minutes or until the onion is transparent, stirring frequently. Add the mushrooms and continue to fry for 1–2 minutes.
2 In a large bowl, combine the vegetable mixture with the remaining ingredients until evenly mixed. Season with salt and pepper. Turn into a 1.6 litre (2¾ pint) ovenproof dish. Cover with foil and bake at 190°C (375°F) mark 5 for 40 minutes. About 15 minutes before the end of cooking, remove the foil to brown the top. Serve straight from the dish.
SERVES 6

ꞱIMBALLO DI RISO

Timballo is an Italian dish from the region around Naples and there are many different versions. The basic risotto mixture which forms the case for the filling is usually the same, but the filling varies from one cook and one occasion to another – you literally fill your timballo with whatever you have to hand! Sautéed vegetables or cooked pulses of your choice can all be used, and the tomato sauce for serving suggested here can be changed to a cream, cheese or herb sauce, whichever complements the filling best. It can also be made with leftover risotto.

75 g (3 oz) vegetable margarine or butter	*2 garlic cloves, skinned and crushed*
1 onion, skinned and finely chopped	*10 ml (2 tsp) chopped fresh basil or 5 ml (1 tsp) dried*
400 g (14 oz) arborio (risotto) rice	*60 ml (4 tbsp) dried breadcrumbs*
180 ml (12 tbsp) dry white wine	*50 g (2 oz) freshly grated Parmesan cheese*
about 1.1 litres (2 pints) hot vegetable stock	*2 free-range eggs, beaten*
salt and pepper	*3 hard-boiled free-range eggs, shelled and sliced*
30 ml (2 tbsp) olive oil	*225 g (8 oz) Mozzarella cheese, sliced*
225 g (8 oz) mushrooms, wiped and sliced	*Tomato Sauce (see page 190), to serve*

1 First make the risotto. Melt 50 g (2 oz) of the margarine or butter in a heavy-based saucepan. Add the onion and fry gently for 5 minutes or until soft but not coloured.

2 Add the rice and stir until coated in the fat, then pour in 150 ml (¼ pint) of the wine and bring to the boil. Simmer, stirring, until the rice has absorbed all the liquid.

3 Pour in about 150 ml (¼ pint) stock, add 5 ml (1 tsp) salt and simmer and stir as before until all the liquid is absorbed. Continue adding stock in this way until the rice is just tender; this should take 15–20 minutes.

4 Meanwhile, heat the oil in a separate pan, add the mushrooms and garlic and fry gently until the juices run. Stir in the remaining wine and the basil. Season with salt and pepper and remove from the heat.

5 Sprinkle the breadcrumbs over the base and up the sides of a well-buttered 20.5 cm (8 inch) spring-release cake tin or mould,

making sure there are no gaps.

6 Remove the risotto from the heat and stir in the Parmesan cheese with the beaten eggs, the remaining margarine or butter and salt and pepper to taste.

7 Press three-quarters of the risotto over the base and up the sides of the lined tin. Arrange about one-third of the hard-boiled egg slices in the bottom, then sprinkle over about one-third of the mushrooms. Top with one-third of the Mozzarella slices.

8 Repeat these layers until all the eggs, mushrooms and Mozzarella are used up, then press the remaining risotto firmly on top.

9 Cover the tin with foil and bake in the oven at 190°C (375°F) mark 5 for 1 hour or until firm. Leave to rest in the tin for 5 minutes, then turn out on to a warmed serving platter. Serve immediately, with Tomato Sauce.

SERVES 8

Overleaf, from left to right, Tomato Herb Foccacia *(page 151),* Bulgar-stuffed Tomatoes *(page 103)*
Baby Vegetable and Pasta Salad *(page 45)*
Creamy Hummus *(page 14),* Guacamole *(page 23),* Spanakopittes *(page 80),* Sesame and Cumin Bread Sticks *(page 150)*

$\mathcal{V}$EGETABLE AND NUT ROAST

This recipe makes a 'loaf' which slices well and can be served hot or cold. Any type of chopped nuts can be used, such as almonds, Brazils or unsalted peanuts, but it's worth buying mature Cheddar specially, as it adds a mouthwatering depth of flavour.

175 g (6 oz) long-grain brown rice
salt and pepper
15 g (½ oz) vegetable margarine or butter
1 medium onion, skinned and chopped
1 garlic clove, skinned and crushed
2 carrots, trimmed, peeled and grated

125 g (4 oz) mushrooms, wiped and finely chopped
125 g (4 oz) fresh wholemeal breadcrumbs
125 g (4 oz) nuts, finely chopped
125 g (4 oz) mature Cheddar cheese, grated
2 free-range eggs, beaten
Tomato Sauce (see page 190) or chutney, to serve

1 Cook the rice in boiling salted water for 30–35 minutes or until tender. Drain well.
2 Meanwhile, heat the margarine or butter in a frying pan and fry the onion, garlic, carrots and mushrooms for 5–10 minutes or until softened, stirring frequently. Remove from the heat, then stir in the breadcrumbs, nuts, cooked rice, cheese and eggs. Season with salt and pepper and mix thoroughly together.
3 Pack the mixture into a greased 1.7 litre (3 pint) loaf tin and bake in the oven at 180°C (350°F) mark 4 for 1–1¼ hours or until firm to the touch and brown on top. Serve sliced, hot or cold, with Tomato Sauce or chutney.
SERVES 4–6

$\mathcal{T}$IAN DE COURGETTES

Use up leftover cooked rice or pre-cooked frozen rice to make this simple supper dish.

2 thick slices of white bread
300 ml (½ pint) milk
125 g (4 oz) long-grain rice
salt and pepper
2 free-range eggs
olive oil

50 g (2 oz) Gruyère cheese, grated
1 small garlic clove, skinned and crushed (optional)
700 g (1½ lb) small courgettes, trimmed and thinly sliced
freshly grated Parmesan cheese (optional)

1 Remove the crusts from the bread and discard. Tear the bread into small pieces and place in a large bowl. Pour over the milk and leave to soak.
2 Meanwhile, cook the rice in boiling salted water until tender. Drain well.
3 Beat the eggs and 30 ml (2 tbsp) olive oil into the bread mixture with about a quarter of the cheese and the garlic, if using. Season generously with salt and pepper.
4 Carefully fold the courgettes and rice into the milk and bread mixture, and pour into a greased gratin dish. Sprinkle with the remaining Gruyère cheese and a little Parmesan, if using. Drizzle with a little extra olive oil. Bake in the oven at 200°C (400°F) mark 6 for 35–40 minutes or until golden brown and firm to the touch. Leave to cool in the dish for 10 minutes before serving.
SERVES 3–4

BULGAR-STUFFED TOMATOES

Serve these stuffed tomatoes as part of a summer lunch with a selection of salads. They are equally delicious served hot.

125 g (4 oz) bulgar wheat	*45 ml (3 level tbsp) chopped fresh basil*
4 large beefsteak tomatoes, each weighing about 175 g (6 oz)	*salt and pepper*
	To serve
25 g (1 oz) nuts, such as hazelnuts, peanuts or cashews, toasted and chopped	*natural yogurt*
50 g (2 oz) stoned black olives, roughly chopped	*Pesto (see page 193), Creamy Hummus (see page 14) or Guacamole (see page 23)*
30 ml (2 tbsp) Pesto (see page 193)	*chopped fresh basil*

1 Put the bulgar wheat in a bowl and pour over 150 ml (¼ pint) boiling water. Leave to soak for 30 minutes or until the water has been absorbed and the bulgar has softened.
2 Cut the tops off the tomatoes and reserve. Scoop out the tomato centres with a spoon and finely chop half the tomato flesh. (Discard the remainder.)

3 Add the chopped tomato to the bulgar wheat with the remaining ingredients and season with salt and pepper. Use to fill the tomato shells. To serve, top each tomato with a spoonful of yogurt and a little Pesto or a spoonful of hummus or Guacamole. Sprinkle with basil and replace the tomato tops.
SERVES 4

GRATIN DAUPHINOISE

For this unorthodox version of a classic dish, it is vital that the potatoes are sliced wafer-thin, so that they cook until melt-in-the-mouth tender. Cooking them in milk first speeds up the oven cooking time (without this they can take up to 4 hours to cook properly). Use potatoes with a 'waxy' texture or they will break up when boiled.

900 g (2 lb) waxy potatoes, such as Maris Bard or Wilja, peeled	*600 ml (1 pint) double cream*
	salt and pepper
1.1 litres (2 pints) milk	*freshly grated nutmeg*
1 small garlic clove, skinned and halved	*125 g (4 oz) Gruyère cheese, grated*

1 Cut the potatoes into very thin slices, using a very sharp knife. Put them in a large saucepan and add the milk. Bring to the boil and simmer very gently for 10–12 minutes or until just soft. Drain well and reserve the milk.
2 Grease a large gratin dish and rub the bottom and sides of the dish with garlic. Put the cream in a saucepan and bring to the boil.
3 Arrange the potatoes in the prepared dish

in an even layer. Cover the potatoes with the cream, adding a little of the reserved milk. Season generously and sprinkle with the nutmeg and grated cheese.
4 Bake, uncovered, in the oven at 180°C (350°F) mark 4 for 1–1½ hours or until the potatoes are very tender and the top is brown. Leave to stand for 15 minutes before serving.
SERVES 6

BAKED POTATOES AND FILLINGS

Baked potatoes are the perfect informal meal, providing hot and filling high-fibre food with minimum effort. They are delicious topped simply with grated or cottage cheese, a spoonful of natural yogurt and a generous sprinkling of black pepper, or piled high with one of the fillings suggested below. Alternatively, serve them with Ratatouille (see page 96), Creamy Hummus (see page 14) or Vegetable Chilli (see page 93).

If you have a microwave cooker, save time by cooking the pricked potatoes on HIGH for 12–14 minutes or until the potatoes feel soft when squeezed, turning them over once during cooking. To crisp the skins, put them into a very hot oven for about 10 minutes.

4 large potatoes, each weighing about 175 g (6 oz)
vegetable oil (optional)
Avocado and Smoked Cheese Filling
2 large ripe avocados
150 ml (¼ pint) Greek yogurt
lemon juice, to taste
125 g (4 oz) smoked hard cheese, cubed
salt and pepper
Carrot, Peanut and Alfalfa Filling
75 ml (5 tbsp) natural yogurt
45 ml (3 tbsp) peanut butter
45 ml (3 tbsp) mayonnaise
4 large carrots, trimmed, peeled and coarsely grated
75 g (3 oz) roasted peanuts

75 g (3 oz) alfalfa sprouts
a squeeze of lemon juice
black pepper
Hot Chilli Bean Filling
397 g (14 oz) can chopped tomatoes
10 ml (2 level tsp) tomato purée
2 garlic cloves, skinned and crushed
2.5 ml (½ level tsp) chilli powder
2.5 ml (½ level tsp) dried oregano
425 g (15 oz) cooked red kidney beans (see page 10) or 400 g (14 oz) can red kidney beans, drained and rinsed
30 ml (2 level tbsp) chopped fresh coriander or parsley
salt and pepper

1 Wash and scrub the potatoes and prick all over with a fork. If you prefer baked potatoes with softish skins, rub the potatoes all over with a little oil; for very crunchy skins, put them into the oven while still wet.

2 Bake the potatoes in the oven at 230°C (450°F) mark 8 for about 1 hour or at 200°C (400°F) mark 6 for about 1½ hours or until the potatoes feel soft when gently squeezed, turning them over once during cooking. (They can be cooked at a lower temperature if, for example, you are cooking a casserole in the oven at the same time, but of course they will take much longer.)

3 While the potatoes are cooking, make the required filling (see right).

4 When the potatoes are cooked, cut them in half and mash the flesh lightly with a fork. Pile the prepared filling on top and serve.
SERVES 4

FILLINGS
Avocado and Smoked Cheese Cut one of the avocados in half, remove the stone and scoop out the flesh. Mash with a fork or purée in a blender or food processor with the yogurt and lemon juice. Halve, stone and peel the remaining avocado and cut into cubes. Fold into the puréed mixture with the cheese, and season with salt and pepper. Use to fill the potatoes.

Carrot, Peanut and Alfalfa Beat the yogurt, peanut butter and mayonnaise together, then gradually fold in the carrots, peanuts and alfalfa. Season with lemon juice and black pepper, and use to fill the potatoes.

Hot Chilli Bean Put all the ingredients into a saucepan, season with salt and pepper, and bring to the boil. Cook vigorously for 15–20 minutes or until reduced and thickened. Use to fill the potatoes.

$\mathcal{I}$MAM BAYILDI

This traditional Turkish dish is usually served cold, but it could be served lukewarm if you prefer. Serve with crusty bread or toasted pitta bread, and perhaps a Greek Salad (see page 45).

6 small aubergines	60 ml (4 tbsp) chopped fresh parsley
salt and pepper	3.75 ml (¾ level tsp) ground allspice
200 ml (7 fl oz) olive oil	5 ml (1 level tsp) sugar
450 g (1 lb) onions, skinned and finely sliced	30 ml (2 tbsp) lemon juice
3 garlic cloves, skinned and crushed	chopped fresh parsley, to garnish
400 g (14 oz) can tomatoes, drained or 450 g (1 lb) tomatoes, skinned and chopped	

1 Halve the aubergines lengthways. Scoop out the flesh and reserve. Leave a substantial shell so they do not disintegrate.
2 Sprinkle the insides of the aubergine shells with salt and put upside-down on a plate. Leave for 30 minutes to drain away the juices.
3 Heat 45 ml (3 tbsp) olive oil in a saucepan, add the onions and garlic and fry gently for about 15 minutes or until soft but not coloured. Add the tomatoes, reserved aubergine flesh, parsley and allspice. Season with salt and pepper. Simmer gently for about 20 minutes or until the mixture has reduced.
4 Rinse the aubergines and pat dry with absorbent kitchen paper. Spoon the filling into each half and place them side by side in a shallow ovenproof dish. They should fit quite closely together.
5 Mix the remaining oil with 150 ml (¼ pint) water, the sugar and lemon juice. Season with salt and pepper. Pour around the aubergines, cover and bake in the oven at 150°C (300°F) mark 2 for about 1 hour or until tender.
6 When cooked, remove from the oven, uncover and leave to cool for 1 hour. Chill in the refrigerator for at least 2 hours before serving garnished with parsley.
SERVES 6

LENTIL LOAF

This makes a soft-textured, mildly flavoured loaf. Serve with a crisp salad.

175 g (6 oz) split red lentils	1 garlic clove, skinned and chopped (optional)
450 ml (¾ pint) vegetable stock or water	175 g (6 oz) farmhouse Cheddar cheese, grated
1 bay leaf	225 g (8 oz) wholemeal breadcrumbs
15 ml (1 tbsp) vegetable oil	30 ml (2 level tbsp) chopped fresh parsley
1 medium onion, skinned and finely chopped	15 ml (1 tbsp) lemon juice
2 celery sticks, trimmed and finely chopped	1 free-range egg, beaten
1 red pepper, cored, seeded and finely chopped	salt and pepper
125 g (4 oz) mushrooms, wiped and finely chopped	Tomato Sauce (see page 190), to serve

1 Put the lentils, stock or water and bay leaf in a saucepan, bring to the boil, then reduce the heat, cover and simmer gently for 15–20 minutes or until the lentils are very soft.
2 Meanwhile, grease and line a 1.1 litre (2 pint) loaf tin. Heat the oil in a large saucepan, add all the vegetables and the garlic, if using, and fry for 2–3 minutes, stirring all the time. Reduce the heat, cover the pan and cook for 10 minutes or until the vegetables are softened.
3 Mix the vegetables with the lentil mixture. Add half the cheese and the remaining ingredients and season generously with salt

and pepper. The mixture should be moist but not sloppy.
4 Spoon the mixture into the prepared tin and bake in the oven at 180°C (350°F) mark 4 for about 1 hour or until firm to the touch in the centre. Sprinkle over the remaining cheese. Increase the oven temperature to 200°C (400°F) mark 6 and cook for a further 8–10 minutes or until the cheese melts. Cool in the tin for 10 minutes before turning out. Serve hot or cold, thickly sliced and accompanied by Tomato Sauce.
SERVES 4–6

SUMMER GRATIN

The cheese and oats are sprinkled around the edges of the dishes to produce an attractive border for the gratin.

175 g (6 oz) dried butter beans, soaked overnight in cold water, or 425 g (15 oz) can butter beans, drained and rinsed	30 ml (2 tbsp) vegetable oil
	1 medium onion, skinned and thinly sliced
450 g (1 lb) tomatoes, skinned and quartered	1 garlic clove, skinned and crushed
30 ml (2 level tbsp) tomato purée	125 g (4 oz) button mushrooms, wiped and halved
2.5 ml (½ level tsp) ground cumin	50 g (2 oz) red Leicester cheese, grated
salt and pepper	25 g (1 oz) rolled oats
400 g (14 oz) calabrese, trimmed and cut into small florets	

1 If using soaked dried beans, drain them and place in a saucepan. Cover with fresh water, bring to the boil and boil rapidly for 10 minutes, then reduce the heat, cover and simmer for about 30 minutes. Drain well.
2 Place half the beans, the tomatoes, tomato purée and cumin in a food processor. Season with salt and pepper and purée until smooth.
3 Cook the calabrese in boiling salted water for about 5 minutes or until just tender. Drain.
4 Heat the oil in a large frying pan, add the onion, garlic, mushrooms and remaining

beans, and stir over a high heat for 3–4 minutes or until beginning to soften.
5 Gently stir in the calabrese and cook for a further 1 minute, then spoon the mixture into six individual ovenproof serving dishes and spoon over the puréed mixture.
6 Mix the cheese and oats together, then sprinkle around the edge of each dish. Bake at 200°C (400°F) mark 6 for about 25 minutes or until thoroughly hot, golden brown and bubbling.
SERVES 6

$\mathscr{S}$PINACH AND LENTIL ROULADE

Make sure that the spinach is really thoroughly drained before adding it to the sauce. It's a good idea to wrap it in a double thickness of muslin or a clean tea towel and to wring it out over the sink to remove all traces of water.

75 g (3 oz) vegetable margarine or butter	*175 g (6 oz) split red lentils, rinsed*
125 g (4 oz) frozen chopped spinach, thawed and thoroughly drained	*50 g (2 oz) spring onions, trimmed and chopped*
	salt and pepper
50 g (2 oz) plain flour	*30 ml (2 level tbsp) tomato ketchup*
300 ml (½ pint) milk	*15 ml (1 level tbsp) creamed horseradish*
2 free-range eggs, separated	

1 Grease and line a 33 × 23 cm (13 × 9 inch) Swiss roll tin with non-stick baking parchment.
2 Melt 50 g (2 oz) margarine or butter in a saucepan and stir in the spinach and flour. Cook for 1 minute, then add the milk. Bring to the boil, stirring, and simmer for 2–3 minutes. Remove from the heat and beat in the egg yolks. Stiffly whisk the egg whites and fold into the mixture. Spoon into the prepared tin and spread evenly. Bake in the oven at 220°C (425°F) mark 7 for about 15 minutes or until well risen and firm to the touch.

3 Meanwhile, cook the lentils and spring onions in boiling salted water for 15–20 minutes or until tender. Drain well, then beat in the tomato ketchup, horseradish and remaining margarine or butter. Season with salt and pepper.
4 Turn out the roulade on to a sheet of non-stick baking parchment and peel off the lining paper. Spread the lentil mixture over the surface and roll up like a Swiss roll, using the paper to help. Serve immediately.
SERVES 4

JERUSALEM ARTICHOKE GRATIN

Serve this warming supper dish with a salad and some crusty bread.

900 g (2 lb) Jerusalem artichokes	1.25 ml (¼ level tsp) grated nutmeg
salt and pepper	3 medium leeks, trimmed and thickly sliced
225 g (8 oz) small button or pickling onions	225 g (8 oz) shelled fresh or frozen peas
75 g (3 oz) vegetable margarine or butter	150 ml (¼ pint) double cream
15 ml (1 tbsp) olive oil	75 g (3 oz) Gruyère cheese, grated
2 garlic cloves, skinned and crushed	75 g (3 oz) Cheddar cheese, grated
150 ml (¼ pint) dry white wine or vegetable stock	50 g (2 oz) breadcrumbs

1 Parboil the Jerusalem artichokes in salted water for 10 minutes. Remove with a slotted spoon and leave until cool enough to handle. Peel off the skins and slice the flesh thickly.

2 Add the button onions to the water and boil for 2 minutes, then remove with a slotted spoon. Peel off the skins, leaving the root ends intact so that the onions remain whole.

3 Heat 50 g (2 oz) of the margarine or butter with the oil in a heavy-based saucepan, add the onions and garlic and toss over a moderate heat until the onions are well coated in the fat.

4 Pour in the wine or stock and 150 ml (¼ pint) water and bring to the boil. Add the nutmeg, cover and simmer for 10 minutes. Add the artichokes, leeks and peas and continue simmering for 5 minutes or until all the vegetables are tender. With a slotted spoon, transfer the vegetables to a flameproof gratin dish.

5 Boil the cooking liquid rapidly until reduced to about half of its original volume. Reduce the heat and stir in the cream. Mix the two cheeses together. Stir half into the sauce. Season with salt and pepper and stir until the cheeses have melted.

6 Pour the cheese sauce over the vegetables in the dish. Mix the remaining cheese with the breadcrumbs, then sprinkle on top.

7 Dot the remaining margarine or butter over the gratin, then bake in the oven at 220°C (425°F) mark 7 for about 10 minutes or until the topping is golden brown.

SERVES 4

STUFFED PEPPERS

For extra flavour, stir a little Hazelnut and Coriander Pesto (see page 193) into the cooked rice mixture. Alternatively, serve the finished peppers with Harissa Sauce (see page 184).

3 green peppers	450 ml (¾ pint) vegetable stock
3 red peppers	15 ml (1 level tbsp) tomato purée
50 g (2 oz) vegetable margarine or butter	125 g (4 oz) mushrooms, wiped and sliced
1 onion, skinned and finely chopped	salt and pepper
1 garlic clove, skinned and crushed	75 g (3 oz) pine nuts or flaked almonds, roasted and
2.5 cm (1 inch) piece of fresh root ginger, peeled and	chopped
chopped	10 ml (2 tsp) soy sauce
125 g (4 oz) long-grain rice	30 ml (2 tbsp) vegetable oil

1 Cut a 2.5 cm (1 inch) lid from the stem end of each pepper. Scoop out the seeds and membranes and discard. Blanch the shells and lids in boiling water for about 2 minutes. Drain and cool.

2 Melt the margarine or butter in a saucepan and gently fry the onion, garlic and ginger for 5 minutes or until softened. Stir in the rice and cook for 1–2 minutes.

3 Add the stock, tomato purée and mushrooms. Bring to the boil and simmer for 13–15 minutes or until the rice is tender and all the stock has been absorbed.

4 Season well with salt and pepper, and stir in the nuts and soy sauce. Use this mixture to fill the peppers.

5 Replace the lids, then put the peppers in a deep ovenproof dish and pour over the oil. Cover with foil and bake in the oven at 190°C (375°F) mark 5 for 30 minutes or until tender.
SERVES 6

MELANZANA PARMIGIANA

Salting the aubergine draws out some of the moisture, thus reducing the amount of oil absorbed during cooking. (It is also thought to extract any bitterness, but the quality of aubergines has improved so much that salting for this reason is no longer necessary.) However, if you are short of time, or not concerned about calories, this step can be omitted. Serve with a crisp mixed green salad and plenty of crusty bread.

900 g (2 lb) long medium aubergines	*225 g (8 oz) Mozzarella cheese, drained and cubed*
salt and pepper	*a handful of fresh basil leaves, marjoram or oregano*
olive oil	*(optional)*
450 ml (¾ pint) Tomato Sauce (see page 190)	*freshly grated Parmesan cheese*

1 Trim off the ends of the aubergines and discard. Cut the aubergines lengthways into thin slices. Sprinkle the slices generously with salt and leave to drain in a colander for at least 30 minutes.

2 Rinse the aubergines and pat dry with absorbent kitchen paper. Heat a little olive oil in a non-stick frying pan and fry the aubergines, in batches, for 3–4 minutes each side, or until golden brown and just cooked through, brushing the frying pan with more olive oil between each batch. Drain well on crumpled absorbent kitchen paper.

3 Spread half the tomato sauce in the base of a large gratin dish. Cover with half the aubergine slices and scatter over the Mozzarella. Cover with the remaining aubergine slices and sprinkle with herbs, if using. Season with salt and pepper.

4 Spread the remaining tomato sauce over the aubergines and sprinkle with Parmesan cheese. Bake in the oven at 200°C (400°F) mark 6 for 30–35 minutes or until golden brown and bubbling. Leave to cool for 5 minutes before serving.
SERVES 4–6

POTATO AND SPINACH ROLL

This is another filling Italian dish. The method is rather laborious, but the finished product is well worth the effort.

450 g (1 lb) old potatoes, peeled	*50 g (2 oz) freshly grated Parmesan cheese*
salt and pepper	*pinch of freshly grated nutmeg*
900 g (2 lb) fresh spinach, trimmed and washed or	*2 free-range eggs*
450 g (1 lb) packet frozen spinach	*5 ml (1 level tsp) baking powder*
30 ml (2 tbsp) olive oil	*about 200 g (7 oz) plain white flour*
1 large onion, skinned and chopped	*50 g (2 oz) vegetable margarine or butter*
125 g (4 oz) curd cheese	*Tomato Sauce (see page 190), to serve*

1 Cook the potatoes in boiling salted water for about 20 minutes or until tender.

2 Meanwhile, make the filling. Put the spinach in a saucepan with a very little water and cook gently for 5–10 minutes (or until thawed if using frozen spinach). Drain well and chop finely.

3 Heat the oil in a frying pan, add the onion and fry gently for 3–4 minutes or until soft but not coloured. Add the spinach and cook for a further 2 minutes.

4 Turn the spinach into a bowl and add the curd cheese, 25 g (1 oz) Parmesan cheese, the nutmeg and one egg. Season with salt and pepper and beat well together.

5 Drain the potatoes, then push them through a sieve into a bowl. Make a well in the centre and add the remaining egg, the baking powder and most of the flour. Beat well together.

6 Knead the mixture on a work surface, adding more flour if necessary, for about 5 minutes. The dough should be smooth and slightly sticky. Shape into a ball.

7 Roll out the dough to a rectangle measuring about 35.5 × 30.5 cm (14 × 12 inches). Spread the spinach mixture over the dough, leaving a 2.5 cm (1 inch) border.

8 Roll up the dough like a Swiss roll. Wrap tightly in a muslin cloth and tie the ends with string.

9 Bring a large flameproof casserole, roasting tin or fish kettle of salted water to the boil and place the roll in it. Return to the boil, then reduce the heat and simmer, partially covered, for 30 minutes. Remove the roll from the water, unwrap and leave to cool for 2 hours.

10 Cut the roll into 2.5 cm (1 inch) thick slices and arrange the slices, slightly overlapping, in an ovenproof dish.

11 Melt the margarine or butter and pour over the slices. Sprinkle with the remaining Parmesan cheese and bake in the oven at 200°C (400°F) mark 6 for about15 minutes or until golden. Serve hot, with Tomato Sauce.
SERVES 8

—EIGHT—

GRILLED AND FRIED

DISHES

There has been a marked decline in the popularity of deep-fat frying in recent years as we all strive for lower-fat, healthier diets. However, providing it is done correctly, the amount of fat absorbed during cooking can be kept to a minimum. It's preferable to use oil that is high in polyunsaturates; safflower, sunflower, corn, grapeseed or soya oil are all suitable. Cooking oils are stable at high temperatures but some molecular changes do take place when oil is heated, so change it after two or three uses.

An electric deep-fat fryer is a good investment since it ensures that the fat reaches the correct temperature and it has a lid to keep smells to a minimum.

Pans of hot oil are notoriously dangerous, so, of course, never leave a pan unattended on the hob. Push the pan to the back of the hob and leave it to cool completely before straining the oil. Thoroughly drain the fried food on crumpled absorbent kitchen paper.

Grilling is a healthier option. Always preheat the grill until hot before cooking to ensure that the food has a good crisp surface. Anything suitable for grilling can be cooked on the barbecue in summer.

This eclectic collection of dishes meets all requirements. Some, like Felafel (see page 114), and Onion Pakoras (see page 116), are suitable starters or could also be served as part of a tapas-style meal, with salad and vegetable based dishes, chunks of bread and chilled lager or red wine.

$\mathcal{B}$EAN BURGERS WITH MANGO CHUTNEY

Make sure that you mash the beans thoroughly in step 3 or the mixture will not hold together when it is cooked. The chutney makes a delicious and unusual accompaniment.

125 g (4 oz) brown rice	1 cm (½ inch) piece of fresh root ginger, peeled and grated
salt and pepper	40 g (1½ oz) medium oatmeal
225 g (8 oz) cooked beans, such as red kidney, black-eyed or aduki (see page 10), or a 425 g (15 oz) can of beans, drained and rinsed	vegetable oil for frying or grilling
	For the Mango Chutney
	1 small ripe mango
1–2 garlic cloves, skinned and crushed	30 ml (2 level tbsp) desiccated or shredded coconut
2.5 ml (½ level tsp) curry paste	finely grated rind and juice of 1 lime
10 ml (2 level tsp) tomato purée	

1 Cook the rice in boiling salted water for about 30 minutes or until tender.
2 Meanwhile, make the mango chutney. Peel the mango and cut the flesh away from the stone. Cut the flesh into small pieces and mix with the remaining ingredients. Set aside.
3 When the rice is cooked, drain and leave it to cool slightly. Put the beans in a bowl and mash thoroughly with a potato masher. Add the garlic, curry paste, tomato purée, ginger and rice. Season with salt and pepper and beat thoroughly until the mixture clings together.
4 Shape the mixture into eight burgers. Spread the oatmeal on a plate and press the burgers into it to coat lightly.
5 Heat some vegetable oil in a frying pan and fry the burgers for 2–3 minutes on each side or until golden brown. Alternatively, brush the burgers lightly with oil and grill for 2–3 minutes on each side or until golden brown. Serve with the chutney.
SERVES 4

Curried Tofu Burgers *left*, Wild Rice and Thyme Salad *right (page 51)*

CURRIED TOFU BURGERS

Adding tofu to vegetarian burgers ensures that they remain moist. It also produces burgers that are lower in fat than those based entirely on nuts.

15 ml (1 tbsp) vegetable oil	5 ml (1 level tsp) tomato purée
1 large carrot, trimmed, peeled and finely grated	225 g (8 oz) packet original tofu
1 large onion, skinned and finely grated	25 g (1 oz) wholemeal breadcrumbs
10 ml (2 level tsp) coriander seeds, finely crushed (optional)	25 g (1 oz) mixed nuts, finely chopped
1 garlic clove, skinned and crushed	salt and pepper
	plain flour
5 ml (1 level tsp) curry paste	vegetable oil for frying or grilling

1 Heat the 15 ml (1 tbsp) oil in a large frying pan. Add the carrot and onion and fry for 3–4 minutes or until the vegetables are softened, stirring all the time. Add the coriander seeds, if using, garlic, curry paste and tomato purée. Increase the heat and fry for 2 minutes, stirring all the time.
2 Mash the tofu with a potato masher, then stir into the vegetables with the breadcrumbs and nuts. Season with salt and pepper, and beat thoroughly until the mixture starts to

stick together. With floured hands, shape the mixture into eight burgers.
3 Heat some oil in a frying pan and fry the burgers for 3–4 minutes on each side or until golden brown. Alternatively, to grill the burgers, brush them lightly with oil and cook under a hot grill for about 3 minutes on each side or until golden brown. Drain on absorbent kitchen paper and serve hot.
MAKES 8

FELAFEL

Serve these spicy chick-pea balls as a main course with Tzatziki (see page 54) and a fruit and nut pilaff, or as an appetiser with a bowl of yogurt flavoured with chopped fresh coriander or mint for guests to dip the felafel into.

225 g (8 oz) chick-peas, soaked overnight in cold water, then drained and cooked (see page 10) or two 425 g (15 oz) cans chick-peas, drained and rinsed	*1 garlic clove, skinned and crushed*
5 ml (1 level tsp) ground cumin	*30 ml (2 tbsp) tahini (see page 14)*
5 ml (1 level tsp) ground turmeric	*50 g (2 oz) fresh breadcrumbs*
5 ml (1 level tsp) cayenne pepper	*45 ml (3 level tbsp) chopped fresh coriander*
5 ml (1 level tsp) salt	*plain flour for coating*
	vegetable oil for frying

1 Put all the ingredients, except the flour and oil, in a food processor or blender and process until the chick-peas are finely chopped but not puréed.
2 Turn the mixture into a large bowl and add about 30 ml (2 tbsp) water. Knead the mixture with your hands until it begins to cling together, adding a little extra water, if necessary.
3 With floured hands, shape the mixture into 20 walnut-sized balls. Slightly flatten each ball with the palm of your hand and coat in flour.
4 Heat the oil in a deep-fat fryer to 190°C (375°F) or until a 2.5 cm (1 inch) cube of bread will brown in the hot oil in 40 seconds. Fry the felafel in the hot oil, a few at a time, for 2–3 minutes or until golden brown. Drain on crumpled absorbent kitchen paper and serve hot.
SERVES 4–6

GRILLED GOATS' CHEESES WITH LAVENDER

Serve as a starter, a light lunch or as part of a barbecue menu with a tomato, olive and onion salad.

5 ml (1 level tsp) chopped fresh lavender blossom	*eight 25–40 g (1–1½ oz) fresh soft goats' cheeses*
15 ml (1 level tbsp) chopped fresh herbs, such as parsley and thyme	*8 fresh vine leaves*
	olive oil

1 Mix together the lavender and herbs, then roll the goats' cheeses in the mixture until lightly coated.
2 Drop the vine leaves in boiling water and leave for 1–2 minutes. Drain and refresh under cold running water. Dry with absorbent kitchen paper.
3 Brush both sides of the leaves with olive oil. Wrap each cheese in a leaf and secure with a wooden cocktail stick.
4 Cook the parcels under a medium grill for 4–5 minutes, keeping them 7.5–10 cm (3–4 inches) from the heat. The leaves should be just beginning to turn brown. Serve immediately.
SERVES 8

CRISP FRIED ONIONS

These delicious, flavoursome morsels are invaluable for adding extra colour, texture and flavour to pilaffs, birianis, curries, salads and casseroles. They can be stored for up to 2 weeks in an airtight container in the refrigerator.

2 medium onions, skinned	*vegetable oil for frying*

1 Cut the onions in half lengthways, then cut into thin slices.
2 Heat about 0.5 cm (¼ inch) oil in a frying pan. When hot, add the onions and fry for about 10 minutes or until golden brown, stirring all the time. Remove the onions from the pan with a slotted spoon and drain on absorbent kitchen paper. Leave to cool and become crisp before using as desired.

VEGETABLE TEMPURA

This dish of crisp, raw vegetables, quickly fried in a light, semi-transparent batter, sums up the Japanese feeling for food. Ingredients should be at their natural best and cooking should be kept to a minimum, so that flavour, texture and aroma can all be enjoyed to the full.

25 g (1 oz) fresh root ginger, peeled and grated	*125 g (4 oz) cauliflower florets*
60 ml (4 tbsp) sake or dry sherry	*2 large carrots, trimmed*
45 ml (3 tbsp) soy sauce	*16 button mushrooms*
125 g (4 oz) plain flour, plus 30 ml (2 level tbsp)	*2 medium courgettes*
30 ml (2 level tbsp) cornflour	*2 red peppers*
30 ml (2 level tbsp) arrowroot	*vegetable oil for deep-frying*
salt and pepper	

1 First make the dipping sauce. Put the ginger in a bowl and add the sake or sherry, the soy sauce and 200 ml (7 fl oz) boiling water. Stir well to mix, then set aside while preparing the vegetables and batter.
2 Sift the 125 g (4 oz) plain flour, the cornflour and arrowroot into a large bowl with a pinch each of salt and pepper. Gradually whisk in 300 ml (½ pint) ice cold water to form a smooth, thin batter. Chill.
3 Divide the cauliflower into tiny sprigs, discarding any thick, woody stalks. Peel the carrots and cut into thin sticks. Wipe the mushrooms and trim the stalks, if necessary. Trim and slice the courgettes.

4 Cut the red peppers in half, remove the cores and seeds and slice the flesh into thin strips. Toss the vegetables in the 30 ml (2 level tbsp) plain flour.
5 Heat the oil in a wok or deep-fat fryer to 190°C (375°F) or until a 2.5 cm (1 inch) cube of bread will brown in the hot oil in 40 seconds. Dip the vegetables in the batter in batches, then remove with a slotted spoon, taking up a lot of the batter with the vegetables. Deep-fry for 3–5 minutes or until crisp, then remove with a slotted spoon. Drain on absorbent kitchen paper. Serve immediately, with the dipping sauce.
SERVES 4

$\mathcal{O}$NION PAKORAS

In northern India, these more-ish morsels are served as a teatime snack, while in southern and western India they are known as *bhaijas* and are served as part of a main meal.

450 g (1 lb) onions, skinned	*5 ml (1 level tsp) chilli powder*
125 g (4 oz) gram or plain wholemeal flour	*5 ml (1 level tsp) ground caradamom*
50 g (2 oz) self-raising flour	*30 ml (2 level tbsp) chopped fresh mint or coriander*
5 ml (1 level tsp) garam masala	*salt and pepper*
5 ml (1 level tsp) ground turmeric	*vegetable oil for frying*

1 Halve the onions, then cut into very thin crescent-shaped slices. Mix the onions with the remaining ingredients, season with salt and pepper, and add 90–120 ml (6–8 tbsp) water, or enough to make a fairly stiff paste. Divide into eight and shape roughly into rounds with your fingers and a tablespoon.

2 Heat some vegetable oil in a frying pan and fry the pakoras in batches for about 3 minutes on each side or until well browned. Drain on absorbent kitchen paper and serve hot.
MAKES 8

~ED DAL CROQUETTES

The moong dal ... ...s are not cooked before being ground to a paste. For this reason, it is ess... ... for the full 24 hours or they will not be soft enough.

225 g (8 oz) moong dal	*salt and pepper*
5 ml (1 level tsp) caraway	*about 60 ml (4 tbsp) vegetable oil*
2.5 ml (½ level tsp) chilli p...	*300 ml (½ pint) natural yogurt*
5 ml (1 level tsp) garam mas...	*...0 ml (2 level tbsp) chopped fresh mint*
2.5 ml (½ level tsp) ground tur...	

1 Pick over the dal and remove any grit discoloured pulses. Put into a sieve and wash thoroughly under cold running water. Drain.
2 Put the dal in a bowl and cover with cold water. Leave to soak for 24 hours.
3 Drain the dal, then process in batches in a food processor until ground to a fine paste. Add the spices and 2.5 ml (½ level tsp) salt and work again until thoroughly mixed in.
4 Heat a little oil in a heavy-based frying pan until smoking hot. Add spoonfuls of the croquette mixture and fry for 2–3 minutes on each side until lightly coloured.

5 Remove the croquettes with a slotted spoon, then drain well on absorbent kitchen paper while frying the remainder.
6 Put the yogurt in a blender or food processor with the mint. Season with salt and pepper, and process to a thin sauce.
7 Put the hot croquettes in a shallow serving dish and pour over the yogurt sauce. Cover the dish and chill for at least 2 hours before serving.
SERVES 4

Muttar Paneer (page 87) left, Onion Pakoras right

STIR-FRIED VEGETABLES

Vegetable stir-fries are delicious made with whatever vegetables you have to hand, though it's important to cut them all into pieces of a similar size. Add tougher, slower-cooking vegetables, such as baby sweetcorn, carrots, green beans, onions, peppers, celery, fennel and radish, first. Delicate fast-cooking vegetables, such as bean sprouts, Chinese leaves, pak choi and spinach, need only 2–3 minutes in the hot oil. Once you've grasped the basic technique, it has endless possibilities. When cooked, the vegetables should be served right away, so make sure that any accompanying noodles or rice are almost cooked when you begin stir-frying.

60 ml (4 tbsp) peanut (groundnut) or vegetable oil	900 g (2 lb) mixed vegetables, prepared as necessary and cut into thin strips or slices
2 garlic cloves, skinned and crushed	
2.5 cm (1 inch) piece of fresh root ginger, peeled and sliced	15 ml (1 tbsp) light soy sauce
	15 ml (1 tbsp) dry sherry
1–2 fresh chillies, seeded and chopped (optional)	5 ml (1 level tsp) sugar
125 g (4 oz) cashew nuts, peanuts or almonds	5 ml (1 level tsp) five-spice powder (optional)

1 Heat the oil in a wok or very large, deep frying pan. Add the garlic, ginger and chillies, if using, and stir-fry for 1–2 minutes. Add the nuts and cook for 2 minutes, stirring all the time. Remove the pan from the heat, remove the nuts with a slotted spoon and set aside.

2 Reheat the oil, then sprinkle in any slow-cooking vegetables. Cook over a very high heat for 3–4 minutes, stirring all the time. Add the remaining vegetables and cook for a further 2–3 minutes or until heated through but still very crisp.

3 Add the soy sauce, sherry, sugar and five-spice powder, if using. Cook for a further 1 minute, then transfer to a warmed serving dish, sprinkle with the nuts and serve immediately.
SERVES 4–6

VARIATIONS

Stir-fried Vegetables with Coconut Milk Omit the nuts, soy sauce, sherry, sugar and five-spice powder. Dissolve 175 g (6 oz) creamed coconut in 450 ml (¾ pint) boiling water. Mix with 5 ml (1 level tsp) ground cumin and 30 ml (2 tbsp) chopped fresh coriander. Cook the vegetables as above, then, when the vegetables are cooked, remove them from the pan with a slotted spoon and set aside. Add the coconut mixture to the hot oil and cook for 1 minute, stirring all the time. Return the vegetables to the pan and reheat for 1–2 minutes. Serve immediately.

Stir-fried Vegetables with Tofu or Quorn Marinate 225 g (8 oz) diced tofu or Quorn in 30 ml (2 tbsp) soy sauce and 30 ml (2 tbsp) dry sherry with 1 skinned and crushed garlic clove for at least 30 minutes before cooking. Drain the Quorn or tofu and stir-fry in hot oil for 2–3 minutes. Remove from the pan and set aside. Cook the vegetables as above and add the soy sauce mixture as in the main recipe, or the coconut mixture. Stir in the Quorn or tofu at the end and reheat for 1–2 minutes before serving.

$\mathscr{S}$PAGHETTI WITH GARLIC

Increase or decrease the quantity of garlic and chilli used in this recipe according to your taste. It's an intensely flavoured dish, so a small amount of spaghetti goes a long way. Serve with a crisp mixed leaf and watercress salad dressed lightly with a sharp vinaigrette.

about 450 g (1 lb) dried spaghetti	1 chilli, seeded and chopped
salt and pepper	30 ml (2 level tbsp) chopped fresh parsley, coriander or basil (optional)
75 ml (5 tbsp) virgin olive oil	
2 garlic cloves, skinned and crushed	

1 Cook the spaghetti in boiling salted water for 8–10 minutes or until *al dente* (tender but still firm to the bite).
2 Meanwhile, heat the oil in a heavy-based saucepan, add the garlic and chilli and fry for 3–4 minutes, stirring occasionally. Don't let the garlic and chilli become too brown or the oil will taste bitter. Remove from the heat and set aside until the pasta is cooked.
3 Drain the pasta thoroughly. Reheat the oil over a very high heat for 1 minute, then pour over the pasta with the herbs, if using. Season with salt and pepper and serve immediately.
SERVES 6

$\mathscr{B}$OLOGNESE SAUCE

This is our vegetarian version of the classic pasta sauce, with apologies to the Italians! Use it to dress pasta, fill lasagne or as a base for shepherd's pie.

30 ml (2 tbsp) olive oil	1 bay leaf
1 celery stick, trimmed and finely chopped	1 bouquet garni
2 carrots, trimmed, peeled and finely chopped	5 ml (1 level tsp) yeast extract
1 medium onion, skinned and finely chopped	5 ml (1 level tsp) sugar
125 g (4 oz) mushrooms, wiped and finely chopped	salt and pepper
2 garlic cloves, skinned and crushed	freshly grated nutmeg
45 ml (3 level tbsp) tomato purée	1 cinnamon stick
two 397 g (14 oz) cans chopped tomatoes	175 g (6 oz) soya mince
300 ml (½ pint) dry red wine	45 ml (3 tbsp) chopped fresh parsley
600 ml (1 pint) vegetable stock	

1 Heat the oil in a large, heavy-based saucepan, add the celery, carrots, onion, mushrooms and garlic and fry for about 5 minutes or until softened. Add the tomato purée and fry for 1 minute, then add all the remaining ingredients except the parsley. Bring to the boil, then reduce the heat, cover and simmer gently for 30–45 minutes or until the soya mince is very tender.
2 Stir in the parsley and season with more salt, pepper and nutmeg, if necessary. Remove the cinnamon stick, bay leaf and bouquet garni before serving.
SERVES 8

SPRING VEGETABLE PASTA

The beauty of this recipe is its versatility. Try experimenting with different combinations of
herbs and vegetables as they come into season. Alternative types of pasta may also be used.

125 g (4 oz) fresh asparagus or French beans, trimmed
225 g (8 oz) leeks, trimmed and thinly sliced diagonally
salt and pepper
175 g (6 oz) creamy goats' cheese or full-fat soft cheese with garlic and herbs
150 g (5 oz) mascarpone cheese or 150 ml (¼ pint) extra-thick double cream
50 g (2 oz) vegetable margarine or butter
30 ml (2 tbsp) olive oil
1 medium onion, skinned and finely chopped
125 g (4 oz) carrots, trimmed, peeled and thinly sliced diagonally

225 g (8 oz) brown-cap (chestnut) mushrooms, wiped and thinly sliced
100 ml (4 fl oz) dry white white
350 g (12 oz) crème fraîche
60 ml (4 level tbsp) chopped fresh herbs, such as parsley, thyme and sage
125 g (4 oz) frozen petits pois
450–700 g (1-1½ lb) dried penne
mascarpone cheese, to serve

1 Cut the asparagus or French beans into
5 cm (2 inch) lengths and blanch with the
leeks in boiling salted water for 3–4 minutes.
Drain thoroughly. Mix together the goats'
cheese and mascarpone cheese or cream.

2 Heat the margarine or butter with the oil
in a large frying pan. Stir in the onion and
cook, stirring, for 3–4 minutes. Add the
carrots and mushrooms and continue to cook
for 2–3 minutes or until beginning to soften.

3 Stir in all the remaining ingredients, except
the cheese mixture, pasta and mascarpone,
and simmer very gently until thickened.

4 Meanwhile, cook the pasta in boiling salted
water for about 10 minutes or until al dente
(tender but still firm to the bite).

5 Remove the sauce from the heat and
gently stir in the cheese mixture. Season with
salt and pepper.

6 Drain the pasta thoroughly and transfer to a
warmed serving dish. Spoon on the hot sauce
and serve immediately, topped with a
spoonful of mascarpone.

SERVES 4

$\mathcal{S}$PINACH AND RICOTTA CANNELLONI

It's much easier to make cannelloni using sheets of lasagne than it is to make it with cannelloni tubes. If you cannot buy sheets of fresh lasagne, use dried, but cook them first according to packet instructions and reduce the final cooking time to about 20 minutes.

60 ml (4 tbsp) olive oil	salt and pepper
2 small onions, skinned and finely chopped	1 garlic clove, skinned and crushed
30 ml (2 level tbsp) tomato purée	450 g (1 lb) frozen leaf spinach, thawed and drained
5 ml (1 level tsp) mild paprika	450 g (1 lb) ricotta cheese
two 397 g (14 oz) cans chopped tomatoes	freshly grated nutmeg
pinch of dried oregano	18 small sheets of fresh lasagne
300 ml (½ pint) dry red wine or vegetable stock	freshly grated Parmesan cheese or a few breadcrumbs
large pinch of sugar	

1 To make the sauce, heat half the oil in a heavy-based saucepan, add half the onion and fry for 5–10 minutes or until very soft. Add the tomato purée and paprika and fry for 2–3 minutes. Add the tomatoes, oregano, red wine or stock and sugar, and season with salt and pepper. Simmer for 20 minutes.
2 Heat the remaining oil in a large saucepan, add the garlic and remaining onion and cook for 5 minutes, stirring all the time. Add the spinach and cook for 2 minutes. Cool slightly,

then add the ricotta cheese. Season with nutmeg, salt and pepper.
3 Lay the lasagne sheets on a work surface and divide the spinach mixture between them. Roll up the sheets to enclose the filling and arrange, seam-side down in a single layer, in a greased ovenproof dish. Pour the sauce over and sprinkle with Parmesan cheese or breadcrumbs. Bake in the oven at 200°C (400°F) mark 6 for 30 minutes.
SERVES 4–6

$\mathcal{P}$ASTA WITH MUSHROOM AND HUMMUS SAUCE

Commercially prepared hummus makes the basis for a very quick and easy pasta sauce.

30 ml (2 tbsp) olive oil	225 g (8 oz) hummus
225 g (8 oz) button mushrooms, wiped and sliced	30 ml (2 tbsp) milk
1 bunch of spring onions, trimmed and chopped	225 g (8 oz) dried spaghetti or tortellini
pinch of cumin seeds	salt and pepper

1 Heat the oil in a saucepan. Add the vegetables and cumin seeds and fry for 2–3 minutes, stirring constantly.
2 Add the hummus and milk. Cover and simmer for 5–10 minutes.

3 Meanwhile, cook the pasta in boiling salted water for 8–10 minutes or until al dente (tender but still firm to the bite). Drain well.
4 Stir the pasta into the sauce and season.
SERVES 2

TAGLIATELLE WITH SUN-DRIED TOMATO SAUCE

For an occasional treat, serve the pasta and sauce topped with a spoonful of crème fraîche and a generous amount of coarsely grated Pecorino or Parmesan cheese. The sauce is equally good served with spaghetti or another type of pasta.

25 ml (1 fl oz) olive oil (preferably from the jar of sun-dried tomatoes)	1 garlic clove, skinned and crushed
	397 g (14 oz) can chopped tomatoes
25 g (1 oz) vegetable margarine or butter	125 g (4 oz) drained sun-dried tomatoes, finely chopped
1 small onion, roughly chopped	100 ml (4 fl oz) dry white wine
75 g (3 oz) celery, roughly chopped	salt and pepper
75 g (3 oz) carrot, roughly chopped	450–700 g (1–1½ lb) dried tagliatelle

1 Heat the oil and margarine or butter in a large saucepan. Add the onion, celery, carrot and garlic and cook, stirring, for 8–10 minutes or until beginning to soften.

2 Stir in the canned tomatoes, sun-dried tomatoes and wine. Season with salt and pepper, cover and simmer for about 30 minutes, stirring occasionally.

3 Meanwhile, cook the tagliatelle in boiling salted water for 8–10 minutes or until *al dente* (tender but still slightly firm to the bite).

4 Pour about half the sauce into a food processor or blender and purée until quite smooth. Stir into the remaining sauce and reheat if necessary.

5 Drain the tagliatelle thoroughly and transfer to a warmed serving bowl. Pour over the sauce and serve immediately.

SERVES 4

$\mathscr{P}$ASTA WITH LEEKS AND FROMAGE FRAIS

Use a hot variety of horseradish relish to give the sauce a good 'kick'.

45 ml (3 tbsp) olive oil	salt and pepper
225 g (8 oz) leeks, trimmed, washed thoroughly and sliced	300 ml (½ pint) fromage frais
150 ml (¼ pint) vegetable stock	15 ml (1 tbsp) horseradish relish
225–275 g (8–10 oz) pasta of your choice	chopped fresh parsley, to garnish

1 Heat the oil in a saucepan. Add the leeks and cook over a low heat for 4–5 minutes or until the leeks begin to soften. Add the stock, bring to the boil, then reduce the heat, cover and simmer for 15–20 minutes or until the leeks are very soft.

2 Meanwhile, cook the pasta in boiling salted water for 8–12 minutes or until *al dente* (tender but still firm to the bite).

3 Stir the fromage frais and horseradish into the leek mixture. Season with salt and pepper and heat gently, without boiling and stirring all the time. Drain the pasta and transfer to a warmed serving bowl. Pour over the sauce, toss together and serve immediately, sprinkled with parsley.
SERVES 2

$\mathscr{S}$TUFFED BAKED PASTA SHELLS

You will need very large pasta shells for this recipe, measuring about 4 cm (1½ inches) long before cooking; once cooked they are even bigger. Don't be tempted to use smaller shells – you will run out of patience trying to stuff them! Serve with a mixed salad.

90 g (3½ oz) vegetable margarine or butter	24 large dried pasta shells
175 g (6 oz) salted cashew nuts, roughly chopped	35 g (1¼ oz) plain flour
175 g (6 oz) button mushrooms, wiped and roughly chopped	750 ml (1¼ pints) milk
	1 bay leaf
1 small onion, skinned and roughly chopped	275 g (10 oz) Lancashire cheese, coarsely grated
50 g (2 oz) celery, trimmed and roughly chopped	45 ml (3 level tbsp) chopped fresh parsley
225 g (8 oz) fresh spinach	1 free-range egg
salt and pepper	

1 Melt 50 g (2 oz) margarine or butter in a large frying pan. Add the cashew nuts, mushrooms, onion and celery, and fry for about 10 minutes or until golden and any excess liquid has evaporated, stirring occasionally.

2 Wash the spinach, put in a saucepan, cover and cook over a low heat until just wilted.

Drain well, then roughly chop. Stir into the mixture, season and leave to cool.

3 Cook the pasta shells in boiling salted water for about 10 minutes or until just tender. Drain well. Fill the shells with the nut mixture and place in a single layer in a large, shallow ovenproof dish.

4 Melt the remaining margarine or butter in

a small saucepan. Add the flour and cook, stirring, for 1–2 minutes, then remove from the heat and gradually blend in the milk. Add the bay leaf, then bring to the boil and simmer, stirring, for 2–3 minutes. Remove from the heat and discard the bay leaf, then beat in the cheese, parsley and egg. Season with salt and pepper and spoon evenly over the pasta.

5 Bake at 180°C (350°F) mark 4 for about 40 minutes or until golden and bubbling.
SERVES 4–6

MUSHROOM LASAGNE

The preparation of lasagne is always lengthy, but the benefit is that it can be frozen or finished a day ahead ready for last-minute baking.

225 g (8 oz) frozen leaf spinach, thawed	*30 ml (2 tbsp) lemon juice*
salt and pepper	*75 g (3 oz) plain flour*
olive oil	*600 ml (1 pint) milk*
about 350 g (12 oz) fresh lasagne or 225 g (8 oz) dried lasagne	*600 ml (1 pint) vegetable stock*
900 g (2 lb) mixed mushrooms, such as button, flat and brown-cap (chestnut), wiped	*freshly grated nutmeg, to taste*
	2 large garlic cloves, skinned and crushed
	175 g (6 oz) Gruyère cheese, grated
125 g (4 oz) vegetable margarine or butter	*50 g (2 oz) fresh white breadcrumbs*

1 Drain the spinach and squeeze out any excess liquid. Chop finely.

2 Bring a large saucepan of salted water to the boil. (Use two if necessary.) Add a dash of olive oil to each, followed by the lasagne. Cook according to packet instructions, stirring occasionally. When the pasta is tender, drain it in a colander and immediately run cold water over it. This will stop the pasta from cooking further and will rinse off some of the starch. Spread the pasta out on clean tea-towels and cover with a damp tea-towel until required.

3 Quarter or slice the mushrooms, or leave them whole, depending on their size. Melt half the margarine or butter in a large saucepan. Add the mushrooms and lemon juice, and season with salt and pepper. Cover and cook over a fairly high heat for 4–6 minutes or until the mushrooms are tender. Remove from the pan with a slotted spoon, then bubble the juices to evaporate any excess moisture until there is only fat left in the saucepan.

4 Melt the remaining margarine or butter in the same saucepan. Carefully stir in the flour and cook for 1–2 minutes before slowly blending in the milk and stock. Gradually bring to the boil, making sure that you keep stirring all the time, and cook for 1–2 minutes or until boiling and thickened. Mix in the nutmeg, garlic and spinach. Taste and adjust the seasoning if necessary.

5 Spoon a little of the sauce into the base of a 2.8 litre (5 pint) ovenproof dish. Top with a layer of pasta followed by a layer of mushrooms. Spoon over more of the sauce, then continue layering the ingredients, finishing with the sauce, making sure that it completely covers the ingredients underneath. Sprinkle over the Gruyère cheese and breadcrumbs.

6 Stand the dish on a baking tray and cook at 200°C (400°F) mark 6 for 45 minutes– 1 hour.
SERVES 6

$\mathscr{P}$ENNE WITH TOMATO AND CHILLI

This simple sauce is equally delicious if made in advance, cooled and then reheated when required. It is also good served with baked potatoes, nut roasts, burgers or a different type of pasta. Should you need to make it in a hurry, from storecupboard ingredients, some or all of the vegetables may be omitted.

30 ml (2 tbsp) olive oil	1–2 fresh red chillies, seeded and chopped
2 celery sticks, trimmed and finely chopped	two 397 g (14 oz) cans chopped tomatoes
1 small carrot, trimmed, peeled and finely chopped	150 ml (¼ pint) dry red wine or vegetable stock
1 medium onion, skinned and finely chopped	a handful of fresh parsley (including some stalks), chopped
1–2 garlic cloves, skinned and crushed	salt and pepper
30 ml (2 level tbsp) tomato purée	450 g (1 lb) dried penne
5 ml (1 level tsp) dried herbes de Provence	

1 Heat the oil in a large heavy-based saucepan. Add the celery, carrot, onion and garlic and cook over a high heat for 2–3 minutes, stirring all the time. Lower the heat and continue cooking for about 5 minutes or until the vegetables are beginning to soften without browning.
2 Add the tomato purée, dried herbs and chillies, increase the heat and fry for 1–2 minutes. Add the tomatoes, red wine or stock and half the parsley. Season with salt and pepper and bring to the boil, then lower the

heat, cover and simmer for 45 minutes.
3 Cook the pasta in boiling salted water for about 10 minutes or until al dente (tender but still firm to the bite).
4 While the pasta is cooking, remove the lid from the sauce, increase the heat and cook vigorously until it is reduced and thickened. Add the remaining parsley, taste and adjust the seasoning, if necessary.
5 Drain the pasta and tip it into the sauce. Toss together to mix and serve immediately.
SERVES 4

$\mathscr{V}$EGETABLE LASAGNE

Sheets of fresh lasagne are available in the chilled cabinet of most supermarkets these days. If using pre-cooked dried lasagne sheets, add a little extra liquid (stock or water) to the vegetable mixture. Serve with a crisp green salad.

30 ml (2 tbsp) olive oil	2 large courgettes, trimmed and sliced
1 garlic clove, skinned and crushed	two 397 g (14 oz) cans chopped tomatoes
1 carrot, trimmed, peeled and chopped	30 ml (2 level tbsp) tomato purée
1 large onion, skinned and sliced	2 bay leaves
1 red pepper, cored, seeded and chopped	about 350 g (12 oz) fresh lasagne or 225 g (8 oz) dried
15 ml (1 level tbsp) mild paprika	salt and pepper
10 ml (2 level tsp) dried oregano or marjoram	900 ml (1½ pints) Béchamel Sauce (see page 189)
1 large aubergine, trimmed and cut into large chunks	Parmesan or Cheddar cheese, grated (optional)
225 g (8 oz) button mushrooms, wiped and sliced	

1 Heat the oil in a large saucepan. Add the garlic, carrot, onion and pepper and fry for 1–2 minutes or until beginning to soften. Add the paprika, herbs and aubergine and fry for a few minutes more.

2 Add the remaining vegetables to the pan with the tomatoes, tomato purée and bay leaves. Bring to the boil, then reduce the heat, cover and simmer for 30 minutes.

3 Meanwhile, if using dried lasagne that needs pre-cooking, cook it in boiling salted water according to packet instructions. Drain and leave to dry on a clean tea-towel.

4 Spread a small amount of the tomato sauce in the base of a 2.8 litre (5 pint) ovenproof dish. Cover with a layer of lasagne and top with a layer of Béchamel Sauce. Continue layering in this way, ending with a layer of Béchamel Sauce that covers the pasta completely. Sprinkle with the cheese, if using.

5 Bake the lasagne in the oven at 200°C (400°F) mark 6 for 45 minutes–1 hour or until the lasagne is piping hot and well browned. Leave to stand for 15 minutes before serving.

SERVES 6

Vegetable Lasagne

Potato Gnocchi

POTATO GNOCCHI

Gnocchi are little dumplings, made in this recipe from potatoes although there are other versions made with semolina, spinach and ricotta cheese. The Italians always eat gnocchi as a first course, sometimes simply sprinkled with melted butter and grated Parmesan cheese, at other times coated in a rich and pungent tomato sauce. The type of gnocchi and the way in which they are served is purely regional; these potato gnocchi are fairly typical of the regions of northern Italy. In Lombardy and Veneto, chopped fresh sage would be added to the melted butter and cheese, whereas in Liguria they like to serve their gnocchi with pesto sauce.

900 g (2 lb) old floury potatoes, such as King Edward or Maris Piper	*225–275 g (8–10 oz) plain flour*
salt	***To serve***
50 g (2 oz) vegetable margarine or butter	*1 quantity Pesto (see page 193) or Tomato Sauce (see page 190)*
1 free-range egg, beaten	*freshly grated Parmesan cheese*

1 Cook the potatoes in their skins in boiling salted water for about 20 minutes or until tender. Drain well, cool slightly and peel.
2 While the potatoes are still warm, push them through a sieve into a large bowl. Add 5 ml (1 tsp) salt, the margarine or butter, egg and half the flour. Mix well to bind together.
3 Turn the mixture out on to a floured surface and knead gently, gradually adding more flour, until the dough is soft, smooth and slightly sticky.
4 With floured hands, roll the dough into 2.5 cm (1 inch) thick ropes. Cut the ropes into 2 cm (¾ inch) pieces.
5 Press a finger into each piece of dough to flatten, then draw your finger towards you to curl the sides of the gnocchi. Alternatively,

make a decorative shape by using the same rolling technique, but roll each dumpling over the end of the prongs of a fork. Spread the dumplings out on a floured tea-towel.
6 Bring a large pan of salted water to the boil and reduce to barely simmering. Drop in a few gnocchi at a time and cook gently for 2–3 minutes or until they float to the surface.
7 With a slotted spoon, remove the gnocchi from the pan, then place them in a greased serving dish. Cover and keep warm while cooking the remaining gnocchi.
8 When all the gnocchi are cooked, toss them in the chosen sauce. Serve immediately, sprinkled with Parmesan.
SERVES 4 AS A STARTER OR LIGHT MEAL

RICOTTA GNOCCHI

Gnocchi made with ricotta cheese are light and easy to make. Taleggio is a semi-soft Italian cheese; use Gouda or Edam instead if you can't find it.

For the gnocchi	For the sauce
150 g (5 oz) ricotta cheese	50 g (2 oz) vegetable margarine or butter
25 g (1 oz) vegetable margarine or softened butter	1 garlic clove, skinned and crushed
15 ml (1 level tbsp) plain flour	30 ml (2 level tbsp) plain flour
1 free-range egg	568 ml (1 pint) milk
freshly grated nutmeg	225 g (8 oz) taleggio, coarsely grated
salt and pepper	salt and pepper

1 Beat together all the gnocchi ingredients until smooth, adding nutmeg, salt and pepper to taste. Cover and chill for 30 minutes.
2 Meanwhile, make the sauce. Melt the margarine or butter with the garlic and stir in the flour. Cook, stirring, for 1–2 minutes, then gradually add the milk. Bring slowly to the boil, stirring occasionally, then reduce the heat and simmer for 3–4 minutes or until thickened. Remove from the heat and beat in the taleggio. Season with salt and pepper. Cover with damp greaseproof paper.
3 Bring a large pan of salted water to the boil

and reduce to barely simmering. Drop in teaspoonfuls of the gnocchi mixture and cook for 4–5 minutes or until they float to the surface. Lift out with a slotted spoon and transfer to one large, or four individual, buttered flameproof dishes. Coat with the sauce.
4 Bake in the oven at 200°C (400°F) mark 6 for 25–30 minutes (15–20 minutes for individual dishes). Brown under a hot grill if necessary, then serve immediately.
SERVES 4 AS A STARTER OR LIGHT MEAL

$\mathscr{S}$PINACH GNOCCHI

If serving this as a starter, serve a light main course and dessert to follow.

900 g (2 lb) washed fresh spinach or 450 g (1 lb) frozen spinach	*1.25 ml (¼ level tsp) freshly grated nutmeg*
225 g (8 oz) curd cheese	*125 g (4 oz) freshly grated Parmesan cheese*
2 free-range eggs, beaten	*salt and pepper*
225 g (8 oz) plain flour	*125 g (4 oz) vegetable margarine or butter*

1 Place the spinach in a saucepan without any water, cover and cook gently for 5–10 minutes or until tender, or thawed if using frozen spinach. Drain very well and chop finely.

2 Mix together the curd cheese, eggs, flour, spinach, nutmeg and half the Parmesan. Season with salt and pepper.

3 With floured hands, form the mixture into cork-sized croquettes, or balls the size of large marbles. Chill in the refrigerator for at least 1 hour.

4 Bring a large pan of salted water to the boil and reduce to barely simmering. Drop in a few gnocchi at a time and cook for 8–10 minutes or until they float to the surface.

5 With a slotted spoon, remove the gnocchi from the pan, then place them in a greased serving dish. Cover and keep warm while cooking the remaining gnocchi.

6 Melt the margarine or butter in a small saucepan and pour it over the gnocchi. Sprinkle with the remaining cheese and serve immediately.

SERVES 4 AS A STARTER OR LIGHT MEAL

$\mathscr{P}$ASTA GRATIN

To make this a vegan dish, omit the cheese and make the Béchamel Sauce with soya milk.

75 g (3 oz) Gruyère cheese, grated	*225 g (8 oz) dried conchiglie or farfalle*
1.25 ml (¼ level tsp) freshly grated nutmeg	*1 quantity Tomato Sauce (see page 190)*
1 quantity hot Béchamel Sauce (see page 189)	*60 ml (4 level tbsp) freshly grated Parmesan cheese*
salt and pepper	*45 ml (3 level tbsp) dried breadcrumbs*

1 Add the Gruyère cheese and nutmeg to the Béchamel Sauce, season with salt and pepper and stir until the cheese has melted.

2 Cook the pasta in boiling salted water for about 10 minutes or until *al dente* (tender but still firm to the bite).

3 Drain the pasta and mix with the Tomato Sauce. Spread half this mixture in the bottom of a buttered ovenproof dish and pour over half the Béchamel Sauce. Repeat the layers, then sprinkle evenly with the Parmesan and breadcrumbs.

4 Bake in the oven at 190°C (375°F) mark 5 for 20 minutes, then brown under a hot grill for 5 minutes. Serve immediately.

SERVES 3–4

—Ten—

Rice, Grains and Noodles

Rice is the staple food for about half of the world's population. Infinitely versatile, it is easy to cook, convenient and relatively low in calories.

Cooking rice isn't difficult, providing you use a large enough pan (as when cooking pasta) and plenty of fast boiling salted water. As soon as the water boils, sprinkle the rice into the pan and keep the heat high until the water returns to the boil. Stir with a fork to loosen any grains that have sunk to the bottom of the pan, then lower the heat and simmer (quite vigorously) for a minimum of 10 minutes or until the rice is tender. Providing you have sufficient water, and a large enough pan, the rice will not stick. There are so many varieties of rice on the market today that it's impossible to give an exact cooking time. Test the rice as it cooks.

While the rice is cooking, fill a kettle with water and bring it to the boil. As soon as the rice is cooked, drain it through a sieve and rinse it with boiling water. Stir the grains with a fork and tip into a heated serving dish.

Brown rice is the whole grain with only the tough outer husk removed. Because the bran is retained, the rice has a chewy texture and nutty flavour. It is less refined than white rice so it takes longer to cook. It can be used in any recipes which call for long-grain rice, but if the dish is cooked by the absorption method, you should allow extra liquid. Basmati and Arborio rice are distinctive varieties.

Grains, such as barley, bulgar wheat, corn, cracked wheat and millet, are the edible seeds of different grasses. They are high in vitamins and can be used whole, cracked or flaked. Bulgar wheat is a useful ingredient to keep in the storecupboard. It requires a mere 30 minutes' soaking in boiling water before it is ready as an accompaniment to stews or casseroles, or for flavouring with herbs, garlic and vegetables to make a quick nutritious salad (see page 48). Corn grain is ground into cornmeal for making polenta (see page 142), cornbread (see page 58), tortillas and muffins.

Like pasta, noodles are now available in all shapes and sizes. Oriental noodles are most widely available dried and compressed into square packages. Allow about 75–125 g (3–4 oz) per person.

FRAGRANT COCONUT RICE

Lemon grass lends a unique flavour and smell to anything it's cooked with. If you cannot find any in the shops (but it really is worth looking for), add the finely grated rind of one lemon instead. This is not comparable, but adds a delicious flavour of its own. Galangal is a root that looks very similar to ginger. If you're lucky enough to find it fresh in an oriental shop, use it in place of dried in this recipe.

25 g (1 oz) creamed coconut, chopped	*1 cinnamon stick*
5 ml (1 level tsp) salt	*1 piece of lemon grass, split*
2.5 ml (½ level tsp) freshly grated nutmeg	*1 bay leaf*
freshly ground black pepper	*2 slices of dried or fresh galangal*
2 cloves	*350 g (12 oz) basmati rice*

1 Put all the ingredients, except the rice, in a heavy-based saucepan with 600 ml (1 pint) water. Bring slowly to the boil. Add the rice, stir with a fork, then cover and simmer gently for 20 minutes or until the water has been absorbed and the rice is tender.

2 Leave to stand for 2 minutes before serving.
SERVES 4–6

 USHROOM RISOTTO

To make a proper risotto, you will need to buy Arborio rice, a special variety from the Arborio region of Italy. It has the ability to absorb a large quantity of liquid during cooking without turning mushy. The perfect risotto is light and creamy, but not stodgy. Butter is traditionally added in copious quantities. It lends the best flavour, but vegetable margarine or olive oil can be used instead.

about 1.3 litres (2¼ pints) Mushroom, Brown Onion or vegetable stock (see pages 41–42)	*225 g (8 oz) mushrooms, wiped and sliced*
125 g (4 oz) butter or vegetable margarine	*350 g (12 oz) Arborio (risotto) rice*
1 medium onion, skinned and very finely chopped	*50 g (2 oz) freshly grated Parmesan cheese*
1 garlic clove, skinned and crushed	*salt and pepper*
10 g (¼ oz) packet dried porcini (cep) mushrooms, soaked in 300 ml (½ pint) warm water for 30 minutes	

1 Put the stock in a large saucepan and bring to the boil. Reduce the heat and keep at barely simmering point.

2 Meanwhile, melt half of the butter or margarine in a large heavy-based saucepan. Add the onion and garlic, and cook for about 5 minutes or until soft. Do not let them burn.

3 Drain the soaked dried mushrooms, reserving the soaking liquid. Chop any large mushrooms. Add to the onion and garlic with the fresh mushrooms and cook for 3–4 minutes, stirring all the time. Add the rice and cook for 1 minute.

4 Slowly pour the mushroom soaking liquid into the pan (being careful to leave any grit from the mushrooms in the bowl). Add about one-third of the stock. Cook gently, stirring occasionally, until the stock has been absorbed. Continue cooking and adding more stock, using a ladle, as soon as each addition has been absorbed, stirring frequently. You may not need all the stock, but continue cooking for about 20 minutes or until the rice is soft. When ready, add three-quarters of the Parmesan cheese, with the remaining butter or margarine, and season with salt and pepper. Serve sprinkled with the remaining Parmesan.

SERVES 6 AS A STARTER OR 4 AS A MAIN COURSE

VARIATIONS

Pea and Saffron Risotto Omit the mushrooms. Shell 700 g (1½ lb) fresh peas. Soak a large pinch of saffron strands in a little of the warm stock for about 10 minutes. Add to the onions in step 3 with 150 ml (¼ pint) dry white wine and the peas. Continue as above. (Alternatively, use 350 g (12 oz) frozen petits pois and add them about 5 minutes before the end of the cooking time.)

Asparagus Risotto Cook as Pea and Saffron Risotto, but substitute 225 g (8 oz) asparagus tips for the peas. Steam until just tender (see page 00 for a foolproof method) and stir into the risotto about 5 minutes before the end of the cooking time.

Almond and Courgette Risotto If making a vegan risotto, use vegetable margarine. Cook as Pea and Saffron Risotto but substitute 450 g (1 lb) courgettes, trimmed and thinly sliced, for the peas. Add them about 5 minutes before the end of the cooking time with 45 ml (3 tbsp) ground almonds. Continue as above but omit the cheese. Serve the risotto sprinkled with toasted flaked almonds and sesame seeds.

$\mathscr{S}$ESAME PILAFF WITH FENNEL

If Florence fennel is not available, use only 1.1 litres (2 pints) stock and stir in 30 ml (2 level tbsp) chopped fresh parsley or spring onion tops just before serving. It's important to use one of the suggested varieties of rice as it soaks up the liquid, becoming plump and tender rather than mushy.

60 ml (4 level tbsp) sesame seeds	pinch of ground turmeric
175 g (6 oz) Florence fennel	350 g (12 oz) Arborio, Carolina or pudding rice
50 g (2 oz) vegetable margarine or butter	about 1.3 litres (2¼ pints) vegetable stock
1 medium onion, skinned and finely chopped	salt and pepper
1 large green pepper, cored, seeded and chopped	

1 Toast the sesame seeds under a hot grill until golden brown, then leave to cool. Trim and finely chop the fennel, reserving the feathery tops. Finely chop the tops and set aside.
2 Melt the margarine or butter in a saucepan and add the onion, pepper, fennel and turmeric. Fry for 2–3 minutes or until beginning to soften, stirring constantly. Stir in the rice and continue to cook, stirring, for

1 minute, then add the stock and toasted sesame seeds. Season with salt and pepper.
3 Bring to the boil, cover and simmer very slowly for about 45 minutes or until all the liquid has been absorbed and the rice is tender. Taste and adjust the seasoning, if necessary, and stir in the fennel tops just before serving.
SERVES 4

$\mathscr{V}$EGETABLE BIRYANI

Serve with Curry Sauce (see page 188), Raita (see page 54) and Nan-style Bread (see page 155).

350 g (12 oz) basmati rice	5 ml (1 level tsp) ground turmeric
salt and pepper	2.5 ml (½ level tsp) chilli powder
50 g (2 oz) ghee or clarified butter	3 medium carrots, trimmed, peeled and thinly sliced
1 large onion, skinned and chopped	225 g (8 oz) French beans, trimmed and halved
2.5 cm (1 inch) piece of fresh root ginger, peeled and grated	225 g (8 oz) small cauliflower florets
1–2 garlic cloves, skinned and crushed	5 ml (1 level tsp) garam masala
5 ml (1 level tsp) ground coriander	juice of 1 lemon
10 ml (2 level tsp) ground cumin	hard-boiled egg slices and coriander sprigs, to garnish

1 Put the rice in a sieve and rinse under cold running water until the water runs clear.
2 Put the rice in a saucepan with 600 ml (1 pint) water and 5 ml (1 level tsp) salt. Bring to the boil, then reduce the heat and simmer for 10 minutes or until only just tender.

3 Meanwhile, melt the ghee or butter in a large heavy-based saucepan, add the onion, ginger and garlic and fry gently for 5 minutes or until soft but not coloured. Add the coriander, cumin, turmeric and chilli powder and fry for 2 minutes more, stirring constantly

$\mathcal{S}$INGAPORE NOODLES

Broccoli, green beans, baby sweetcorn, water chestnuts and mooli are also suitable.

225 g (8 oz) thin round egg noodles	*2 carrots, trimmed, peeled and thinly sliced*
salt	*a handful of mustard greens, pak choi or 2 Chinese*
60 ml (4 tbsp) vegetable oil	* leaves, shredded*
2 garlic cloves, skinned and crushed	*125 g (4 oz) mangetouts, trimmed*
1 medium onion, skinned and chopped	*4 spring onions, trimmed and chopped*
2.5 cm (1 inch) piece of fresh root ginger, peeled and	*5 ml (1 level tsp) curry powder*
* chopped*	*30 ml (2 tbsp) light soy sauce*
1 fresh green chilli, seeded and chopped	*30 ml (2 tbsp) hoisin sauce*

1 Cook the noodles in boiling salted water following the instructions on the packet. Drain and toss in 15 ml (1 tbsp) of the oil.
2 Heat the remaining oil in a wok or very large frying pan. Add the garlic, onion, ginger and chilli and stir-fry for 2–3 minutes.

3 Add the vegetables and sprinkle with the curry powder. Stir-fry for 3–4 minutes or until the vegetables are softened but still crisp. Add the noodles with the soy and hoisin sauces and stir-fry for 1–2 minutes until hot.
SERVES 4

Singapore Noodles

*E*GG FRIED RICE

Vegans can omit the eggs and make plain Fried Rice. If serving this as a main meal rather than an accompaniment, add a few more vegetables and increase the nuts to 125 g (4 oz).

450 g (1 lb) long-grain rice	*4 spring onions, trimmed and chopped*
salt	*50 g (2 oz) unsalted cashew nuts or peanuts (optional)*
about 30 ml (2 tbsp) vegetable oil	*2 free-range eggs, beaten*
1 large onion, skinned and chopped	*5 ml (1 level tsp) sugar*
1 green chilli, seeded and chopped	*30 ml (2 tbsp) light soy sauce*
2 large carrots, trimmed, peeled and coarsely grated	*Crisp Fried Onions (see page 115), to serve (optional)*
1 green pepper, cored, seeded and finely chopped	

1 Cook the rice in boiling salted water for about 10 minutes or until just tender. Do not overcook it or the fried rice will be mushy. Drain the rice, rinse with boiling water, then spread out on a large plate or tray while cooking the vegetables.
2 Heat the oil in a wok or very large frying pan. Add the onion, chilli, carrots and green pepper and stir-fry for 3–4 minutes or until the vegetables are softened. Add the spring

onions and nuts, if using, and fry for 1 minute. Pour in the egg in a thin stream, stirring all the time so that it breaks up into small pieces. When all of the egg has set, add the rice, sugar and soy sauce and continue cooking, stirring all the time, until the rice is heated through. Add a little extra oil if the rice starts to stick. Serve immediately, sprinkled with Crisp Fried Onions, if liked.
SERVES ABOUT 6

*V*EGETABLE COUSCOUS

Couscous is produced by moistening grains of semolina and forming them into tiny pellets. It's a staple food in North African countries where it is served with a meat or vegetable stew. The couscous grains are steamed above the stew in a *couscousière* or steamer. Serve this vegetable couscous with Harissa Sauce (see page 184).

125 g (4 oz) chick-peas, soaked overnight in cold water	*1.1 litres (2 pints) vegetable stock*
350 g (12 oz) couscous (not pre-cooked)	*30 ml (2 level tbsp) tomato purée*
2 medium leeks, trimmed, thickly sliced and thoroughly washed	*chilli sauce, to taste*
	salt and pepper
125 g (4 oz) vegetable margarine or butter	*1 medium red pepper, cored, seeded and diced*
1 medium carrot, trimmed, peeled and thickly sliced	*1 medium green pepper, cored, seeded and diced*
1 medium parsnip, trimmed, peeled and roughly chopped	*450 g (1 lb) tomatoes, skinned and quartered*
225 g (8 oz) swede, peeled and roughly chopped	*225 g (8 oz) courgettes, trimmed and sliced*
5 ml (1 level tsp) ground cumin	*1 small cauliflower, divided into florets*
5 ml (1 level tsp) ground coriander	*chopped fresh parsley, to garnish*
2.5 ml (½ level tsp) paprika	

1 Drain the chick-peas and put in a large saucepan. Cover with fresh water, bring to the boil and cook for 1 hour. Drain well.

2 Place the couscous in a bowl and pour over 200 ml (7 fl oz) warm water. Work the water into the couscous with your fingertips, using a 'rubbing-in' motion to ensure all the grains are separate. Leave to stand for 15 minutes, then repeat the process twice more, using a total of 600 ml (1 pint) water.

3 Melt 50 g (2 oz) margarine or butter in a large saucepan with a capacity of at least 4 litres (7 pints), over which a perforated steamer will fit snugly. Add the prepared vegetables and sprinkle over the spices. Fry gently until lightly browned, then add the chick-peas with the stock, tomato purée and chilli sauce. Season with salt and pepper and bring to the boil.

4 Line a steamer with a double thickness of muslin and spoon in the couscous, seasoning well with salt and pepper. Place over the vegetables and cover the steamer tightly. Bring the vegetables to a fast boil, then lower the heat and simmer gently for about 30 minutes.

5 Take the pan and steamer off the heat and spoon the couscous into a large bowl. Cut the remaining margarine or butter into small pieces and add to the couscous. Stir well until the butter has melted and every grain is separate. Season again, if necessary.

6 Add the remaining prepared vegetables to the pan and stir well. Add a little extra chilli sauce, if liked. Return to the heat and bring slowly to the boil. Spoon the couscous back into the lined steamer and place over the pan. Cover the steamer tightly, lower the heat and simmer for another 15 minutes.

7 Turn the couscous into a dish and fork through. Serve the vegetable mixture separately, sprinkled with parsley.
SERVES 6

*M*USHROOM FRICASSEE WITH LEMON COUSCOUS

Flat mushrooms give a delicious flavour to the fricassee, but can make the sauce very dark – a half-and-half mixture of cup and flat mushrooms is best.

125 g (4 oz) couscous	*10 ml (2 level tsp) plain flour*
grated rind and juice of 1 lemon	*150 ml (¼ pint) milk*
salt and pepper	*10 ml (2 level tsp) Dijon mustard*
75 g (3 oz) vegetable margarine or butter	*25 g (1 oz) pine nuts*
225–275 g (8–10 oz) flat or cup mushrooms, wiped and sliced	

1 Bring 150 ml (¼ pint) water to the boil and pour over the couscous. Add the lemon rind, season with salt and pepper and leave to soak for about 5 minutes, stirring occasionally.

2 Heat 50 g (2 oz) of the margarine or butter in a frying pan, add the mushrooms and fry quickly until just beginning to soften.

3 Stir in the flour and milk and bring to the boil. Cook for 1–2 minutes, adding a little more milk if it's too thick. Remove from the heat and stir in the mustard and 10 ml (2 tsp) lemon juice. Taste and adjust the seasoning.

4 Meanwhile, heat the remaining margarine or butter in a separate frying pan. Add the pine nuts and couscous and cook over a high heat, stirring occasionally, until piping hot. Season and serve with the mushrooms.
SERVES 2

Toasted Polenta

Polenta, or ground corn, is a staple of northern Italian cooking. It's often eaten hot, like porridge, but it can also be cooled, cut into squares and then fried or grilled as here. Different types require varying cooking times; always ensure the mixture is tender and the liquid well reduced. The polenta squares can be prepared the day before you wish to serve them. Serve as an accompaniment to casseroles, stews or Grilled Vegetable Salad (see page 50).

5 ml (1 level tsp) salt	1 garlic clove, skinned and crushed (optional)
200 g (7 oz) polenta	freshly ground black pepper
25 g (1 oz) vegetable margarine or butter	

1 Pour 1.1 litres (2 pints) cold water into a large saucepan and bring to the boil. Add the salt, then pour in the polenta in a very fine stream, stirring vigorously all the time with a wooden spoon. Simmer for about 15 minutes or until the polenta is very thick and no longer grainy. Stir to prevent it sticking.
2 Remove the pan from the heat and stir in the margarine or butter, garlic, if using, and black pepper.

3 Turn out on to a wooden board or a plate and spread to a thickness of about 1–2 cm (½–¾ inch). Cool, cover and chill in the refrigerator for at least 1 hour. Cut into 5 cm (2 inch) squares.
4 When ready to serve, toast the polenta squares on both sides under a hot grill for 7–10 minutes. Serve at once or cover loosely and keep warm.
SERVES ABOUT 6

Barley with Spinach and Ginger

Barley was one of the first grains to be cultivated in this country but it is now seldom used. This simple dish makes the most of the humble grain. Serve it with rice and natural yogurt .

225 g (8 oz) pot or pearl barley	salt and pepper
700 ml (1¼ pints) vegetable stock	15 ml (1 tbsp) vegetable oil
225 g (8 oz) frozen chopped spinach	5 ml (1 level tsp) cumin seeds
1 garlic clove, skinned and crushed	
2.5 cm (1 inch) piece of fresh root ginger, peeled and chopped	

1 Wash the barley, then put it in a large saucepan with the stock. Bring to the boil, then reduce the heat, cover and simmer for 35–40 minutes or until most of the stock has been absorbed and the barley is tender. Stir occasionally to prevent the barley sticking.
2 Add the frozen spinach and stir over a low heat for about 10 minutes or until the spinach

has thawed. Add the garlic and ginger, lower the heat, re-cover and cook for a further 5–7 minutes, stirring occasionally. Season with salt and pepper, then spoon into a serving dish.
3 Heat the oil in a small saucepan, add the cumin and cook for about 1 minute, stirring. Pour over the barley and spinach, and serve.
SERVES 4

—Eleven—

Pizzas, Breads and Rolls

Pizza at its best is wholesome, nourishing and simply delicious. Don't spoil it with doughs that are dry, burnt or soggy, and toppings too sparse or too overpowering to enjoy. These pitfalls can be avoided if you follow our recipe for a soft yeasty dough, or the quicker, more scone-like, alternative. Then add the topping of your choice – from a simple tomato and cheese mixture to a more flamboyant pepper and garlic creation.

Yeast gives pizzas, breads and rolls their characteristic smell and texture. It is available in several forms. Fresh yeast, also known as compressed yeast, is sold in blocks. It is creamy fawn in colour, and has a faint winy smell. It should have a smooth, compact texture and crumble easily. The best results are obtained when the yeast is very fresh, but it can be stored, tightly wrapped to prevent it from drying out, in the refrigerator for up to a month. It can also be frozen for up to 3 months, but it is advisable to divide it into usable 25 g (1 oz) portions. Thaw at room temperature for a couple of hours before using.

Dried yeast should be mixed with a tepid liquid and left in a warm place for 15–20 minutes to become frothy, before being mixed with flour. If the liquid is water, add a pinch of sugar. This isn't necessary if you're using milk, because milk already contains lactose, a form of sugar. If the yeast fails to froth after 15–20 minutes, it's no longer active. Unfortunately it cannot be resurrected, so throw it away and start again.

Fast-action dried yeast is a revolutionary new form of yeast which is mixed straight into the flour without any pre-blending. When used to make a plain dough, fast-action yeast has the added advantage of rising the dough in a much shorter time; the dough needs to be left to rise only once.

Bread freezes very well. Wrapped tightly, it will keep for several months. Refresh it in a hot oven before serving. Unbaked bread dough can also be frozen. The best time to freeze dough is when it has been shaped and is in the tin ready to rise. Just place the dough and tin in a good-sized, oiled plastic bag, squeeze out the air, leaving a space above the dough, and freeze it (preferably on fast freeze). Thaw, still wrapped, in a warm place and leave to rise until doubled in size.

We tried freezing and reheating the completed pizzas, but we didn't feel the results did justice to the original recipe, so only resort to this if you really need to.

PIZZA

This basic pizza dough can be rolled out to almost any size or shape you fancy, but, as a rough guide, it will make one large rectangular pizza measuring about 38 × 30.5 cm (15 × 12 inches), two 30.5 cm (12 inch) round pizzas or four thin 20 cm (8 inch) round pizzas. Be guided by the size of your baking equipment – special round pizza pans are available but not essential. A very large, flat baking sheet, or even a large roasting tin, works just as well. Packet bread mix also makes a good, quick base. You will need two 284 g (10 oz) packets (or the equivalent) to make the same quantity. When making up the mix, substitute 30 ml (2 tbsp) olive oil for some of the liquid.

When it comes to toppings for pizza, it is difficult, and unnecessary, to suggest exact quantities since it depends on the size of the pizza(s) made and your personal taste. Whichever combinations you choose, be generous! In addition to the toppings, sprinkle thinly sliced garlic, fresh or dried herbs, such as oregano, marjoram or basil, or capers, chopped chillies, olives, pine nuts or raisins on to the pizza for extra flavour.

450 g (1 lb) strong white or wholemeal flour

5 ml (1 level tsp) fast-action dried yeast

salt and pepper

olive oil

three 397 g (14 oz) cans chopped tomatoes

1 Put the flour, yeast and 5 ml (1 level tsp) salt in a bowl and mix together. Make a well in the centre and add 300 ml (½ pint) tepid water with 30 ml (2 tbsp) olive oil. Beat thoroughly with your hand until the dough leaves the sides of the bowl clean. You may need to add more tepid water, particularly if using wholemeal flour.

2 Turn the dough on to a lightly floured surface and knead for about 10 minutes or until smooth and elastic. Roll out to the size and shape of your choice and place on a baking sheet(s). Spread with the tomatoes and add the topping(s) of your choice (see right). Season with salt and pepper and drizzle over a little olive oil. Leave in a warm place for 20–30 minutes or until the dough looks puffy around the edges.

3 Bake in the oven at 220°C (425°F) mark 7 for 20–30 minutes (depending on size) or until golden brown and bubbling. Serve hot.

TOPPINGS

Roasted Pepper Roast four large peppers under a hot grill until the skin is blackened. Leave to cool, then remove the skin and seeds, and cut the flesh into strips. Scatter over the pizza(s) before cooking.

Artichoke Slice some drained bottled or canned artichoke hearts, and add to the pizza(s) before cooking.

Mushroom Thinly slice some mushrooms. Fry in olive oil with a little garlic, then drain well. Scatter over the pizza(s) before cooking.

Cheese Most firm cheeses with good melting properties are suitable for topping pizzas. Mozzarella is traditional, but try Bel Paese, Fontina, Taleggio, Gruyère or Parmesan.

Vegetable Almost any vegetable is good on a pizza; steamed fresh spinach (or well drained frozen leaf spinach); aubergine, courgettes or baby onions, cut into chunks or sliced and sautéed in olive oil; fresh tomatoes, sliced.

QUICK PIZZA BASE

This makes the same quantity as the recipe above.

450 g (1 lb) self-raising flour

5 ml (1 level tsp) salt

125 g (4 oz) vegetable margarine or butter

300 ml (½ pint) milk

1 Sift the flour and salt into a bowl, then rub in the margarine or butter until the mixture resembles fine breadcrumbs. Add the milk and mix to a soft dough. Turn out on to a lightly floured surface and knead until smooth. Roll out the dough and use as above.

PANZEROTTI

These deep-fried stuffed pizzas are delicious served hot as a snack or starter, or served cold as part of a picnic or *al fresco* buffet. You will only need about 16 teaspoons of tomato sauce for the filling. We suggest that you make up one quantity of the recipe on page 190 and freeze the remainder or serve it with the panzerotti instead of Pesto.

1 quantity pizza dough (see page 144)	*salt and pepper*
Tomato Sauce (see page 190) or tomato purée	*vegetable oil for deep-frying*
about 175 g (6 oz) Mozzarella or goats' cheese, roughly chopped	*Pesto (see page 193) or leftover Tomato Sauce, to serve*

1 Make the pizza dough following the instructions on page 145 and leave in a warm place to rise.
2 Turn the risen dough out on to a floured surface, knead lightly and divide into 16 equal pieces. Using a rolling pin, roll each piece to a rough circle measuring about 10 cm (4 inches) in diameter.
3 Spread about 5 ml (1 tsp) Tomato Sauce or purée on to each circle, leaving a border around the edge (don't be over-generous or it will leak out during cooking). Sprinkle the cheese over the tomato and season.

4 Brush the edges of the dough with water, then fold in half to enclose the filling. Press the edges firmly together, then crimp to seal in the filling. Make sure that you do this thoroughly to prevent the filling leaking out.
5 Heat the oil in a deep-fat fryer to 180°C (350°F) or until a 2.5 cm (1 inch) cube of bread browns in the hot oil in 1 minute. Deep-fry the panzerotti in batches for 2–3 minutes or until golden brown. Drain on absorbent kitchen paper, then serve hot, topped with Pesto or Tomato Sauce.
MAKES 16

SODA BREAD

Round loaves of soda bread were traditionally baked on a hot griddle over an open fire, and had a lovely crisp crust. The bread is moist, close-textured and delicious.

450 g (1 lb) plain wholemeal flour	*5 ml (1 level tsp) bicarbonate of soda*
125 g (4 oz) plain white flour	*5 ml (1 level tsp) salt*
50 g (2 oz) rolled oats	*about 450 ml (¾ pint) buttermilk*

1 Put the flours, oats, bicarbonate of soda and salt in a large bowl and mix together. Add enough buttermilk to mix to a soft dough.
2 Knead very lightly, then shape into a large round and place on a greased baking sheet. Cut a deep cross in the top. Bake in the oven

at 230°C (450°F) mark 8 for 15 minutes, then reduce the oven temperature to 200°C (400°F) mark 6 and bake for a further 20–25 minutes or until the loaf sounds hollow when tapped on the bottom. Eat while still warm.
MAKES 1 LARGE LOAF

BASIC BREAD AND ROLLS

Shape and flavour this basic bread dough as desired.

15 g (½ oz) fresh yeast, or 7.5 ml (½ level tsp) dried
yeast, or one 7 g sachet fast-action dried yeast
about 300 ml (½ pint) tepid milk
450 g (1 lb) strong wholemeal or white flour

5 ml (1 level tsp) salt
1 free-range egg, beaten
poppy, caraway, fennel or sesame seeds

1 Dissolve the fresh yeast in the milk. If using dried yeast, sprinkle it into the milk and leave in a warm place for 15 minutes or until frothy. If using fast-action dried yeast, this stage is not necessary.

2 Put the flour and salt in a bowl. Add the fast-action dried yeast, if using. Make a well in the centre, then pour in the yeast liquid, or just the milk if using fast-action dried yeast. Beat well together until the dough leaves the sides of the bowl clean. If using wholemeal flour, you will need to add a little extra milk. Turn on to a lightly floured surface and knead for about 10 minutes or until smooth and elastic.

3 If using fresh or dried yeast, place the dough in an oiled bowl, cover with a clean tea-towel and leave in a warm place for about 1 hour or until doubled in size. Turn the dough on to a floured surface and knead lightly. (This first rising and second kneading stage is not necessary if fast-action yeast has been used.)

4 Shape the dough into the desired shape or divide into eight and shape into rolls. Cover with a clean tea-towel, and leave in a warm place for about 30 minutes or until doubled in size.

5 Brush with beaten egg to glaze and sprinkle with seeds. Bake in the oven at 230°C (450°F) mark 8 for 10 minutes, then reduce the temperature to 200°C (400°F) mark 6 and bake the loaves for a further 20–25 minutes or rolls for a further 10 minutes. Cool on a wire rack.

VARIATIONS

Nut Bread Add 125 g (4 oz) roughly chopped shelled walnuts or toasted hazelnuts to the basic mixture (step 2).

Cheese Bread Add 125 g (4 oz) grated well flavoured Cheddar cheese and 5 ml (1 level tsp) dried mustard powder to the basic mixture (step 2). Sprinkle with a little extra cheese 15 minutes before the end of the cooking time.

MAKES 1 LARGE LOAF OR 8 ROLLS

OLIVE SOURDOUGH BREAD

If you make bread regularly, a sourdough starter is a convenient way of leavening bread.
Providing it is replenished as it is used, it will keep indefinitely.
After making the olive sourdough bread, blend about 75 g (3 oz) strong flour with about
150 ml (¼ pint) water to make a runny paste. Stir it into the remaining starter, re-cover as
before and leave for at least 24 hours before using.
Providing it is nourished every 4 days with a paste made from at least 25 g (1 oz) strong
flour and water, the starter will always be ready to use. If you do not use it for a few days,
store it in the refrigerator.

For the sourdough starter	75 g (3 oz) strong wholemeal flour
15 g (½ oz) fresh yeast, or 7.5 ml (1½ level tsp) dried yeast and a pinch of sugar	5 ml (1 level tsp) salt
	45 ml (3 level tbsp) chopped mixed fresh herbs
225 g (8 oz) strong white flour	45 ml (3 tbsp) virgin olive oil
For the bread	225 g (8 oz) mixed stoned black and green olives, roughly chopped
400 g (14 oz) strong white flour	
75 g (3 oz) rye flour	

1 To make the sourdough starter, blend the fresh yeast with 150 ml (¼ pint) tepid water in a large bowl. If using dried yeast, sprinkle it on to 150 ml (¼ pint) water, add the sugar and leave in a warm place until frothy.

2 Mix in a further 300 ml (½ pint) tepid water and enough of the flour to form a thick, pourable mixture. Don't worry if it's not perfectly smooth; the yeast will break down any lumps. Tightly cover the bowl with a damp cloth and leave at warm room temperature for 3 days to ferment and develop the sourdough flavour. (Wring out the cloth in cold water if it dries out.)

3 To make the bread, put the flours, salt and herbs in a bowl and mix together. Add 200 ml (7 fl oz) of the starter and the olive oil and 225 ml (8 fl oz) tepid water, or enough to make a soft dough.

4 On a lightly floured surface, knead the dough for about 10 minutes or until smooth and elastic. Put the dough in a large oiled bowl, cover with a clean tea-towel and leave in a warm place for about 1 hour or until doubled in size.

5 Knock back the dough on a lightly floured surface, then carefully knead in the olives. Shape into a long sausage, then curl it round to form a coil. Wrap one end of the dough over the other and pinch with your fingers to mould them together into a circle.

6 Transfer the dough to a greased baking sheet and cover loosely with a clean tea-towel. Leave in a warm place for about 20 minutes or until doubled in size.

7 Remove the tea-towel and, with a sharp pair of scissors, snip around the top of the loaf to make a zig-zag pattern. Brush with water and bake in the oven at 230°C (450°F) mark 8 for 15 minutes. Reduce the temperature to 190°C (375°F) mark 5 and bake for a further 20–25 minutes or until the loaf sounds hollow when tapped on the base. Cool on a wire rack.

MAKES 1 LARGE LOAF

POTTED HERB BREAD

Small terracotta flowerpots are available from garden centres. Soak them overnight in cold water, then dry thoroughly before using. Alternatively, shape the dough into six neat rounds and place on a baking sheet. Leave to rise and bake as directed.

white vegetable fat, melted, for greasing	*7.5 ml (1½ level tsp) salt*
15 g (½ oz) fresh yeast, or 7.5 ml (1½ level tsp) dried yeast and 5 ml (1 level tsp) sugar, or one 7 g sachet fast-action dried yeast	*50 g (2 oz) vegetable margarine or butter*
	150 ml (10 level tbsp) finely chopped fresh herbs, such as basil, parsley, thyme or marjoram
450 g (1 lb) strong white or wholemeal flour	

1 Brush six 9 cm (3½ inch) diameter terracotta flowerpots with melted fat. Blend the fresh yeast with 300 ml (½ pint) tepid water. If using dried yeast, sprinkle it into the water with the sugar and leave in a warm place for 15 minutes or until frothy. If using fast-action dried yeast, this stage is not necessary.

2 In a large bowl, mix together the flour and salt. Add the fast-action dried yeast, if using. Rub in the margarine and stir in the herbs.

3 Make a well in the centre of the flour mixture and pour in the yeast liquid, or 300 ml (½ pint) tepid water if using fast-action dried yeast. Mix well (adding a little extra water if using wholemeal flour) and turn on to a floured surface. Knead for 10 minutes or until smooth.

4 If using fresh or dried yeast, put the dough in a large oiled bowl and cover with a clean tea-towel. Leave to stand in a warm place until doubled in size. Knead the dough again for 2–3 minutes. (If fast-action dried yeast has been used, this first rising and second kneading stage is not necessary.)

5 Cut the dough into six pieces. Shape the pieces into elongated balls and drop them into the prepared pots. Leave in a warm place until the dough rises to the tops of the pots.

6 Brush the loaves with salt water and bake in the oven at 200°C (400°F) mark 6 for 10 minutes. Reduce the temperature to 180°C (350°F) mark 4 and bake for a further 20 minutes. Turn the loaves out of the pots and return them to the oven for 5 minutes to crisp the outsides, then cool slightly on a wire rack. Serve warm.

MAKES 6

SESAME AND CUMIN BREAD STICKS

These crisp, slightly spicy bread sticks are perfect for serving with hummus or your favourite dip.

15 g (½ oz) fresh yeast, or 7.5 ml (1½ level tsp) dried yeast and 5 ml (1 level tsp) sugar, or one 7 g sachet fast-action dried yeast	*50 g (2 oz) vegetable margarine or butter*
	30 ml (2 tbsp) sesame oil
	30 ml (2 tbsp) vegetable oil
450 g (1 lb) strong white flour	*1 free-range egg, beaten*
7.5 ml (1½ level tsp) salt	*45 ml (3 level tbsp) sesame seeds*
5 ml (1 level tsp) ground cumin	*30 ml (2 level tbsp) cumin seeds*

1 Blend the fresh yeast with 200 ml (7 fl oz) tepid water. If using dried yeast, sprinkle it into the water with the sugar and leave in a warm place for 15 minutes or until frothy. If using fast-action dried yeast, this stage is not necessary.

2 Put the flour, salt and ground cumin in a large bowl. Add the fast-action dried yeast, if using. Put the margarine or butter and oils in a small saucepan and heat gently until the butter has melted. Make a well in the centre of the dry ingredients and pour in the fat with the yeast liquid or 200 ml (7 fl oz) tepid water if using fast-action dried yeast. Mix to make a dough, adding a little extra water if necessary. Turn the dough out on to a floured surface and knead for 10 minutes or until smooth and elastic.

3 If using fresh or dried yeast, put the dough in an oiled bowl, cover with a clean tea-towel and leave in a warm place for 1 hour or until doubled in size. Knead the dough for 2–3 minutes. (If fast-action dried yeast has been used, this first rising and second kneading is not necessary.)

4 Divide the dough into 32 pieces. Roll each piece into a sausage shape about 20.5 cm (8 inches) long and place on greased baking sheets.

5 Brush the dough sticks with beaten egg and sprinkle with the sesame and cumin seeds. Bake in the oven at 200°C (400°F) mark 6 for 15–20 minutes or until golden brown. Turn off the oven and leave the bread sticks to cool in the oven. When cold they should be crisp. Store in an airtight container.

MAKES ABOUT 32

$\mathcal{T}$OMATO HERB FOCACCIA

Sun-dried tomatoes lend a delicious flavour and a distinctive colour to this Italian bread.

50 g (2 oz) sun-dried tomatoes in olive oil, drained and chopped	*15 ml (1 level tbsp) chopped fresh thyme or rosemary*
450 g (1 lb) strong white flour	*45 ml (3 tbsp) olive oil*
2.5 ml (½ level tsp) salt	*1 free-range egg*
50 g (2 oz) vegetable margarine or butter	*coarse salt (optional)*
one 7 g sachet fast-action dried yeast	*chopped fresh thyme or rosemary, to serve*

1 Put the tomatoes in a bowl and pour over 200 ml (7 fl oz) boiling water. Leave to soak for 15 minutes.

2 Put the flour and salt in a bowl and rub in the margarine or butter. Stir in the yeast.

3 Drain the tomatoes, reserving the liquid, and stir into the flour with the herbs.

4 Beat together the reserved liquid, the olive oil and egg. Make a well in the centre of the flour mixture, pour in the egg mixture and mix to a dough.

5 Turn the dough on to a floured surface and knead for 5 minutes or until smooth.

6 Put the dough on a greased baking sheet and press into a square measuring at least 25.5 cm (10 inches) across. Cover with a clean tea-towel and leave in a warm place for about 30 minutes or until doubled in size. Brush with salt water. Slash the top with a sharp knife, or make indentations with a wooden spoon, and sprinkle with salt, if using.

7 Bake in the oven at 220°C (425°F) mark 7 for 15–20 minutes or until golden brown. Sprinkle with chopped fresh thyme or rosemary before serving.

MAKES 1 LOAF

HERBED GRANARY BREAD

This is one recipe in which dried herbs are no substitute for fresh.

15 g (½ oz) fresh yeast, or 7.5 ml (1½ level tsp) dried yeast and a pinch of sugar, or one 7 g sachet fast-action dried yeast	30 ml (2 level tbsp) chopped mixed fresh herbs, such as mint, thyme, marjoram, rosemary and chives
450 g (1 lb) Granary flour	1 garlic clove, skinned and crushed (optional)
5 ml (1 level tsp) salt	10 ml (2 tsp) runny honey
30 ml (2 level tbsp) chopped fresh parsley	fine oatmeal for sprinkling

1 Blend the fresh yeast with 300 ml (½ pint) warm water. If using dried yeast, sprinkle it into 300 ml (½ pint) warm water with the sugar and leave in a warm place for 15 minutes or until frothy.

2 Put the flour, salt and herbs in a bowl and mix together. Add the fast-action dried yeast, if using. Make a well in the centre. Stir the garlic, if using, and the honey into the yeast liquid (or 300 ml/½ pint warm water if using

fast-action dried yeast), then pour into the centre of the dry ingredients. Beat together until the dough leaves the sides of the bowl clean. Turn the dough on to a lightly floured surface and knead well for about 10 minutes.

3 If using fresh or dried yeast, put the dough in a clean bowl. Cover with a clean tea-towel and leave in a warm place for about 1 hour or until doubled in size. Turn the dough on to a floured surface and knead lightly. (If fast-action dried yeast has been used, this first rising and second kneading stage is not necessary.)

4 Shape the dough into a sausage shape about 40.5 cm (16 inches) long and place on a greased baking sheet. Cut several slashes on the top of the loaf. Cover and leave in a warm place for 30 minutes or until doubled in size.

5 Brush with a little milk and sprinkle with oatmeal. Bake in the oven at 230°C (450°F) mark 8 for 10 minutes, then reduce the oven temperature to 200°C (400°F) mark 6 and bake for a further 15–20 minutes or until the loaf sounds hollow when tapped on the base. Leave to cool on a wire rack.
MAKES 1 LOAF

CHEESE AND HERB SCONES

Scones are quick to throw together at a moment's notice if you run short of bread. Serve them as an accompaniment to salads and soups, or for lunch, split and filled with salad, cheese or hummus. They really are best served fresh and warm from the oven.

225 g (8 oz) self-raising flour
pinch of salt
5 ml (1 level tsp) mustard powder
5 ml (1 level tsp) baking powder
40 g (1½ oz) vegetable margarine or butter
125 g (4 oz) strong Cheddar cheese, finely grated
about 150 ml (¼ pint) milk

1 Grease a baking sheet. Sift the flour, salt mustard powder and baking powder together into a bowl. Rub in the margarine or butter until the mixture resembles fine breadcrumbs. Stir in half the cheese and enough milk to give a fairly soft, light dough.

2 On a lightly floured surface, roll out to about 2 cm (¾ inch) thick and cut into rounds with a 5 cm (2 inch) plain cutter. Put on the baking sheet, brush the tops with milk and sprinkle with the remaining cheese.

3 Bake in the oven at 220°C (425°F) mark 7 for about 10 minutes. Cool on a wire rack.
MAKES ABOUT 12

VARIATIONS

Olive and Herb Scones Omit the cheese and mustard. Finely chop 25 g (1 oz) stoned black or green olives, or a mixture, and stir into the rubbed-in ingredients with 30 ml (2 level tbsp) chopped mixed fresh herbs.

Push half of an olive into the top of each scone and sprinkle with a few herbs before baking.

Tomato and Garlic Scones Omit the cheese and mustard. Finely chop 25 g (1 oz) sun-dried tomatoes and stir into the rubbed-in ingredients. Add ½ a small garlic clove, skinned and crushed, to the milk. Sprinkle the scones with a few herbs or a little grated Parmesan cheese before baking.

Nut Scones Omit the mustard. The cheese may be omitted or left in as preferred. Add 50 g (2 oz) chopped mixed nuts to the rubbed-in ingredients. Sprinkle the scones with sesame or poppy seeds before baking.

Plain Scones To make plain scones, for serving with jam and cream, follow the basic recipe but omit the herbs, cheese and mustard (you should add salt to sweet scones).

Sweet Fruit Scones Add 50 g (2 oz) dried mixed fruit to the plain scone mixture above.

POTATO SCONES

Potato scones should be made from floury potatoes, such as Pentland Squire or Maris Piper, which will mash well without lumps.

450 g (1 lb) floury potatoes, peeled	*25 g (1 oz) vegetable margarine or butter*
salt	*about 125 g (4 oz) plain flour*

1 Cook the potatoes in boiling salted water for about 20 minutes or until tender. Drain and mash until smooth. Add 5 ml (1 level tsp) salt and the margarine or butter, then work in enough flour to make a stiff dough.
2 Turn on to a floured surface, knead lightly and roll out until 0.5 cm (¼ inch) thick. Cut into about twelve 6.5 cm (2½ inch) rounds.
3 Cook on a greased griddle or in a heavy-based frying pan for 4–5 minutes on each side or until golden brown. Serve hot with butter, or as an accompaniment to stews, casseroles, omelettes, and poached or fried eggs.
MAKES ABOUT 12

CORNBREAD

15 g (½ oz) fresh yeast, or 7.5 ml (1½ level tsp) dried yeast, or one 7 g sachet fast-action dried yeast	*125 g (4 oz) soft light brown sugar*
	10 ml (2 level tsp) salt
about 375 ml (13 fl oz) tepid milk	*50 g (2 oz) vegetable margarine or butter*
350 g (12 oz) cornmeal	*corn or maize meal for sprinkling*
450 g (1 lb) strong white flour	

1 Blend the fresh yeast with the milk. If using dried yeast, sprinkle it into the milk and leave in a warm place for 15 minutes or until frothy. If using fast-action dried yeast, this stage is not necessary.
2 Put the cornmeal, flour, sugar and salt in a bowl. Add the fast-action dried yeast, if using. Rub in the margarine or butter. Make a well in the centre, then pour in the yeast liquid (or 375 ml/13 fl oz tepid milk if using fast-action dried yeast) to make a soft dough, adding a little more milk if necessary. Knead on a floured surface for 10 minutes or until smooth and elastic.
3 If using fresh or dried yeast, put the dough in an oiled bowl, cover with a clean tea-towel and leave to rise in a warm place for about 1 hour or until doubled in size. Turn the dough on to a floured surface and knead for 5 minutes. (If fast-action dried yeast has been used, this first rising and second kneading stage is not necessary.)
4 Divide the dough into two, shape each piece into a 15 cm (6 inch) round and place on two greased baking sheets. Cover and leave in a warm place until doubled in size.
5 Using a sharp knife, mark the top of each loaf in squares. Brush with water, then sprinkle generously with corn or maize meal. Bake in the oven at 230°C (450°F) mark 8 for 15 minutes, then reduce the temperature to 190°C (375°F) mark 5 for 15 minutes or until well risen and the loaves sound hollow if tapped on the bottom. Cool on a wire rack.
MAKES 2 LOAVES

NAN-STYLE BREAD

This flat, tear-drop shaped bread is traditionally baked on the side of a tandoor oven. This version is not entirely authentic but it does produce a soft, puffy nan-style bread that's perfect for mopping up curries and Indian foods.

15 g (½ oz) fresh yeast, or 7.5 ml (1½ level tsp) dried yeast, or one 7 g sachet fast-action dried yeast	10 ml (2 level tsp) caster sugar
200 ml (7 fl oz) tepid milk	1 free-range egg, beaten
450 g (1 lb) plain flour	30 ml (2 tbsp) vegetable oil
5 ml (1 level tsp) baking powder	60 ml (4 tbsp) natural yogurt
5 ml (1 level tsp) salt	vegetable ghee or melted butter, for brushing

1 Blend the fresh yeast and 150 ml (¼ pint) of the milk together. If using dried yeast, sprinkle it into 150 ml (¼ pint) of the milk and leave in a warm place for 15 minutes or until frothy. If using fast-action dried yeast, this stage is not necessary.

2 Sift the flour, baking powder and salt into a large bowl. Add the fast-action dried yeast, if using. Make a well in the centre and stir in the sugar, egg, oil and yogurt.

3 Add the yeast liquid, or 200 ml (7 fl oz) tepid milk if using fast-action dried yeast, and mix to a soft dough, adding more milk if necessary. Turn the dough on to a lightly floured surface and knead for 10 minutes or until smooth and elastic.

4 Put the dough in a bowl, cover with a clean cloth and leave to rise in a warm place for about 1 hour or until doubled in size.

5 Knead the dough on a lightly floured surface for 2–3 minutes, then divide into six equal pieces. Roll out each piece and shape into a large tear-drop about 25 cm (10 inches) long.

6 Place one nan on a baking sheet and put under a preheated hot grill. Cook for 1½–2

minutes on each side or until golden brown and puffy. Brush the cooked nan with melted ghee or butter. Cook the remaining nan in the same way. Serve warm.

VARIATION

Peshawari Nan (Nan with Sultanas and Almonds) Follow the recipe above to the beginning of step 5. To make the filling, mix together 125 g (4 oz) sultanas, 125 g (4 oz) ground almonds, 60 ml (4 tbsp) vegetable ghee or butter and 45 ml (3 tbsp) chopped fresh coriander. Knead the dough on a lightly floured surface and divide into six equal pieces. Roll each piece into a round about 15 cm (6 inches) in diameter. Spoon the filling into the centre of each nan and fold over the dough to enclose the filling completely. Press the edges well together to seal. Cook for 1½ minutes on one side, turn over, brush with plenty of melted ghee or butter and sprinkle with a few flaked almonds. Cook for 1½–2 minutes or until golden brown and puffy. Serve warm, sprinkled with chopped fresh coriander.

MAKES 6

AJOWAN PARATHAS

Parathas are surprisingly easy to make once you've mastered the procedure. Ajowan is a spice with a strong thyme-like flavour. Use cumin instead if you can't find it in the shops.

350 g (12 oz) plain wholemeal flour
15 ml (1 level tbsp) ajowan seeds
5 ml (1 level tsp) salt

3.75 ml (¾ level tsp) chilli powder
vegetable ghee, butter or vegetable margarine, melted, for brushing

1 Put the flour, ajowan seeds, salt and chilli powder in a bowl and mix well together. Add about 300 ml (½ pint) cold water and bind to a soft pliable dough – it may be slightly sticky.

2 Turn the dough on to a lightly floured surface and knead with floured hands for 6–8 minutes or until smooth and elastic. Cover the dough with a clean damp cloth and leave to rest for about 15 minutes.

3 Divide the dough into 12 pieces. Take a piece of dough and shape it into a smooth ball. Roll it out on a lightly floured surface into a round about 15 cm (6 inches) across.

4 Brush a little ghee, butter or margarine over the paratha, then roll it into a long sausage shape. Hold the rolled paratha upright and place one end in the centre of your hand. Wind the rest of the roll carefully around the centre point to form a small fat disc.

5 Press the disc lightly together and roll out on a floured surface to a round about 15 cm (6 inches) in diameter. Cover with a clean damp cloth and roll out the remaining dough to make 12 parathas altogether.

6 Heat a heavy frying pan or griddle. Place one paratha in the pan and cook over a low heat until small bubbles appear on the surface. Turn the paratha over and brush the top with melted ghee, butter or margarine. Cook for about 30 seconds or until golden brown.

7 Turn the paratha again and brush with more fat. Press down the edges of the paratha with a spatula to ensure even cooking, and cook the other side until golden brown.

8 Brush with more fat and serve at once or wrap in foil and keep warm while cooking the remainder.

MAKES 12

— T WELVE —

If you live on your own or often eat alone, or if there is just one vegetarian in the family, this chapter will be useful. Here are delicious recipes, scaled down to make just enough for one.

Don't be shy about buying in small quantities. Family units are becoming progressively smaller than they have traditionally been, and suppliers are prepared to market their goods accordingly. Avoid supermarkets where everything is pre-packaged and geared to buying in quantity; instead opt for markets and delicatessens where you can pick out exactly what and how much you want. Try to be organised and plan your shopping and meals for the week.

When buying fresh fruit and vegetables, it is particularly important to choose sound, good quality produce. If you're cooking meals for one it is likely that you will want to store them whole or in part for several days. Obviously, fruit and vegetables in peak condition will keep for much longer than those that are bruised or shrivelled. To prolong storage, keep them in the refrigerator. With fruit, watch out for pieces that are ripening more quickly than the others in the bag. Remove the ripe fruit

immediately and cook or eat it since it will encourage the others to deteriorate. Use this natural process to your advantage if you want something to ripen quickly (particularly avocados) by putting the under-ripe fruit in a sealed paper bag with a fully ripe fruit.

As well as the recipes in this chapter, other recipes throughout the book make suitable meals for one, particularly omelettes, soups, baked potatoes and pasta. It's sensible to make soups in larger quantities and to freeze them in individual portions. Similarly, beans and lentils can be soaked, cooked and frozen or stored in the refrigerator for future use. If you cook too much pasta or rice by mistake, toss it with a well-flavoured dressing and a few vegetables or beans to serve as a salad later in the week. It's worth noting that cooked boiled rice freezes well (as long as it's not overcooked) and it reheats in minutes in the microwave.

Apart from the puddings in this chapter, baked apples or poached pears (cooked in the oven or the microwave) are obvious puddings for one. Raspberry Rose Ice Cream (see page 219) or Coconut Ice Cream (see page 217) are also worth making as they can be stored in the freezer for up to 3 months and used as required.

$\mathscr{S}$OUFFLÉED CAULIFLOWER

This makes a generous meal for one served with steamed or boiled green vegetables. Use fromage frais labelled '8 per cent fat' (rather than 1 per cent) for the best result.

125 g (4 oz) cauliflower florets	*5 ml (1 level tsp) Dijon mustard*
salt and pepper	*1 free-range egg, separated*
75 ml (5 tbsp) fromage frais	*50 g (2 oz) Cheddar cheese, grated*

1 Cook the cauliflower florets in boiling salted water for about 5 minutes or until tender but still slightly crisp. Drain well. Grease a small, shallow ovenproof dish and put the cauliflower in the bottom.
2 Put the fromage frais and mustard in a bowl and stir in the egg and half the cheese. Season.

3 Put the egg white in a separate bowl and whisk until stiff. Fold carefully into the cheese mixture and spoon over the cauliflower. Sprinkle with the remaining cheese and bake in the oven at 190°C (375°F) mark 5 for about 25 minutes or until risen and golden.
SERVES 1

$\mathscr{M}$ANGETOUT AND MUSHROOM MAYONNAISE

This is a really simple, light and healthy lunch dish. If you're not in a hurry to eat it, the dressing is improved if left to stand for 30 minutes to allow the flavours to develop.

50 g (2 oz) mangetouts	*15 ml (1 level tbsp) chopped fresh parsley*
salt and pepper	*15 ml (1 level tbsp) chopped chives*
30 ml (2 tbsp) mayonnaise	*50 g (2 oz) button mushrooms, wiped and sliced*
15 ml (1 tbsp) natural yogurt	

1 Trim the mangetouts and cut into diamond-shaped pieces. Blanch in boiling salted water for 1 minute, then drain and refresh under cold running water.
2 Beat together the mayonnaise, yogurt, parsley and half the chives. Season.
3 Arrange the mangetouts and mushrooms on a plate and top with the mayonnaise mixture. Sprinkle with the remaining chives.
SERVES 1

Mangetout and Mushroom Mayonnaise

MIXED VEGETABLE AND EGG SUPPER

Make a similar dish with leftover Ratatouille (see page 96). Serve with lots of crusty bread
or toast smeared with Dijon mustard, to mop up the juices.

15 ml (1 tbsp) olive oil	*a pinch of dried rosemary*
1 large courgette, trimmed and sliced	*2 tomatoes, chopped*
½ small green pepper, cored, seeded and roughly chopped	*salt and pepper*
1 small onion, skinned and sliced	*1 free-range egg*
½ small garlic clove, skinned and crushed	*25 g (1 oz) Cheddar or Gruyère cheese, grated*

1 Heat the oil in a small saucepan. Add the
courgette, pepper and onion and cook for
about 5 minutes or until beginning to soften
and brown, stirring occasionally.
2 Stir in the garlic, rosemary and tomatoes.
Season with salt and pepper and simmer,
uncovered, for 3–5 minutes or until the
vegetables are tender and the liquid has been
well reduced. Transfer the mixture to an

individual flameproof dish.
3 Make a slight hollow in the vegetable
mixture and break the egg carefully into it.
Season the egg with salt and plenty of pepper.
Sprinkle with the cheese.
4 Cook under a preheated grill for 8–10
minutes (depending on how well done you
like your eggs). Eat straight away!
SERVES 1

PASTA WITH SAUTÉED MUSHROOMS

This dish is everything that a weekday supper for one should be – it's quick to make,
requires little effort, yet it's delicious. Have ready a glass of robust Italian red wine and
perhaps a green salad (if you have the time or the inclination to make it) to complete
the feast.

125–175 g (4–6 oz) dried pasta	*1 garlic clove, skinned and crushed*
salt and pepper	*a large knob of butter*
30 ml (2 tbsp) olive oil	*a few chopped fresh herbs (optional)*
175 g (6 oz) mushrooms (medium-sized open-cup or	*a few spoonfuls of double cream (optional)*
oyster mushrooms are best), wiped and thickly sliced	*freshly grated Parmesan cheese, to serve*

1 Cook the pasta in boiling salted water
according to the packet instructions or until *al
dente* (tender but still firm to the bite).
2 Meanwhile, heat the oil in a frying pan and
fry the mushrooms over a high heat for 2–3
minutes or until slightly browned. Lower the
heat, add the garlic and continue cooking the
mushrooms until the pasta is cooked.
3 When the pasta is cooked, drain and return

it to the saucepan with the butter and plenty
of black pepper.
4 Season the mushrooms with salt and pepper
and add the herbs and cream, if using. Tip the
pasta on to a plate, top with the mushrooms
and serve immediately with freshly grated
Parmesan cheese.
SERVES 1

FRENCH BREAD PIZZA

Try spreading the toasted bread with a little Pesto (see page 193), or whole grain mustard, or rubbing it with a cut clove of garlic, for extra flavour.

about 175 g (6 oz) ripe tomatoes, chopped	*½ small French loaf*
4 black olives, stoned	*olive oil for brushing*
50 g (2 oz) Mozzarella or Bel Paese cheese, grated	*dried oregano or marjoram*
freshly ground black pepper	

1 In a bowl, combine the tomatoes, olives and half of the cheese. Season with pepper.
2 Trim the end off the French bread and split the loaf in half lengthways. Toast both pieces on each side, then brush the cut sides with a little olive oil.

3 Spoon on the tomato mixture, then top with the remaining grated cheese. Sprinkle with the herbs and cook under a hot grill for 2 minutes or until the cheese melts. Serve immediately.
SERVES 1

MARINATED TOFU KEBABS

Pressed tofu is firmer for grilling, and because it contains less liquid, it will absorb more marinade, and therefore more flavour. You will only need 75 g (3 oz) tofu (weighed before pressing) to make enough for one meal, but it is worth pressing and marinating the whole 225 g (8 oz) packet for use in other recipes. Follow this basic idea to vary as you like – chunks of courgette, baby sweetcorn, aubergines and small onions all work well. Peanut Sauce (see page 24) is a good accompaniment, as is Harissa Sauce (see page 184) or Curry Sauce (see page 188).

75 g (3 oz) firm tofu	*30 ml (2 tbsp) dry sherry*
1 garlic clove, skinned and crushed	*15 ml (1 tbsp) vegetable oil*
2.5 cm (1 inch) piece of fresh root ginger, peeled and	*1 small green pepper, cored, seeded and cut into chunks*
* grated*	*a few cherry tomatoes*
30 ml (2 tbsp) soy sauce	*a few small mushrooms*

1 To press the tofu, put it on a plate or board, cover with a second plate or board and weight this down (cans of tomatoes or beans are useful for this). Leave for 1 hour, draining off the liquid as necessary.
2 Cut the tofu into bite-sized chunks. Mix together the garlic, ginger, soy sauce, sherry and vegetable oil. Add the tofu, pepper, tomatoes and mushrooms and stir so that

everything is coated in the marinade. Cover and leave in the refrigerator to marinate for at least 1 hour or overnight.
3 Thread all the ingredients on to two bamboo kebab skewers. Grill under a hot grill for 5–8 minutes or until the vegetables are cooked, turning frequently and brushing with the marinade.
SERVES 1

CATALAN RED PEPPERS

If you prefer to eat this hot, keep the pepper in the oven until the filling is ready. Rinse the rice with boiling, not cold, water, pile it into the hot pepper, pour over the dressing and serve immediately.

1 red pepper	a few mixed black and green stoned olives, chopped
olive oil	10 ml (2 tsp) capers
40 g (1½ oz) mixed long-grain and wild rice	10 ml (2 tsp) white wine vinegar
salt and pepper	½ small garlic clove, skinned and crushed
2 tomatoes	lettuce, to serve
2 spring onions, trimmed and chopped	

1 Rinse and dry the pepper, then put it on a baking sheet and brush lightly with oil. Bake in the oven at 220°C (425°F) mark 7 for 15–20 minutes or until just tender. Cool, halve and remove the core and seeds. (The skin can also be removed, if wished, but the pepper will not hold its shape so well.) Pat dry with absorbent kitchen paper.
2 Meanwhile, cook the rice in boiling salted water according to the packet instructions or until tender. Drain and rinse under cold running water, then drain well again. Quarter the tomatoes, discard the seeds and roughly chop the flesh. Mix into the rice with the spring onions, olives and capers.
3 Whisk together 30 ml (2 tbsp) olive oil, the vinegar and garlic, and season with salt and pepper. Stir into the rice mixture.
4 Pile the rice into the pepper halves and arrange on a serving plate. Cover and chill for 30 minutes before serving on a bed of lettuce.
SERVES 1

*E*GG AND SPINACH CROÛTE

If you keep a bag of chopped spinach spheres in your freezer, add one or two to the hot sauce and simmer until thawed – much quicker and easier than cooking spinach from scratch.

2.5 cm (1 inch) thick slice of bread, toasted	*150 ml (¼ pint) milk*
½ garlic clove, skinned	*freshly grated nutmeg*
50 g (2 oz) fresh spinach, trimmed and washed	*salt and pepper*
15 g (½ oz) vegetable margarine or butter	*a few drops of vinegar*
15 ml (1 level tbsp) plain flour	*1 free-range egg*

1 With a 7.5 cm (3 inch) pastry cutter, stamp out one round from the slice of toast, rub with the garlic clove and set aside.

2 Cook the spinach with only the water that clings to the leaves for 3–4 minutes or until wilted. Drain well and chop finely.

3 Melt the margarine or butter in a small saucepan, add the flour and cook gently, stirring, for 1–2 minutes. Remove from the heat and gradually blend in the milk. Bring to the boil, stirring constantly, then simmer for 3 minutes. Stir in the spinach and season with nutmeg, salt and pepper.

4 Meanwhile, half fill a frying pan with water and a few drops of vinegar, and bring to the boil. Break the egg into a cup, then slide it into the simmering water. Cook gently for 3–4 minutes or until lightly set, then lift out of the water with a slotted spoon. (Alternatively, use an egg poacher if you have one).

5 Top the toasted croûte with the poached egg and spoon over the spinach sauce. Serve immediately.

SERVES 1

*I*NDIVIDUAL BREAD AND BUTTER PUDDING

If you prefer a very crisp top, brown the cooked pudding under a hot grill for about 2 minutes. This makes a generous serving for one.

1 large slice of bread, crusts removed	*15 ml (1 level tbsp) caster sugar*
vegetable margarine or butter	*1 small free-range egg*
50 g (2 oz) currants or sultanas	*150 ml (¼ pint) milk*

1 Thickly spread the bread with margarine or butter and cut into fingers or small squares. Put half into a greased 450 ml (¾ pint) ovenproof dish and sprinkle with all the fruit and half the sugar. Top with the remaining bread, buttered side up, and sprinkle with the remaining sugar.

2 Beat the egg with the milk and strain over the bread. Leave to stand for 30 minutes, so that the bread absorbs some of the liquid.

3 Bake the pudding in the oven at 170°C (325°F) mark 3 for 35–45 minutes or until set and the top is crisp and golden.

SERVES 1

CINNAMON BANANA

Serve with chilled cream or vanilla ice cream. Alternatively, if you prefer the combination of sweet and tart flavours, serve with Greek yogurt, Quark or fromage blanc.

15 g (½ oz) vegetable margarine or butter	1.25 ml (¼ level tsp) ground cinnamon
15 ml (1 tbsp) soft brown sugar	1 banana
30 ml (2 tbsp) orange juice	a few no-soak dried prunes, halved
30 ml (2 tbsp) sherry	

1 Melt the margarine or butter in a heavy-based frying pan. Add the remaining ingredients, except the banana and prunes, and heat gently, stirring, until the sugar has dissolved.
2 Peel the banana, then cut in half lengthways. Place in the pan with the prunes and cook over a gentle heat for 5–10 minutes or until hot but still retaining its shape. Baste the banana frequently with the sauce and turn the pieces over once during cooking. Serve immediately.
SERVES 1

PLUM CROÛTE

This recipe works equally well with firm nectarines or peaches. Omit the cinnamon and flavour the sugar with a little grated orange rind and a pinch of ground mixed spice instead.

1 large slice of white bread	25 g (1 oz) demerara sugar
15 g (½ oz) vegetable margarine or butter, melted	1.25 ml (¼ level tsp) ground cinnamon
2 ripe plums	

1 Cut the crusts off the slice of bread and discard. Brush both sides of the bread with the melted margarine or butter, making sure the bread is coated right to the edges.
2 Place the bread in an individual Yorkshire pudding tin, pressing it down well, but leaving the four corners protruding over the edge.
3 Bake the croûte in the oven at 200°C (400°F) mark 6 for 15–20 minutes or until crisp and golden brown.
4 Meanwhile, halve and stone the plums, then place in a pan with the sugar and cinnamon. Sprinkle in 5–10 ml (1–2 tsp) water, then cook gently for about 5 minutes or until the plums are tender and juicy but still retaining their shape.
5 When the croûte is cooked, transfer to a serving plate. Spoon the plums in the centre and serve immediately.
SERVES 1

—THIRTEEN—

From around the age of two, children can eat much the same as the rest of the family (although most dislike highly spiced, very garlicky food). Nevertheless, they should be encouraged to eat and become familiar with a wide variety of foods. By all means, cook them meals to eat with the family using recipes from throughout the book, but in this chapter you will find a selection of recipes written specifically with young vegetarians in mind. Because all but the most steadfast children are influenced by their peer group, we've included vegetarian sausages and burgers to be enjoyed while non-vegetarian friends eat meaty versions. Soup makes a warming, nutritious meal for youngsters, too; most of the recipes in Chapter Two are suitable. Purée very chunky soups, to make them more manageable for children.

A very high fibre diet is unsuitable for young children because it is so bulky. Young children have small appetites and they fill up on these foods quickly before eating sufficient quantity to get the nutrients they need. For the same reason, do not give young children uncooked bran. Similarly, skimmed and semi-skimmed milk and low-fat foods should be avoided until around the age of two . They don't contain the high concentration of calories young children need and they contain less of the vitamins A and D than their full-fat counterparts. So, when making cheese- and milk-based sauces, use full-fat milk. Vegan children should be given fortified soya milk.

Aim to present most meals with a selection of vegetables (if fresh are unavailable, frozen are almost as good), cucumber slices, halved cherry tomatoes or carrot sticks.

BEANY PIES

You need a very small can of beans for these pies; if you can only buy a large can, transfer the remaining beans to a clean container, cover and keep in the refrigerator. Follow this procedure with all opened cans – once exposed to the air, any acids in the food react with the metal lining of the can and contaminate it.

8 thin slices of wholemeal bread cut from a small loaf	*150 g (5 oz) can baked beans in tomato sauce*
40 g (1½ oz) vegetable margarine or butter, melted	*25 g (1 oz) Cheddar cheese, grated*

1 Using a large round pastry cutter, cut four circles from half of the bread slices, just large enough to line four 10 cm (4 inch) patty tins. Brush some of the margarine or butter over both sides of the bread.
2 Line four patty tins with the bread, pressing down well. Divide the baked beans between the bread-lined patty tins.
3 Cut four circles from the remaining bread, just large enough to cover the prepared pies. Brush both sides with the remaining margarine or butter and place on top of the pies, pressing firmly around the edges to seal.
4 Sprinkle with the cheese and bake at 200°C (400°F) mark 6 for 20–25 minutes or until golden brown and crisp. Remove from the tins, leave to cool slightly, then serve.
MAKES 4

GLAMORGAN SAUSAGES

For adult-sized sausages, shape the mixture into eight instead of 16.

175 g (6 oz) fresh breadcrumbs	salt and pepper
125 g (4 oz) Caerphilly or Cheddar cheese, grated	1 free-range egg
1 small leek, trimmed, washed and very finely chopped	about 30 ml (2 tbsp) milk
15 ml (1 level tbsp) very finely chopped fresh parsley	plain flour for coating
a large pinch of mustard powder	vegetable oil for frying or grilling

1 In a large bowl, mix together the breadcrumbs, cheese, leek, parsley and mustard, and season with salt and pepper. Add the egg and mix thoroughly, then add enough milk to bind the mixture together.

2 Divide the mixture into 16 and shape into small sausages.

3 If shallow frying, roll the sausages in the flour to coat. Heat a little oil in a frying pan, add the sausages and fry for about 5 minutes or until golden brown. To grill, lightly brush the sausages with oil and cook under a hot grill for 3–4 minutes or until golden brown, turning occasionally. Serve hot immediately, or leave to cool and serve cold.

MAKES 16

BURGERS

Shape this mixture into burgers that are a manageable size for your children. Older children will probably prefer larger burgers which can be served in buns with lettuce and ketchup, while younger children will prefer smaller burgers with peas or beans and oven chips. The ingredients include Worcestershire sauce; check the labels in the supermarket for a brand that does not contain anchovies.

225 g (8 oz) packet original tofu	15 ml (1 tbsp) Worcestershire sauce
125 g (4 oz) carrots, trimmed, peeled and finely grated	10 ml (2 tsp) yeast extract
125 g (4 oz) fresh breadcrumbs	1 free-range egg
1 small onion, skinned and finely chopped	salt and pepper
5 ml (1 level tsp) mixed dried herbs	vegetable oil for frying

1 Put the tofu in a bowl and mash with a potato masher. Add the carrots, breadcrumbs, onion, herbs, Worcestershire sauce, yeast extract and egg. Season with salt and pepper and mix well.

2 Divide the mixture into eight or less, and shape each into a round flat cake.

3 Heat some oil in a large frying pan and cook the burgers for 4–5 minutes on each side or until golden brown and cooked through. To grill, lightly brush the burgers with oil and cook under a hot grill for about 4 minutes each side or until golden brown. Drain on absorbent kitchen paper. Serve hot.

MAKES ABOUT 8

$\mathscr{M}$INI QUICHES

These freeze well so it's worth making a batch for quick lunches or teatime meals. To freeze, cool, then pack in a rigid container, interleaved with greaseproof paper. Freeze for up to 3 months. Reheat from frozen at 180°C (350°F) mark 4 for 10–15 minutes or until warmed through.

1 quantity Shortcrust Pastry (see page 69)	about 40 g (1½ oz) sweetcorn kernels
2 free-range eggs, size 3	2 small tomatoes, chopped
225 ml (8 fl oz) milk	25 g (1 oz) Cheddar cheese, finely grated
2 spring onions, trimmed and sliced	25 g (1 oz) frozen petits pois, thawed

1 Thoroughly grease two 12-hole bun trays. Roll out the pastry on a floured surface and cut out twenty-four 7 cm (2¾ inch) rounds with a fluted cutter. Press a round of pastry into each hole in the bun tin.
2 Beat the eggs with the milk in a jug. Put a few spring onion slices and a few sweetcorn kernels in eight of the pastry cases. Divide the tomato and cheese between a further eight

cases. Divide the petits pois amongst the remaining cases.
3 Carefully pour the custard into the pastry cases and bake in the oven at 200°C (400°F) mark 6 for 35 minutes or until the filling is just set and the pastry lightly browned. Serve warm or cold.
MAKES 24

$\mathscr{P}$OTATO NESTS

Much of a potato's goodness is in the skin, which serves here as an edible container. If you have a microwave cooker, save time by cooking the pricked potatoes on HIGH for 12–15 minutes (depending on their size). Turn them over halfway through cooking. The final cooking in the oven makes them crisp.

4 small baking potatoes, each weighing about 200 g (7 oz), scrubbed	salt and pepper
	1 tomato, finely chopped
30–45 ml (2–3 tbsp) Greek yogurt, mayonnaise or fromage frais	45 ml (3 tbsp) sweetcorn kernels
	75 g (3 oz) hard cheese, finely grated

1 Prick each potato several times with a fork. Bake in the oven at 200°C (400°F) mark 6 for about 1½ hours or until tender.
2 Cut a thin slice horizontally from the top of each potato, then carefully scoop most of the potato into a bowl, leaving shells about 0.5 cm (¼ inch) thick.
3 Mix the scooped-out potato with the yogurt, mayonnaise or fromage frais. Season

with salt and pepper and mix in the tomato, sweetcorn and half the cheese. Spoon back into the potato shells and place in a shallow ovenproof dish.
4 Sprinkle the filling with the remaining cheese and return to the oven for about 20 minutes or until melted and lightly browned.
MAKES 4

$\mathcal{V}$EGETABLE TOAD IN THE HOLE

This works well with most vegetables. It is also a good way of using up leftovers. You will need a Yorkshire pudding tin with four 10 cm (4 inch) compartments. Serve with Tomato Sauce (see page 190) or chutney.

175 g (6 oz) prepared mixed vegetables, such as carrots, courgettes, green beans and broccoli	*50 g (2 oz) plain flour*
4 cherry tomatoes	*a pinch of salt*
white vegetable fat	*1 free-range egg*
	175 ml (6 fl oz) full-fat milk and water mixed

1 Depending on the ages of the children you are cooking for, cut the vegetables into small or large chunks. Steam or boil the vegetables until just tender. Prick the tomatoes with a fork.

2 Put a knob of fat into each compartment of a four-hole Yorkshire pudding tin. Put the tin in the oven at 220°C (425°F) mark 7 for about 5 minutes to heat the oil.

3 Meanwhile, sift the flour and salt into a bowl and make a well in the centre. Break the egg into the well, then add half the liquid.

Gradually mix the flour into the liquid to make a smooth, thick paste, then gradually work in the remaining liquid. Beat until smooth. If necessary, remove any lumps with a balloon whisk.

4 Divide the vegetables between the compartments in the pudding tin and pour over the batter. Bake on the top shelf in the oven for 30–35 minutes or until well risen and golden brown. Serve with Tomato Sauce (see page 190) or chutney.

SERVES 4

$\mathscr{M}$ACARONI CHEESE

This makes a fairly large amount (in children's terms), but it is a good idea to make a lot and freeze the extra in portion sizes ready for reheating in the microwave. Serve with halved cherry tomatoes, or steamed or boiled carrots, peas, beans or courgettes.

225 g (8 oz) short-cut macaroni or small pasta shapes	*a pinch of freshly grated nutmeg or 2.5 ml (½ level tsp)*
65 g (2½ oz) vegetable margarine or butter	*prepared mustard (optional)*
65 g (2½ oz) plain flour	*225 g (8 oz) mature Cheddar cheese, grated*
900 ml (1½ pints) full-fat milk	*45 ml (3 level tbsp) fresh wholemeal breadcrumbs*
salt and pepper	

1 Cook the macaroni in boiling salted water for about 10 minutes or until just tender. Drain well.

2 Meanwhile, melt the margarine or butter in a saucepan, stir in the flour and cook gently for 1 minute. Remove the pan from the heat and gradually stir in the milk. Bring to the boil and continue to cook, stirring, until the sauce thickens, then remove from the heat, season with salt and pepper and add the nutmeg or mustard, if using, most of the cheese and the macaroni.

3 Pour into an ovenproof dish and sprinkle with the remaining cheese and the breadcrumbs.

4 Brown under a hot grill or place on a baking sheet and bake in the oven at 200°C (400°F) mark 6 for 25–30 minutes or until golden and bubbling.

VARIATION

Cauliflower Cheese Omit the macaroni. Trim 1 large cauliflower and cut into very small florets (you will need about 800 g/1¾ lb florets). Cook the florets in fast boiling salted water for about 10 minutes or until just tender, then drain. If making cauliflower cheese for very young children, chop the florets into tiny pieces. Place in an ovenproof dish. Make the sauce and pour over the cauliflower. Sprinkle with the remaining cheese and breadcrumbs and brown under a hot grill or bake in the oven as for Macaroni Cheese.

SERVES ABOUT 4 ADULTS OR 8 CHILDREN

$\mathcal{L}$ENTIL POTATO PIES

Put the cooked mixture straight into individual foil (or china if you plan to reheat it in the microwave) containers ready for freezing.

75 g (3 oz) split red lentils	*salt and pepper*
1 onion, skinned and halved	*450 g (1 lb) old potatoes, cooked*
1 large carrot, trimmed, peeled and coarsely grated	*about 45 ml (3 tbsp) milk or a large knob of vegetable margarine*
2.5 ml (½ level tsp) yeast extract	*vegetable oil for brushing*
225 g (8 oz) mixed vegetables, such as sweetcorn, green beans, courgettes and parsnips, prepared and finely diced (if necessary)	

1 Put the lentils, onion, carrot, yeast extract, mixed vegetables and 300 ml (½ pint) water in a saucepan. Bring to the boil, cover and simmer gently for 20–25 minutes or until the lentils are very soft and mushy and all of the water has been absorbed, adding a little extra water if necessary. Season with salt and pepper and discard the onion halves. Divide the mixture between four or six individual ovenproof dishes.

2 Mash the potatoes with the milk or margarine or a little water to make it very soft. Spoon the potato on top of the lentil mixture, covering it completely. Brush with a little vegetable oil. Stand the pies on a baking sheet and bake in the oven at 220°C (425°F) mark 7 for 15–20 minutes or until golden brown. Alternatively, brown the pies under a hot grill (better for younger children who prefer their food lukewarm).
MAKES 4–6 PIES

$\mathcal{C}$HOCOLATE MUESLI BARS

For young children, cut into small squares and save as an occasional treat. The chocolate and syrup mixture could be melted in the microwave. It will take about 3–4 minutes on LOW. Stir occasionally to prevent it burning.

25 g (1 oz) vegetable margarine or butter	*75 g (3 oz) plain chocolate, broken into pieces*
15 ml (1 tbsp) golden syrup	*225 g (8 oz) no-added-sugar muesli*

1 Grease an 18 cm (7 inch) square tin. Heat the margarine or butter, syrup and chocolate in a heavy-based saucepan until the butter and chocolate have melted. Stir in the muesli and mix thoroughly together.

2 Spoon the mixture into the tin and level the surface. Chill in the refrigerator until set, then cut into 14 bars.
MAKES 14

OATY BARS

These oaty bars are ideal as a lunch-box filler or a mid-morning snack for younger children. If you have a microwave cooker, melt the margarine, milk and honey on HIGH for 1–2 minutes.

75 g (3 oz) vegetable margarine	2.5 ml (½ level tsp) bicarbonate of soda
30 ml (2 tbsp) milk	2.5 ml (½ level tsp) light muscovado sugar
15 ml (1 tbsp) runny honey	75 g (3 oz) rolled oats
75 g (3 oz) plain wholemeal flour	75 g (3 oz) no-soak dried apricots, chopped

1 Grease two baking sheets. In a small saucepan, melt the margarine with the milk and honey.
2 Put the flour, bicarbonate of soda, sugar, oats and apricots in a bowl. Mix together, then make a well in the centre. Pour in the melted mixture and mix well.
3 Divide the mixture into 8 pieces and shape each into a bar about 6.5 cm (2½ inches) long. Place on the baking sheets and bake in the oven at 200°C (400°F) mark 6 for 10–15 minutes or until golden brown. Leave to cool on the baking sheets for 2–3 minutes, then transfer to a wire rack to cool completely.
MAKES 8

ORANGE JELLY

A very simple soft-set jelly made using agar-agar. Serve with a selection of fresh fruit, such as strawberries, tangerines, raspberries or mango.

300 ml (½ pint) orange juice	15 ml (1 level tbsp) sugar
15 ml (1 level tbsp) agar-agar	

1 Mix the orange juice with 300 ml (½ pint) water and pour half into a small saucepan with the agar-agar. Bring to the boil, reduce the heat and simmer for 5 minutes or until dissolved, stirring all the time. Add the remaining juice, stir in the sugar remove from the heat and leave to cool slightly.
2 Pour the jelly mixture into four wetted individual moulds or dishes, then leave in the refrigerator for 1–2 hours or until set. Turn out on to a serving plate just before serving.
SERVES 4

—FOURTEEN—

VEGETABLE ACCOMPANIMENTS

An interesting side dish can transform the dullest of meals into something special. If you've no time to make a spectacular main course but need a vegetable to serve with something, perhaps from the chilled cabinet, or a commercially prepared vegetable, tofu or nut burger or a baked potato, then look no further. Here are vegetable dishes with a twist. Most are quick to cook, but all are full of flavour and character.

Serve Roast Potatoes and Garlic (see page 180) and perhaps Creamed Celeriac and Apple (see page 178) with a nut roast or one of the pies in Chapter Five. Sag Aloo (see page 179) and Okra with Onion and Chilli (below) complement most curry dishes. If your time or energy won't even stretch to one of these accompaniments, steam or boil root vegetables and toss with Pesto (see page 193) or a little herb or lemon butter, or stir-fry Chinese leaves, mangetouts, pak choi or spring greens with a little sesame oil and garlic or ginger. Alternatively, toss a mixture of cooked vegetables in one of the dressings in Chapter Fifteen.

Remember, if you cook vegetables in water, the water soluble vitamins will leach out into the cooking water. So, always use the minimum possible (don't fill the pan right to the top – a couple of inches of water should be enough) and reserve all cooking water for adding to stocks and soups.

If you've got a microwave, it's excellent for cooking small quantities of vegetables in the minimum of water. Ensure that the vegetables are trimmed to an even size and cook them in a large shallow dish in preference to a deep bowl. Time carefully, because unlike when cooked conventionally, you can't see them and they are easily overcooked.

OKRA WITH ONION AND CHILLI

Okra, or ladies' fingers, are long, thin, tapering vegetables which are used extensively in Indian cooking. When trimming the ends in step 1, take care not to cut the flesh or a sticky substance will be released during cooking.

450 g (1 lb) fresh okra	2 small fresh green chillies
45 ml (3 tbsp) vegetable oil	10 ml (2 level tsp) ground cumin
1 medium onion, skinned and finely sliced	salt and pepper

1 Wash the okra and trim off the stalk ends. Dry well on absorbent kitchen paper.
2 Heat the oil in a large, heavy-based frying pan or wok, add the onion and fry over a moderate heat, stirring constantly, for about 5 minutes or until turning golden.
3 Meanwhile, trim the ends off the green chillies and cut the flesh into fine rings with a sharp knife. Remove as many seeds as you like, according to how hot the dish is to be.

4 Add the okra, chillies and cumin to the pan. Season with salt and pepper and continue cooking over a moderate heat for 10–15 minutes, stirring constantly. The okra should be cooked but still quite crisp and the onions a deeper brown. Taste and adjust the seasoning, if necessary, then turn into a warmed serving dish.
SERVES 4

$\mathcal{S}$AUTÉED ARTICHOKES with ORANGE

Jerusalem artichokes are knobbly little roots looking rather like root ginger. They have a soft, sweet, almost earthy flavour. They're quite delicious, but should only be eaten in moderate quantities as they have a well-founded reputation for causing flatulence!

900 g (2 lb) Jerusalem artichokes	*30 ml (2 tbsp) vegetable oil*
salt and pepper	*25 g (1 oz) vegetable margarine or butter*
lemon juice	*chopped fresh parsley (optional)*
1 orange	

1 Scrub the artichokes. If possible, leave them whole; if not, cut them into large chunks about the size of golf balls.

2 Put the artichokes in a saucepan and cover with salted water acidulated with lemon juice. Bring to the boil, then reduce the heat, cover and simmer for 8–10 minutes or until the artichokes are barely tender. Finely grate the orange rind and segment the flesh.

3 Drain the artichokes and refresh under cold running water. Peel off the skins and divide the flesh into good-sized chunks.

4 Heat the oil and margarine or butter in a frying pan and add the artichokes with the orange rind. Fry over a moderate heat, turning frequently, until golden brown.

5 Stir in the orange segments and parsley, if wished. Taste and adjust the seasoning, if necessary, before serving.

SERVES 4

Sautéed Artichokes with Orange

AUBERGINES WITH MUSTARD SEEDS AND YOGURT

Grilling whole aubergines until the skins char gives the flesh a wonderful smoky flavour. If you are making this dish in the summertime, the flavour will be even more accentuated if the aubergines are charred over a barbecue. Serve as a cooling accompaniment to very spicy dishes or as a main meal with pilau rice.

3 medium aubergines, about 900 g (2 lb) total weight	60 ml (4 level tbsp) chopped fresh coriander
60 ml (4 tbsp) vegetable oil	5 ml (1 level tsp) salt
30 ml (2 level tbsp) black mustard seeds, ground	300 ml (½ pint) natural yogurt
2.5 ml (½ level tsp) chilli powder	

1 Put the aubergines under a preheated grill for about 15 minutes, turning occasionally. The skins should be black and charred and the flesh soft.
2 Leave the aubergines until just cool enough to handle, then peel the skins off and discard. Chop the flesh roughly.
3 Heat the oil in a heavy-based frying pan,

add the ground mustard seeds, chopped aubergine flesh and the chilli powder. Stir over a moderate heat for about 5 minutes or until thoroughly hot, then add the coriander.
4 Beat the salt into the yogurt, then stir into the aubergine until evenly blended. Turn into a warmed serving dish and serve immediately.
SERVES 4–6

SUMMER CARROTS IN SPICED DRESSING

Fresh coriander could be substituted for the chives.

450 g (1 lb) young carrots, trimmed and scrubbed	5 ml (1 tsp) honey
50 g (2 oz) vegetable margarine or butter	30 ml (2 level tbsp) roughly chopped chives
25 g (1 oz) flaked almonds	5 ml (1 tsp) lemon juice
5 ml (1 level tsp) ground cumin	salt and pepper
10 ml (2 level tsp) ground coriander	

1 Steam the carrots or cook in boiling salted water for 4–5 minutes or until just tender. Drain well.
2 Melt the margarine or butter in a large frying pan and stir in the almonds and spices. Cook, stirring, for 1–2 minutes or until the

almonds are golden brown. Toss in the carrots, honey, chives and lemon juice. Stir over a high heat until well mixed, then season with salt and pepper and serve.
SERVES 4

Summer Carrots in Spiced Dressing left, Potted Herb Bread (page 150)

CREAMED CELERIAC AND APPLE

Serve this delicate purée with mild-flavoured main courses – it won't cope well with spicy casseroles.

900 g (2 lb) celeriac	*10 ml (2 level tsp) creamed horseradish*
salt and pepper	*30 ml (2 tbsp) single cream*
lemon juice	*chopped fresh parsley*
350 g (12 oz) cooking apple	

1 Peel the celeriac, thinly slice and immediately drop into cold salted water acidulated with lemon juice. Bring to the boil, cover and simmer for 25–30 minutes or until tender.
2 Peel, quarter, core and slice the apple. Add to the pan and simmer for 3–4 minutes longer or until the apple is tender. Drain well.

3 Mash the celeriac and apple, then return to the pan with the horseradish. Season with salt and pepper and reheat, stirring all the time, until all excess moisture has been driven off.
4 Stir in the cream with plenty of chopped parsley, reheat gently, then taste and adjust the seasoning, if necessary, before serving.
SERVES 4

PARNSIP AND GINGER BAKE

This is perfect for mopping up the juices from bean casseroles and stews.

900 g (2 lb) parsnips, trimmed, peeled and thinly sliced	*2 free-range eggs*
salt and pepper	*25 g (1 oz) vegetable margarine or butter*
15 g (½ oz) piece of fresh root ginger, peeled and finely chopped	*finely grated rind and juice of ½ lemon*
	flaked almonds
60 ml (4 tbsp) single cream	

1 Cook the parsnips in boiling salted water for about 15 minutes or until tender. Drain the parsnips, then mash them.
2 Stir the ginger into the parsnip purée with the cream, eggs, margarine or butter, the lemon rind and 15 ml (1 tbsp) lemon juice. Beat well to mix and season.

3 Turn into a lightly greased 1.1 litre (2 pint) shallow ovenproof dish. Sprinkle the surface lightly with almonds.
4 Bake at 200°C (400°F) mark 6 for 20–25 minutes or until golden brown and lightly set. Serve immediately.
SERVES 4

 Sag Aloo

Ghee is a type of clarified butter originally made in India but now produced elsewhere. It has a better flavour than ordinary clarified butter and is particularly useful for frying at high temperatures. Commercially produced vegetarian ghee, made from hydrogenated vegetable oil, is now widely available in large supermarkets.

900 g (2 lb) fresh spinach, or 450 g (1 lb) frozen leaf spinach, thawed and drained	*5 ml (1 level tsp) black mustard seeds*
60 ml (4 tbsp) vegetable ghee or oil	*2.5 ml (½ level tsp) ground turmeric*
1 medium onion, skinned and thinly sliced	*1.25 ml (¼ level tsp) chilli powder*
2 garlic cloves, skinned and crushed	*1.25 ml (¼ level tsp) ground ginger*
10 ml (2 level tsp) ground coriander	*salt*
	450 g (1 lb) old potatoes, peeled and thickly sliced

1 If using fresh spinach, wash well, put in a large saucepan without any water and cook over a very gentle heat for about 15 minutes. If using frozen spinach, cook over a gentle heat for 5 minutes. Drain well and cool.
2 With your hands, squeeze out all the moisture from the spinach. Chop finely.
3 Melt the ghee or oil in a heavy-based saucepan or flameproof casserole, add the onion, garlic, spices and salt to taste and fry gently for about 5 minutes or until the onion

begins to brown, stirring frequently.
4 Add the potatoes and stir gently to mix with the onion and spices. Pour in 150 ml (¼ pint) water and bring to the boil, then lower the heat and simmer, uncovered, for 10 minutes. Stir occasionally and add a few more spoonfuls of water if necessary.
5 Fold the spinach gently into the potato mixture. Simmer for a further 5–10 minutes or until the potatoes are just tender. Serve hot.
SERVES 4–6

 Herb-Glazed Tomatoes

This dish also cooks well in the microwave. Cover the prepared tomatoes with a plate or a lid and cook on HIGH for 5–7 minutes or until tender, rearranging halfway through cooking.

4 beefsteak tomatoes, about 550 g (1¼ lb) total weight	*5 ml (1 tsp) lemon juice*
25 g (1 oz) vegetable margarine or butter	*25 ml (1½ tbsp) shredded fresh basil*
salt and pepper	*basil sprigs, to garnish*
45 ml (3 tbsp) double cream	

1 Cut the tomatoes in half and trim away the cores. Melt the margarine or butter in a large frying pan and gently fry the tomatoes for 1 minute on each side. Arrange the tomatoes in a greased, shallow ovenproof dish and season.
2 Add the cream, lemon juice and half the basil to the juices in the frying pan, mix well

and drizzle over the tomatoes. Sprinkle with more pepper.
3 Bake in the oven at 190°C (375°F) mark 5 for about 8 minutes. Sprinkle with the remaining basil and cook for a further 2–3 minutes. Serve hot, garnished with basil.
SERVES 8

ROAST POTATOES AND GARLIC

Once roasted, garlic is deliciously mild and creamy. Encourage your guests to slip the cloves from their skins and mash them into their gravy or sauce.

1.8 kg (4 lb) potatoes, peeled	*2 whole bulbs of garlic*
salt and pepper	*chopped fresh parsley, to garnish*
olive oil	

1 Cut the potatoes into large even-sized pieces, put them in a saucepan of cold salted water and bring to the boil. Boil for 2 minutes, then drain thoroughly.
2 Heat the oil in a roasting tin in the oven. Add the potatoes and baste with the oil until all sides are coated. Separate the garlic into cloves, and remove the loose papery skins, leaving the inner skins attached. Scatter the garlic over the potatoes. Cook in the oven at 180°C (350°F) mark 4 for about 45 minutes, turning occasionally.
3 Increase the oven temperature to 220°C (425°F) mark 7 and continue cooking the potatoes for a further 20–25 minutes or until crisp and golden brown. Season with salt and pepper and sprinkle with parsley.
SERVES 8

FRIED MASALA POTATOES

These highly spiced potatoes are rather high in calories – but worth every tasty mouthful! Serve as an accompaniment to a simple (preferably low-calorie) main course.

900 g (2 lb) new potatoes	*4 garlic cloves, skinned*
vegetable ghee or oil for deep-frying	*2 medium onions, skinned and chopped*
10 ml (2 level tsp) cumin seeds	*45 ml (3 tbsp) vegetable ghee or oil*
15 ml (1 level tbsp) coriander seeds	*5 ml (1 level tsp) chilli powder*
7.5 ml (1½ level tsp) garam masala	*2.5 ml (½ level tsp) ground turmeric*
2.5 cm (1 inch) piece of fresh root ginger, peeled and roughly chopped	*5 ml (1 level tsp) salt*
	300 ml (½ pint) natural yogurt

1 Wash the potatoes and scrub clean if necessary. Cut into 2.5 cm (1 inch) pieces. Pat dry with absorbent kitchen paper.
2 Heat the oil in a deep-fat fryer to 180°C (350°F) and deep-fry the potatoes in batches for 10 minutes or until golden brown. Remove from the oil and drain on absorbent kitchen paper.
3 Place the cumin and coriander seeds in a blender or food processor with the garam masala, ginger, garlic and onions. Process until smooth, adding a little water if necessary.
4 Heat the ghee or oil in a heavy-based frying pan, add the masala paste and fry gently for about 5 minutes. Add the chilli, turmeric and salt and fry for a further 1 minute.
5 Pour in the yogurt, then add the potatoes. Stir well and cook for another 5 minutes or until completely heated through. Serve piping hot.
SERVES 4–6

-Fifteen-

Sauces and Dressings

Successful sauce making is easy provided a few basic rules are adhered to. Choose a good heavy-based pan to reduce the risk of burning. If the roux does burn, there's no remedy – you'll have to throw it away and start again. A burnt roux makes a bitter sauce (with unappetising black bits in it). Don't despair if the sauce is lumpy – vigorous mixing with a large balloon whisk will usually do the trick, or as a last resort, push it through a sieve. Most sauces can be prepared ahead of time and refrigerated. To prevent a skin forming, lay a piece of damp greaseproof paper on the surface of the sauce. Reheat gently, whisking in more liquid if the sauce has become too thick.

Smooth sauces freeze very well. Freeze in usable quantities as large blocks of sauce take quite a while to thaw. It's preferable to reheat in a double saucepan to prevent scorching, or in a large bowl in the microwave. Sauces containing pieces of tomato, mushroom and so on, don't freeze so well as they're difficult to whisk when reheating.

The foundation of most good dressings is the oil. Virgin oils are those obtained from a first, cold pressing. These unrefined oils have the strongest flavour and are therefore the most expensive. Good virgin olive oil is essential for well flavoured dressings. Rich and mellow walnut, hazelnut and almond oils lend their own characteristic flavours. They're too strong to be used alone, so blend with a blander oil such as sunflower or groundnut. Sesame oil adds interesting oriental tones to salads, but avoid very dark-coloured brands; they are overpowering and cloying.

Oils gradually lose their flavour and become rancid, particularly nut oils, so store them in a cool, dark place and adhere to the use-by date.

Vinegars now come in all sorts of flavours as well. As a change from the familiar wine vinegars, try cider, sherry or raspberry vinegar or varieties flavoured with herbs, spices or garlic. Balsamic vinegar is wonderfully dark with a sweet-sour flavour. Its fine, distinctive flavour turns the humblest salad into something special. Use it in moderation because it is very strong. Both oils and vinegars can be flavoured at home with herbs, spices, garlic or soft fruits such as raspberries, strawberries or blackcurrants.

Use this collection of sauces and dressings to embellish the recipes in this book or your own favourite dishes.

WHITE SAUCE 1

This is one of the basic sauces which has infinite possible variations. The quantities given here make a pouring sauce suitable for serving as an accompaniment to pies, nut roasts, vegetables and pulses. To make a thicker sauce for binding ingredients to fill pancakes, pies, etc, increase the amounts of flour and fat to 50 g (2 oz).

15 g (½ oz) vegetable margarine or butter	*300 ml (½ pint) milk*
15 g (½ oz) plain flour	*salt and pepper*

1 Melt the margarine or butter in a saucepan, stir in the flour and cook gently for 1 minute, stirring.
2 Remove the pan from the heat and gradually stir in the milk. Bring to the boil slowly and continue cooking, stirring all the time, until the sauce comes to the boil and thickens.
3 Simmer very gently for a further 2–3 minutes. Season with salt and pepper.
MAKES 300 ML (½ PINT)

QUICK METHOD
Put the fat, flour, milk, salt and pepper in a saucepan. Heat, whisking continuously, until the sauce thickens and is cooked.

BLENDER OR FOOD PROCESSOR METHOD
Put the fat, flour, milk, salt and pepper in the machine and blend until smooth. Pour into a saucepan and bring to the boil, stirring, until the sauce thickens.

MICROWAVE METHOD
Put all the ingredients in a large bowl and cook on HIGH for 4–5 minutes, or until thickened, whisking every minute.

VARIATIONS
Add the following to the hot sauce with the seasoning:

Cheese Sauce 50 g (2 oz) grated mature Cheddar cheese and a large pinch of mustard powder.

Parsley or Herb Sauce Add about 30 ml (2 tbsp) chopped fresh parsley or herbs of your choice.

Blue Cheese Sauce Add 50 g (2 oz) crumbled Stilton, or other hard blue cheese, and 10 ml (2 tsp) lemon juice.

Mushroom Sauce Add 75 g (3 oz) lightly cooked sliced mushrooms.

Onion Sauce Add 1 medium onion, chopped and cooked.

Egg Sauce Add 1 hard-boiled free-range egg, finely chopped.

Sweet Sauce Add 15–30 ml (1–2 level tbsp) caster sugar.

WHITE SAUCE 2

This white sauce is thickened with cornflour and contains less fat than White Sauce 1. Use it when you want a lower-calorie sauce. Using semi-skimmed milk or a mixture of milk and stock reduces the calorie content even more. Any of the variations for White Sauce 1 can be used with this as a base.

25 ml (5 level tsp) cornflour	*a knob of vegetable margarine or butter*
300 ml (½ pint) milk	*salt and pepper*

1 Put the cornflour in a bowl and blend with 75 ml (5 tbsp) milk to a smooth paste. Heat the remaining milk with the margarine or butter until boiling, then pour on to the blended mixture, stirring all the time to prevent lumps forming.

2 Return the mixture to the saucepan, bring to the boil slowly and continue to cook, stirring all the time, until the sauce comes to the boil and thickens.

3 Simmer gently for a further 2-3 minutes, to make a white, glossy sauce. Season with salt and pepper.

MAKES 300 ML (½ PINT)

ℋARISSA SAUCE

This is a fiery hot sauce, usually served with couscous and rice and bean dishes. It cooks well in the microwave. Simply put everything in a bowl, cover and cook on HIGH for 8–10 minutes or until the pepper is really soft. Add the water, re-cover and cook for 3–4 minutes or until the water is boiling. Complete as below.

15 ml (1 tbsp) vegetable oil	15 ml (1 level tbsp) ground coriander
1 large red pepper, cored, seeded and finely chopped	5 ml (1 level tsp) ground caraway
2 red chillies (or more to taste), seeded and chopped	30 ml (2 level tbsp) tomato purée
2 garlic cloves, skinned and crushed	salt and pepper

1 Heat the oil in a large heavy-based saucepan. Add all the ingredients, except salt and pepper, and cook over a medium heat for about 5 minutes or until the pepper has softened.
2 Add 300 ml (½ pint) water and bring to the boil. Reduce the heat, cover and simmer gently for about 10 minutes or until the pepper is really soft. Purée in a blender or food processor until smooth. Season to taste with salt and pepper. Serve hot or cold.
MAKES ABOUT 300 ML (½ PINT)

𝒮OURED CREAM AND HORSERADISH SAUCE

The strength of commercially prepared horseradish sauce or relish varies considerably. Some are labelled 'hot' and give a considerable 'kick' to the sauce; others are very mild. Add your chosen brand a little at a time to get the desired effect. Serve with beetroot, carrots, mushrooms, baked onions and, of course, nut roasts.

40 g (1½ oz) vegetable margarine or butter	300 ml (10 fl oz) soured cream
45 ml (3 level tbsp) plain flour	about 45 ml (3 level tbsp) horseradish sauce
300 ml (½ pint) vegetable stock	salt and pepper

1 Melt the margarine or butter in a heavy-based saucepan, add the flour and cook for 2 minutes, stirring all the time.
2 Remove from the heat and gradually add the stock, stirring briskly. Bring to the boil and stir until thick. Simmer for 5 minutes.
3 Add the soured cream and mix in well.
4 Stir in the horseradish sauce to taste and season with salt and pepper. Reheat gently without boiling.
MAKES ABOUT 600 ML (1 PINT)

GARLIC CHEESE AND WALNUT SAUCE

Serve this with stuffed baked onions, or peppers, steamed broccoli or Brussels sprouts, or as a topping for baked potatoes.

40 g (1½ oz) vegetable margarine or butter	*150 g (5 oz) full fat soft cheese with garlic and herbs*
40 ml (8 level tsp) plain flour	*25 g (1 oz) walnuts, chopped*
450 ml (¾ pint) milk	*salt and pepper*

1 Melt the margarine or butter in a heavy-based saucepan, add the flour and cook for 2 minutes, stirring all the time.
2 Remove from the heat and gradually add the milk, beating between each addition.
3 Cook until thickened, stirring all the time, then simmer for about 5 minutes.
4 Off the heat, beat in the cheese a little at a time, making sure it melts. Stir in the chopped walnuts. Season with salt and pepper. Reheat but do not boil.
MAKES ABOUT 450 ML (¾ PINT)

VINAIGRETTE DRESSING

Make up a large batch of dressing and store in the refrigerator ready for use when required. Increase or decrease the proportion of oil to vinegar within the suggested range, according to how sharp you like your dressing. The flavour can be varied with any of the suggestions shown below.

175–225 ml (6–8 fl oz) olive oil	*2.5 ml (½ level tsp) caster sugar or honey*
45 ml (3 tbsp) white wine, red wine, garlic or herb vinegar	*10 ml (2 level tsp) Dijon mustard*
	salt and pepper

Whisk together all the ingredients until thoroughly combined. Season with salt and pepper.

VARIATIONS
Herb Whisk into the dressing 30 ml (2 level tbsp) finely chopped, fresh mixed herbs, such as parsley, thyme, marjoram, chives, sage, etc.
Mustard and Parsley Stir in 15 ml (1 level tbsp) whole grain mustard and 30 ml (2 level tbsp) finely chopped fresh parsley

Sweet and Spiced Add 5 ml (1 level tsp) mango chutney, 5 ml (1 level tsp) mild curry paste and 2.5 ml (½ level tsp) ground turmeric.
Roquefort Place the dressing in a liquidiser or food processor. Add 25 g (1 oz) Roquefort cheese and 30 ml (2 tbsp) single cream. Blend until smooth.
Garlic Crush 1–2 garlic cloves into the dressing.
MAKES 200–250 ML (7–9 FL OZ)

*T*ARRAGON AND TOMATO VINAIGRETTE

Use very ripe, bright red tomatoes for the best flavour.

30 ml (2 tbsp) red wine vinegar	*15 ml (1 level tbsp) chopped onion (preferably red)*
60 ml (4 tbsp) olive oil	*a few drops of Tabasco*
15 ml (1 tbsp) mustard oil	*salt and pepper*
5 ml (1 level tsp) tomato purée	*75 g (3 oz) tomatoes, skinned, seeded and chopped*
15 ml (1 level tbsp) each chopped fresh tarragon and parsley	*a pinch of caster sugar (optional)*

1 Whisk together the vinegar, oils, tomato purée, herbs, onion and Tabasco. Season with salt and pepper.
2 Stir in the tomatoes and add caster sugar if wished. Taste and adjust the seasoning, if necessary.
MAKES ABOUT 150 ML (¼ PINT)

*R*ICH GARLIC DRESSING

Balsamic vinegar produces a dark, sweet-sour dressing, ideal with strong-flavoured foods.

50 ml (2 fl oz) balsamic vinegar	*2 garlic cloves, skinned and crushed*
150 ml (¼ pint) olive oil	*salt and pepper*
2.5 ml (½ level tsp) caster sugar	

1 Whisk together the vinegar, oil, sugar and garlic until thoroughly combined.
2 Season with salt and pepper.
MAKES ABOUT 200 ML (7 FL OZ)

*H*ERB PURÉE

This aromatic purée is ideal for stirring into steamed vegetables, pasta, rice or noodles.

50 g (2 oz) fresh mixed herb leaves, such as basil, thyme or marjoram	*150 ml (¼ pint) olive oil*
	60 ml (4 level tbsp) freshly grated Parmesan cheese

Roughly chop the herbs in a food processor. Slowly pour in the oil and blend into a thick purée. Blend in the cheese. Transfer to a jar and store in the refrigerator. The purée will keep for 2–3 weeks.
SERVES 4

A selection of sauces and dressings

CURRY SAUCE

This is a fairly simple curry sauce to serve with hard-boiled eggs, cooked vegetables and pulses. This basic recipe can, of course, be embellished by the addition of chillies, ginger, a few cardamoms or chopped fresh coriander.

30 ml (2 tbsp) vegetable oil	5 ml (1 level tsp) ground cumin
1 large onion, skinned and chopped	50 g (2 oz) split red lentils
1 garlic clove, skinned and crushed	450 ml (¾ pint) vegetable stock
10 ml (2 level tsp) ground coriander	salt and pepper
10 ml (2 level tsp) ground turmeric	150 ml (¼ pint) Greek yogurt
5 ml (1 level tsp) fenugreek seeds	

1 Heat the oil in a heavy-based saucepan. Add the onion and garlic and fry for 5 minutes or until softened. Add the spices and fry for 2 minutes, stirring.

2 Add the lentils and stock, bring to the boil, then reduce the heat, cover and simmer for 30 minutes or until the lentils are very soft. Season with salt and pepper. Stir in the yogurt and reheat gently before serving.

MAKES ABOUT 600 ML (1 PINT)

LEEK SAUCE

Serve with steamed, boiled or roast vegetables.

50 g (2 oz) vegetable margarine or butter	150 ml (5 fl oz) single cream
450 g (1 lb) leeks, trimmed, thoroughly washed and finely chopped	salt and pepper
	10 ml (2 level tsp) green peppercorns in brine, drained and chopped
175 ml (6 fl oz) vegetable stock	
20 ml (4 tsp) lemon juice	

1 Melt the margarine or butter in a saucepan and fry the leeks for 1–2 minutes. Cover with a tight-fitting lid and cook over a low heat for about 5 minutes or until very soft, stirring occasionally. Add the stock and simmer gently, covered, for a further 10 minutes. Leave the stock mixture to cool slightly.

2 In a blender or food processor, purée the leeks and stock with the lemon juice. Sieve the resulting mixture back into the rinsed-out saucepan. Stir in the cream, seasoning and peppercorns. Reheat gently without boiling for 1–2 minutes before serving.

MAKES ABOUT 600 ML (1 PINT)

BÉCHAMEL SAUCE

Flavoured milk gives a delicate aroma to this white sauce. There is a long and short method. The long method is strictly for the purist; this simplified version makes a splendid sauce in half the time. It's delicious served plain or with the addition of mildly flavoured ingredients such as egg or mushroom.

300 ml (½ pint) milk	*1 blade of mace*
1 slice of onion	*15 g (½ oz) vegetable margarine or butter*
1 bay leaf	*scant 15 g (½ oz) plain flour*
6 peppercorns	*salt and pepper*

1 Pour the milk into a saucepan. Add the onion, bay leaf, peppercorns and mace and bring to scalding point. Remove from the heat, cover and leave to infuse for 10–30 minutes. Strain.
2 Melt the margarine or butter in a saucepan. Remove from the heat and stir in the flour until evenly blended. Gradually pour on the warm milk, stirring well. Season lightly with salt and pepper.
3 Bring to the boil, stirring constantly, and simmer for 2–3 minutes.
MAKES ABOUT 300 ML (½ PINT)

HOLLANDAISE SAUCE

Hollandaise should always be served warm. Bear in mind that it curdles easily: if this happens, simply add an ice cube, whisk well and the sauce should come back together again. It's traditionally served with steamed asparagus as a starter, but it makes an excellent accompaniment to most vegetables.

45 ml (3 tbsp) white wine vinegar	*75–100 g (3–4 oz) butter, at room temperature*
6 peppercorns	*2 free-range egg yolks*
1 small bay leaf	*salt*
1 blade of mace	

1 Place the vinegar, peppercorns, bay leaf and mace in a small saucepan. Bring to the boil and boil rapidly until reduced to only 10 ml (2 tsp). Set aside.
2 Soften the butter slightly. In a small heatproof bowl, cream the egg yolks with a small piece of butter and a pinch of salt. Strain the herb and vinegar mixture into the bowl.
3 Place the bowl in a bain-marie over a gentle heat until the mixture becomes thick, stirring constantly.
4 Gradually add the remainder of the butter in small pieces, stirring constantly. When 75 g (3 oz) of the butter has been added, season the sauce lightly with salt. If still too sharp, add a little more butter. The sauce should be lightly piquant. Serve lukewarm.
SERVES 4

$\mathcal{T}$OMATO SAUCE

This makes a deliciously rich, well flavoured sauce for serving with pasta, vegetable bakes or roasts. To make a spicy sauce, add 1–2 chopped fresh chillies and a little chopped fresh coriander. Add other flavourings, such as garlic, bay leaves, thyme or rosemary, to make a sauce to complement whatever it's being served with.

30 ml (2 tbsp) olive oil	a large pinch of dried oregano
1 small onion, skinned and finely chopped	300 ml (½ pint) dry red wine or vegetable stock
30 ml (2 level tbsp) tomato purée	a large pinch of sugar
5 ml (1 level tsp) mild paprika	salt and pepper
two 397 g (14 oz) cans chopped tomatoes	

1 Heat the oil in a heavy-based saucepan, add the onion and fry for 5–10 minutes or until very soft. Add the tomato purée and paprika and fry for 2–3 minutes. Add the tomatoes, oregano, red wine or stock and sugar.

2 Season the sauce with salt and pepper, then bring to the boil and simmer for about 20 minutes or until the sauce is slightly reduced.
MAKES ABOUT 600 ML (1 PINT)

$\mathcal{G}$RAVY

It's not that difficult to make a delicious vegetarian gravy, providing you use a good, well flavoured stock (Brown Onion or Mushroom, pages 41 and 42, both work well) or use a mixture of red wine and stock. Add a dash or two of gravy browning or yeast extract to get a dark brown colour, if necessary.

15 ml (1 tbsp) vegetable oil	30 ml (2 level tbsp) plain flour
1 large onion, skinned and chopped	600 ml (1 pint) stock or stock and red wine
125 g (4 oz) mushrooms, wiped and chopped	a sprig of fresh thyme
1 garlic clove, skinned and crushed (optional)	salt and pepper

1 Heat the oil in a heavy-based saucepan. Add the onion, mushrooms and garlic, if using. Fry over a high heat for about 10 minutes or until the onions start to turn golden brown. Stir all the time so that they brown evenly rather than burn.
2 Add the flour and cook over a low heat for about 5 minutes or until the flour starts to brown, stirring all the time. Take the pan off the heat and leave to cool for 1–2 minutes.
3 Gradually blend in the stock (or stock and wine), return to the heat and bring to the boil. Add the thyme, season with salt and pepper, lower the heat, cover and simmer for 20 minutes. Strain into a clean saucepan. Taste and adjust the seasoning, if necessary, just before serving.
MAKES ABOUT 450 ML (¾ PINT)

 AYONNAISE

The ingredients for Mayonnaise should be at room temperature. Never use eggs straight from the refrigerator or cold larder as this may result in curdling. (See below for rescue remedies.)

1 free-range egg yolk	1.25 ml (¼ level tsp) pepper
2.5 ml (½ level tsp) mustard powder or 5 ml (1 level tsp) Dijon mustard	2.5 ml (½ level tsp) sugar
	15 ml (1 tbsp) white wine vinegar or lemon juice
2.5 ml (½ level tsp) salt	about 150 ml (¼ pint) vegetable oil

Put the egg yolk into a bowl with the
mustard, salt, pepper, sugar and 5 n
the vinegar or lemon juice. Mix th
then add the oil, drop by drop, whi
constantly, until the sauce is thick a
smooth. If it becomes too thick, add
more of the vinegar or lemon juice.
the oil has been added, add the rema
vinegar or lemon juice gradually and
thoroughly.
MAKES ABOUT 150 ML (¼ PINT)

Making Mayonnaise in a blender
processor Most blenders and food
processors need at least a two-egg qua
order to ensure that the blades are cov
Put the yolks, salt and pepper and half
vinegar or lemon juice into the blende
or food processor bowl and blend well.
your machine has a variable speed cont
run it at a slow speed. Add the oil gradu
while the machine is running. Add the
remaining vinegar and season.

Rescue remedies If the Mayonnaise
separates, save it by beating the curdled
mixture into a fresh base. This base can be
any one of the following: 5 ml (1 tsp) hot
water; 5 ml (1 tsp) vinegar or lemon juice;
5 ml (1 level tsp) Dijon mustard or 2.5 ml
(½ level tsp) mustard powder; or an egg yolk.
Add the curdled mixture to the base, beating

hard. When the mixture is smooth, continue
g the oil as above. (If you use an extra
lk you may find that you need to add a
xtra oil.)

g Mayonnaise Home-made
naise does not keep as long as bought
s because it lacks their added
ers, stabilisers and preservatives.
er, Mayonnaise should keep for 3–4
a screw-topped glass jar in the
tor. Allow to come to room
ure before stirring or the Mayonnaise
le.

MAYONNAISE

Tofu Mayonnaise, a vegan
to egg-based Mayonnaise, follow
r or food processor method above.
gg and replace with a 300 g
cket of silken tofu. Reduce the oil
to 90 ml (6 tbsp).
MAKES ABOUT 300 ML (½ PINT)

VARIATIONS
Curried Tofu Mayonnaise Flavour with
5 ml (1 tsp) hot curry paste.
Garlic and Herb Tofu Mayonnaise
Flavour with 1 garlic clove, skinned and
crushed and 30 ml (2 level tbsp) chopped
mixed fresh herbs.

LAVOURED MAYONNAISE

Add one of the following flavourings to 150 ml (¼ pint) home-made or shop-bought mayonnaise.

Curry Cream Sauce Sauté 10 ml (2 level tsp) chopped onion and 1 crushed garlic clove in 15 ml (1 tbsp) oil for 2–3 minutes. Stir in 10 ml (2 level tsp) curry powder and 5 ml (1 level tsp) tomato purée. Add 75 ml (3 fl oz) water, 1 slice of lemon and 10 ml (2 level tsp) apricot jam. Simmer for 5–7 minutes. Strain the mixture and leave to cool. When cold, whisk into the mayonnaise. Taste and adjust the seasoning, if necessary.

Watercress and Lemon Beat 60 ml (4 level tbsp) finely chopped watercress and the finely grated rind of 2 lemons into the mayonnaise. Taste and adjust the seasoning, if necessary.

Thousand Island Stir in 30 ml (2 level tbsp) finely chopped green olives, 10 ml (2 level tsp) each finely chopped parsley and onion, 10 ml (2 level tsp) tomato purée, 30 ml (2 level tbsp) finely chopped green pepper and 1 chopped hard-boiled egg. Taste and adjust the seasoning, if necessary.

Blue Cheese and Toasted Walnut Beat 125 g (4 oz) crumbled Danish Blue cheese, 150 ml (5 fl oz) soured cream, ½ quantity Vinaigrette Dressing (see page 185), 1 skinned and crushed garlic clove, 25 g (1 oz) toasted chopped walnuts and 15 ml (1 level tbsp) chopped fresh parsley into the mayonnaise. Taste and adjust the seasoning, if necessary.

Aïoli (Garlic Mayonnaise) See the recipe on page 22 for Fried Courgettes with Rosemary Aïoli.

OGURT AND TAHINI CREAM

Use to dress coleslaw, or serve with hard-boiled eggs, warm potatoes or vegetable crudités.

90 ml (6 tbsp) natural yogurt	*60 ml (4 level tbsp) thin tahini (see page 14)*
15–20 ml (3–4 tsp) white wine vinegar	*salt and pepper*
90 ml (6 tbsp) olive oil	

1 Whisk together the yogurt and vinegar. Slowly stir in the olive oil until thoroughly combined.

2 Beat in the tahini and then season with salt and pepper.
MAKES ABOUT 200 ML (7 FL OZ)

$\mathcal{P}$ESTO

This is the classic Genoese pasta sauce. It uses copious quantities of fresh basil – dried will not do. Use it to flavour soups, dressings and pizzas as well as pasta.

50 g (2 oz) fresh basil leaves (weighed without stalks)	*salt and pepper*
2 garlic cloves, skinned	*125 ml (4 fl oz) olive oil*
30 ml (2 tbsp) pine nuts	*50 g (2 oz) freshly grated Parmesan cheese*

Put the basil, garlic, pine nuts, salt, pepper and olive oil in a blender or food processor and blend at high speed until very creamy. Transfer the mixture to a bowl, fold in the cheese and mix thoroughly. Store for up to 2 weeks in a screw-topped jar in the refrigerator.

MAKES 300 ML (½ PINT); ENOUGH FOR 4–6 SERVINGS OF PASTA

$\mathcal{H}$AZELNUT AND CORIANDER PESTO

This makes a vibrant green pesto with a pungent smell and a strong flavour. Serve it separately for guests to mix to taste with their individual plates of steaming pasta, dilute it with fromage frais or yogurt and toss with cooked vegetables and pulses, or use in small amounts to flavour vinaigrette dressings for hot or cold salads.

75 g (3 oz) hazelnuts	*finely grated rind and juice of ½ lemon*
1 large bunch of coriander, weighing about 125 g (4 oz)	*about 150 ml (¼ pint) olive oil*
2–3 garlic cloves, skinned and crushed	*salt and pepper*

1 Toast the hazelnuts under a hot grill. Tip them on to a clean tea-towel and rub off the loose skins. Toast again under the grill until golden brown on all sides. Leave to cool, then tip into a blender or food processor.
2 Trim the stalks from the coriander and discard. Put the leaves into the blender with the hazelnuts. Add the garlic and the lemon rind and juice. Process until finely chopped, then, with the machine still running, gradually add the oil in a thin, steady stream until you have a fairly thick sauce-like consistency.
3 Season with black pepper and a little salt. Turn into a bowl or a jar, cover tightly, and use as required. Store in the refrigerator for 1–2 weeks.

MAKES ABOUT 300 ML (½ PINT); ENOUGH FOR 4–6 SERVINGS OF PASTA

*F*RESH PEAR DRESSING

To produce a smooth dressing, choose very ripe pears. Serve with Spinach Ricotta Terrine
(see page 18), salads and fried dishes.

350 g (12 oz) ripe, juicy pears	*a few drops of red wine vinegar*
150 ml (¼ pint) walnut oil	*salt and pepper*
150 ml (¼ pint) olive oil	

Peel, halve and core the pears. Roughly chop
and put in a blender or food processor. Add
the oils and vinegar, and season with salt and
pepper. Purée until smooth, then taste and

adjust the seasoning, if necessary. Whisk the
dressing again just before serving.
MAKES ABOUT 450 ML (¾ PINT)

*B*RANDY AND CELERY SAUCE

If you're nervous about setting the brandy alight (see step 5), make the sauce with double
cream, instead of single, add the brandy to the sauce and boil for 1–2 minutes. Don't try to
boil a sauce containing single cream – it will curdle. The higher fat content of double cream
means it can be boiled without risk of curdling, but it will also increase the calorie content!
Serve with Wild Mushroom Strudel (see page 78), nut roasts and vegetable burgers.

25 g (1 oz) vegetable margarine or butter	*salt and pepper*
4 celery sticks, trimmed and finely chopped	*150 ml (5 fl oz) single cream*
15 ml (1 level tbsp) rice flour or plain flour	*15–30 ml (1–2 tbsp) brandy*
300 ml (½ pint) vegetable stock	
15 ml (1 level tbsp) chopped fresh dill or 5 ml (1 level tsp) dried dill weed	

1 Heat the margarine or butter in a saucepan,
add the celery and cook gently until almost
tender.
2 Stir in the flour and cook for 1 minute.
Remove from the heat, gradually blend in the
stock, and bring to the boil, stirring all the
time. Mix in the dill, season with salt and
pepper and simmer for about 5 minutes. Cool
slightly.

3 Purée the sauce in a food processor, then
sieve into a clean saucepan.
4 Whisk the cream into the sauce and heat
gently without boiling, stirring occasionally.
Taste and adjust the seasoning, if necessary.
5 Gently heat the brandy until warm, but not
boiling. Remove from the heat, set alight and
stir into the sauce to taste.
MAKES ABOUT 450 ML (¾ PINT)

—Sixteen—

Cakes and Teabreads

Vegans and non-egg eating vegetarians can have a hard time finding suitable recipes for cakes and teabreads. Here, we have devised a delicious selection of recipes, many without eggs, milk or dairy produce. In fact the Eggless Chocolate Cake (see page 197) is so moist, rich and delicious that no one will realise that it's egg-free.

Flours vary enormously – look for a finely ground wholemeal flour for cakes, biscuits and teabreads; the coarser types tend to give a much crumblier texture. Wholemeal flour absorbs more liquid than white flour, so when substituting one for the other use slightly more liquid. Cakes made solely with wholemeal flour are denser and heavier – a mixture of half white and half wholemeal gives a lighter result.

Most of these recipes will keep well for several days, and in some cases for up to 2 weeks if wrapped in greaseproof paper and foil and then put into an airtight container. Alternatively, they can be frozen. We recommend that you thaw them, still wrapped, overnight, but if time does not allow, unwrap until thawed, then immediately overwrap again.

Many of the recipes contain dried fruits and nuts. Some manufacturers treat dried fruit with sulphur dioxide gas to prevent it becoming too dark in colour. Choose unsulphured brands if you're interested in reducing your consumption of chemical additives. Buy dried fruit in small quantities and store it in an airtight container.

Nuts contain a high proportion of oil so they tend to become rancid rather quickly. Buy them in small quantities from a shop with a fast turnover, and keep them in the refrigerator or a cool dark place.

FRUIT AND NUT BARS

If you have a microwave, cook the apples and fruit juice on HIGH, covered, for about 5–6 minutes.

450 g (1 lb) eating apples, peeled, cored and chopped	*75 g (3 oz) self-raising wholemeal flour*
75 ml (5 tbsp) unsweetened fruit juice	*25 g (1 oz) desiccated coconut*
225 g (8 oz) mixed dried fruit, such as no-soak dried apricots, dates, sultanas, chopped if necessary	*50 g (2 oz) pumpkin seeds*
	30 ml (2 tbsp) vegetable oil
125 g (4 oz) chopped mixed nuts	*30 ml (2 tbsp) pear and apple spread or apricot conserve*
75 g (3 oz) rolled oats	

1 Put the apples and fruit juice in a heavy-based saucepan, cover and cook gently for 10–15 minutes or until the apple is very soft, shaking the pan occasionally (don't remove the lid). Beat thoroughly to make a smooth purée.
2 Add all the remaining ingredients except the spread or conserve, and beat well together. Oil a 20.5 cm (8 inch) square tin and line the base with greaseproof paper. Oil the paper. Spoon the mixture into the tin and bake in the oven at 180°C (350°F) mark 4 for about 40 minutes or until firm to the touch.
3 Turn out on to a wire rack. Brush with the spread or conserve while still warm and mark into 12 bars. Leave to cool, then cut through into bars.
MAKES 12

$\mathscr{E}$GGLESS CHOCOLATE CAKE

No one will ever guess that there's anything unusual about this cake! It's really moist, chocolaty and irresistible. It also keeps very well, wrapped in foil or in an airtight tin.

125 g (4 oz) creamed coconut	a large pinch of salt
50 g (2 oz) cocoa powder	225 g (8 oz) light soft brown sugar
400 g (14 oz) self-raising flour	200 ml (7 fl oz) sunflower oil
5 ml (1 level tsp) baking powder	icing sugar for dusting (optional)

1 Oil and line a 1.7 litre (3 pint) loaf tin.
2 Pour 650 ml (22 fl oz) boiling water over the coconut and stir until it dissolves. Cool.
3 Sift the cocoa powder, flour, baking powder and salt into a bowl and mix together with the sugar. Make a well in the centre, then pour in the coconut mixture and the oil. Using a wooden spoon, beat the ingredients together thoroughly to make a smooth, batter.
4 Pour into the prepared tin and bake in the oven at 180°C (350°F) mark 4 for 1¼ hours or until well risen and just firm to the touch. Leave to cool in the tin for 10 minutes, then turn out and leave to cool completely. Dust with icing sugar before serving, if liked.
MAKES ABOUT 12 THICK SLICES

$\mathscr{C}$ARROT CAKE

Root vegetables were often used to lend sweetness to 18th-century cakes and puddings. Beetroots, parsnips and carrots were all common ingredients, but of these, only carrot is still favoured today. It makes a very pleasant, moist cake, without any hint of carrot in the taste.

225 g (8 oz) vegetable margarine or butter	5 ml (1 level tsp) baking powder
225 g (8 oz) light soft brown sugar	50 g (2 oz) ground almonds
4 free-range eggs, separated	150 g (5 oz) walnut pieces, chopped
finely grated rind of ½ orange	350 g (12 oz) young carrots, trimmed, peeled and grated
20 ml (4 tsp) lemon juice	225 g (8 oz) cream cheese
175 g (6 oz) self-raising flour	10 ml (2 tsp) runny honey

1 Grease and line a deep 20.5 cm (8 inch) round cake tin.
2 Cream the margarine or butter and sugar together in a bowl until pale and fluffy. Beat in the egg yolks, then stir in the orange rind and 15 ml (3 tsp) of the lemon juice.
3 Sift in the flour and baking powder, then stir in the almonds and 100 g (4 oz) walnuts.
4 Whisk the egg whites until stiff, then fold into the cake mixture with the carrots. Pour into the tin and hollow the centre slightly.
5 Bake at 180°C (350°F) mark 4 for 1½ –2 hours or until a skewer inserted in the centre comes out clean. Cover the top with foil after 1 hour if it starts to brown.
6 Leave to cool slightly, then turn out on to a wire rack and remove the lining paper. Cool.
7 To make the topping, beat together the cheese, honey and remaining lemon juice and spread over the top of the cake. Sprinkle the topping with the remaining walnuts.
MAKES 8–10 SLICES

*H*AZELNUT AND CHOCOLATE FLAPJACKS

Jumbo oats are available from health food stores. They give the flapjacks a crunchier texture.

50 g (2 oz) hazelnuts
125 g (4 oz) soft light brown sugar
125 g (4 oz) vegetable margarine or butter

15 ml (1 tbsp) golden syrup
175 g (6 oz) jumbo or porridge oats
50 g (2 oz) milk chocolate drops

1 Lightly grease a shallow, oblong baking tin measuring 28 × 18 cm (11 × 7 inches) along the top. Roughly chop the hazelnuts.
2 Melt together the sugar, margarine or butter and syrup. Stir in the hazelnuts and oats. Allow to cool slightly, then stir in the chocolate drops.

3 Spoon into the tin and bake at 180°C (350°F) mark 4 for about 30 minutes or until golden and firm.
4 Cool in the tin for a few minutes before cutting into squares. Turn out on to a wire rack to cool completely.
MAKES ABOUT 12

*L*EMON AND COCONUT CAKE

If you prefer to use wholemeal flour, add an extra 2.5 ml (½ level tsp) baking powder and a little extra lemon juice to the creamed mixture.

125 g (4 oz) softened butter or vegetable margarine
200 g (7 oz) caster sugar
2 free-range eggs
2 lemons
125 g (4 oz) self-raising white flour

5 ml (1 level tsp) baking powder
2 free-range egg whites
75 g (3 oz) desiccated coconut
icing sugar, to dust

1 Grease and base-line a shallow, oblong baking tin measuring 28 × 18 cm (11 × 7 inches) along the top.
2 Beat together the butter or margarine, 125 g (4 oz) of the sugar, two eggs, grated rind of one lemon, flour and baking powder.
3 Add about 15 ml (1 tbsp) lemon juice or enough to form a soft dropping consistency. Spoon into the tin.
4 Whisk the egg whites until stiff but not dry. Fold in the remaining sugar, grated rind of one lemon and the coconut. Spoon roughly over the mixture. Bake at 180°C (350°F)

mark 4 for about 30 minutes or until golden.
5 Cool in the tin for a few minutes before turning out on to a wire rack to cool. Dust the sponge squares lightly with icing sugar.
MAKES 12 FINGERS

VARIATION
Coffee and Walnut Omit the lemon rind and juice in the cake mixture and beat in 5 ml (1 level tsp) instant coffee, dissolved in 15 ml (1 tbsp) hot water. For the topping, use soft light brown sugar instead of caster sugar and chopped walnuts instead of coconut.

ORANGE AND POPPY SEED CAKE

The finished loaf could be decorated with a little glacé icing made by blending sifted icing sugar with enough orange juice to give a smooth coating consistency.

225 g (8 oz) vegetable margarine or butter	*5 ml (1 level tsp) baking powder*
175 g (6 oz) golden caster sugar	*a pinch of salt*
3 free-range eggs	*finely grated rind and juice of 2 oranges*
350 g (12 oz) self-raising wholemeal flour	*50 g (2 oz) poppy seeds*

1 Grease and line a 1.4 litre (2½ pint) loaf tin. Put all the ingredients except the poppy seeds in a blender or food processor and process until smooth and well mixed. Fold in the poppy seeds.

2 Spoon the mixture into the prepared tin. Bake at 180°C (350°F) mark 4 for 50 minutes–1 hour or until well risen and firm to the touch. Turn out and cool on a wire rack.
MAKES ABOUT 12 SLICES

$\mathcal{S}$PICED APPLE CAKE

This deliciously moist cake is equally good served with cream and eaten warm as a pudding.
It is best consumed within 2 days of being made.

125 g (4 oz) vegetable margarine or butter	10 ml (2 level tsp) baking powder
175 g (6 oz) dark soft brown sugar	450 g (1 lb) cooking apples, peeled, cored and chopped
2 free-range eggs, beaten	45–60 ml (3–4 tbsp) milk
225 g (8 oz) plain wholemeal flour	15 ml (1 tbsp) runny honey
5 ml (1 level tsp) ground mixed spice	15 ml (1 level tbsp) light demerara sugar
5 ml (1 level tsp) ground cinnamon	

1 Grease and line a deep 18 cm (7 inch) round cake tin with greaseproof paper.
2 Cream the margarine or butter and sugar together until pale and fluffy. Add the eggs, a little at a time, beating well after each addition. Add the flour, spices and baking powder and mix well. Fold in the apples and milk to make a soft dropping consistency.

3 Turn the mixture into the prepared tin and bake at 170°C (325°F) mark 3 for 1½ hours or until well risen and firm to the touch. Turn out on to a wire rack to cool.
4 When the cake is cold, brush with the honey and sprinkle with the demerara sugar.
MAKES ABOUT 10 SLICES

$\mathcal{P}$EANUT AND RAISIN COOKIES

Leave the chopped ingredients in chunks so the cookies retain some bite and texture.

125 g (4 oz) softened butter or vegetable margarine	2.5 ml (½ level tsp) baking powder
150 g (5 oz) caster sugar	2.5 ml (½ level tsp) salt
1 free-range egg	125 g (4 oz) crunchy peanut butter
150 g (5 oz) plain flour	175 g (6 oz) raisins

1 Grease two baking sheets.
2 Beat together all the ingredients except the raisins, until well blended. Stir in the raisins.
3 Spoon large teaspoonfuls of the mixture on to the baking sheets, leaving room to spread. Bake at 190°C (375°F) mark 5 for about 15 minutes, or until golden brown around the edges. Cool slightly before lifting on to a wire rack to cool completely.
MAKES ABOUT 30

VARIATIONS
Chocolate Nut Omit the peanut butter and raisins and add 5 ml (1 tsp) vanilla essence. Stir in 175 g (6 oz) chocolate drops and 75 g (3 oz) roughly chopped walnuts.
Coconut and Cherry Omit the peanut butter and raisins, reduce the sugar to 75 g (3 oz) and stir in 50 g (2 oz) desiccated coconut and 125 g (4 oz) rinsed, roughly chopped glacé cherries.
Oat and Cinnamon Omit the peanut butter and raisins and add 5 ml (1 tsp) vanilla essence. Stir in 5 ml (1 level tsp) ground cinnamon and 75 g (3 oz) rolled oats.

ALTED FRUIT TEABREAD

Fruit loaves keep well and the flavour actually improves if they are kept for a day or two before eating. Malt is the raw material from which beer and malt whisky are made and it's this that makes this sticky cake particularly more-ish. Serve thinly sliced and spread with butter.

225 g (8 oz) self-raising flour	*30 ml (2 tbsp) golden syrup*
a pinch of salt	*45 ml (3 tbsp) malt extract*
30 ml (2 tbsp) dark soft brown sugar	*150 ml (¼ pint) milk*
175 g (6 oz) mixed dried fruit	

1 Grease a 900 ml (1½ pint) loaf tin and line the base and sides with greaseproof paper.
2 Put the flour, salt, sugar and fruit in a bowl and mix together. Make a well in the centre.
3 Put the syrup, malt extract and milk in a saucepan and heat gently until melted. Pour into the well in the centre of the dry ingredients, then beat thoroughly together.

Add a little extra milk, if necessary.
4 Turn the mixture into the prepared tin and bake at 170°C (325°F) mark 3 for about 1–1¼ hours. Turn out and leave to cool on a wire rack. When completely cold, wrap in greaseproof paper and foil and store for 1 day before eating.
MAKES 10 SLICES

ARBLED CHOCOLATE TEABREAD

It's much easier to melt the chocolate in a microwave, if you own one. It will take about 2–3 minutes on LOW. Stir occasionally.

225 g (8 oz) butter or vegetable margarine	*few drops orange flower water (optional)*
225 g (8 oz) caster sugar	*75 g (3 oz) plain chocolate*
3 free-range eggs, beaten	*15 ml (1 level tbsp) cocoa powder*
125 g (4 oz) self-raising white flour	*125 g (4 oz) self-raising wholemeal flour*
finely grated rind of 1 large orange	*15 ml (1 tbsp) milk*
30 ml (2 tbsp) orange juice	

1 Grease a 1.1 litre (2 pint) loaf tin and line the base and sides with greaseproof paper.
2 Cream the fat and sugar together until pale and fluffy, then gradually beat in the eggs, beating well after each addition.
3 Transfer half of the mixture to another bowl and beat in the white flour, orange rind, juice and orange flower water, if using.
4 Break the chocolate into pieces, put into a small bowl and place over a pan of simmering water. Stir until the chocolate melts. Stir into

the remaining cake mixture with the cocoa powder, wholemeal flour and milk.
5 Put alternate spoonfuls of the two mixtures into the prepared tin. Use a knife to swirl through the mixture to make a marbled effect, then level the surface.
6 Bake at 180°C (350°F) mark 4 for 1¼–1½ hours, until well risen nd firm to the touch. Turn out on a wire rack to cool.
MAKES ABOUT 14 SLICES

MIXED FRUIT TEABREAD

This foolproof teabread is really moist and well flavoured. The only catch is that you need to remember to soak the fruit overnight, and it is best if wrapped and stored for 1–2 days before slicing.

175 g (6 oz) raisins	*1 free-range egg, beaten*
125 g (4 oz) sultanas	*225 g (8 oz) plain wholemeal flour*
50 g (2 oz) currants	*7.5 ml (1½ level tsp) baking powder*
175 g (6 oz) soft brown sugar	*2.5 ml (½ level tsp) ground mixed spice*
300 ml (½ pint) strained cold tea (without milk)	

1 Grease and base-line a 900 g (2 lb) loaf tin. Put the dried fruit and sugar in a large bowl. Pour over the tea, stir well to mix and leave to soak overnight.

2 The next day, add the egg, flour, baking powder and mixed spice to the fruit and tea mixture. Beat thoroughly with a wooden spoon until all the ingredients are evenly combined. Spoon into the prepared tin and level the surface.

3 Bake in the oven at 180°C (350°F) mark 4 for about 1¼ hours or until the cake is well risen and a skewer inserted in the centre comes out clean.

4 Turn the cake out of the tin and leave on a wire rack until completely cold. Wrap in greaseproof paper and foil and store in an airtight container for 1–2 days before slicing.
MAKES ABOUT 14 SLICES

BANANA CAKE

Use very ripe bananas for the best flavour. A few chopped nuts or a handful of sultanas or currants can also be added, if liked.

125 g (4 oz) vegetable margarine or butter	*75 g (3 oz) plain wholemeal flour*
125 g (4 oz) caster sugar	*finely grated rind of ½ lemon*
2 free-range eggs, beaten	*2 large ripe bananas*
125 g (4 oz) self-raising flour	

1 Grease a 1.4 litre (2½ pint) loaf tin and line the base with greaseproof paper.

2 Cream together the butter and sugar until pale and fluffy. Gradually beat in the eggs. Sift in the flours, adding any bran left in the sieve. Mash the lemon rind with the bananas and fold into the mixture with the flour.

3 Spoon into the prepared tin and level the surface. Bake in the oven at 170°C (325°F) mark 3 for 1–1¼ hours or until firm to the touch. Leave to cool in the tin for 5 minutes, then turn out and cool on a wire rack.
MAKES ABOUT 14 SLICES

APRICOT PASTRIES

These more-ish pastries look remarkably professional yet they're really quick and easy to make using ready rolled squares of puff pastry (you'll find them in the freezer cabinet in most supermarkets). Serve the pastries fresh from the oven for breakfast or with morning coffee.

420 g (15 oz) can apricot halves in syrup	*250 g (8 oz) packet white almond paste or marzipan*
3 ready-rolled puff pastry sheets, each measuring about	*beaten free-range egg, to glaze (optional)*
20.5 cm (8 inches) square	*a few flaked almonds*

1 Empty the can of apricots into a sieve placed over a small saucepan. Let them drain for a couple of minutes to catch all the syrup. Remove the apricots from the pan and set aside. Bring the syrup to the boil and boil for 2–3 minutes until it is reduced and thickened slightly. Remove from the heat and cool.
2 Trim the edges of the pastry squares and cut each one in half lengthways to make a total of six rectangles. Cut the almond paste lengthways into six equal slices. Using your fingers or a rolling pin, slightly flatten each

slice so that it is slightly smaller than a piece of pastry. Place each piece of marzipan on a piece of pastry.
3 Arrange the pastries on a baking sheet. Brush with egg glaze, if using, then top each with two apricot halves, cut side down. Sprinkle with a few flaked almonds. Bake in the oven at 220°C (425°F) mark 7 for 15–20 minutes or until golden brown. As soon as they come out of the oven, brush with the syrup to glaze.
MAKES 6

ASPBERRY AND APPLE CAKE

A stunning, moist cake, packed with apples and raspberries. It works equally well with frozen raspberries if they're added to the creamed mixture while frozen.

225 g (8 oz) self-raising flour	2 free-range eggs, beaten
a large pinch of salt	45 ml (3 tbsp) milk
175 g (6 oz) vegetable margarine or butter	225 g (8 oz) firm but ripe raspberries, or frozen raspberries
50 g (2 oz) ground almonds	
125 g (4 oz) caster sugar	50 g (2 oz) flaked almonds
225 g (8 oz) eating apples, peeled, cored and chopped	icing sugar, for dusting

1 Grease and base-line a 20.5 cm (8 inch) spring-release cake tin.
2 Sift the flour and salt into a large bowl. Rub in the fat until the mixture resembles fine breadcrumbs. Stir in the almonds, sugar and apples, using a wooden spoon. Beat in the eggs and milk, then carefully fold in half of the raspberries.
3 Spoon the mixture carefully into the tin and level the surface. Sprinkle over the remaining raspberries and the almonds. Bake in the oven at 180°C (350°F) mark 4 for about 1–1¼ hours or until well risen, golden brown and firm to the touch in the centre. Dust with icing sugar and serve warm or cold, on its own or with yogurt, cream or crème fraîche.
MAKES 8–10 SLICES

RUNE AND PEAR TORTE SLICE

Prunes are used extensively in the cooking of southwest France and appear in a variety of cakes and tortes. The French might not approve of ready-made filo pastry, but it does make a delicious torte. If time and motivation allow, you could make your own strudel pastry instead!

225 g (8 oz) no-soak stoned prunes	4 large sheets filo pastry – about 24 × 48 cm (11 × 19 inches) each
300 ml (½ pint) warm tea	
lemon juice	45 ml (3 level tbsp) quince or apricot preserve
450 g (1 lb) ripe dessert pears	50 g (2 oz) walnut pieces
25 g (1 oz) fresh white breadcrumbs	icing sugar to dust
50–75 g (2–3 oz) butter, melted	

1 Very roughly chop the prunes. Place in a medium bowl with the tea and 30 ml (2 tbsp) lemon juice. Cover and leave to soak overnight.
2 The next day, strain soaking liquor into a saucepan. Peel, quarter, core and roughly chop the pears. Stir into the prunes with the breadcrumbs and 15 ml (1 tbsp) lemon juice.
3 Place one sheet of pastry on the work surface, brush with melted butter. Continue to layer up the pastry, buttering each layer.
4 Spoon the filling in a strip along one long

edge of the pastry, leaving 5 cm (2 inches) clear at each end. Fold the ends up over the filling, buttering the underside of each flap; then roll up the pastry to enclose the prune mixture. Lift carefully onto a baking sheet and brush all over with butter.

5 Bake at 200°C (400°F) mark 6 for about 30 minutes or until well browned. Cool for about 20 minutes.

6 Meanwhile, place the quince preserve in the saucepan with the soaking liquor. Bubble down until a syrupy glaze remains, then strain. Grill walnuts until lightly browned.

7 Brush a little glaze over the torte and sprinkle over the nuts. Carefully brush with remaining glaze. Dust with icing sugar. Serve warm, with crème fraîche or yogurt.

SERVES 8

Prune and Pear Torte Slice

CHOCOLATE NUT MUFFINS

These are particularly good served warm, fresh from the oven. If using wholemeal flour, you will need to add a little extra milk. The muffins freeze well; when thawed, warm through for 5 minutes in a hot oven.

125 g (4 oz) plain chocolate
125 g (4 oz) Brazil nuts, roughly chopped
225 g (8 oz) self-raising flour
5 ml (1 level tsp) baking powder
50 g (2 oz) soft dark brown sugar

225 ml (8 fl oz) milk
60 ml (4 tbsp) sunflower oil
5 ml (1 tsp) vanilla flavouring
1 free-range egg (size 1)

1 Grease twelve deep muffin or bun tins. Place a paper case in each.

2 Break up the chocolate into a bowl and melt over a pan of simmering water. Remove the chocolate from the heat and beat in the nuts and all the remaining ingredients.

3 Spoon the mixture into the paper cases and bake at 220°C (425°F) mark 7 for 15–20 minutes. Cool in the tins.

VARIATION

Banana and Honey Omit the chocolate and Brazil nuts. Use 275 g (10 oz) self-raising wholemeal flour instead of white flour. Beat together all the remaining ingredients with 225 g (8 oz) mashed banana, 30 ml (2 tbsp) runny honey, the grated rind of one lemon, and an extra 2.5 ml (½ level tsp) baking powder.

SPICED CITRUS MINCEMEAT

We're always asked for a vegetarian mincemeat recipe – so here it is!

125 g (4 oz) each dried apricots, raisins and flaked almonds
350 g (12 oz) sultanas
225 g (8 oz) carrots, peeled and grated
175 g (6 oz) shredded vegetarian suet
125 g (4 oz) dark brown soft sugar
7.5 ml (1½ level tsp) ground cinnamon

2.5 ml (½ level tsp) grated nutmeg
6 whole green cardamom pods
finely grated rind and juice of 1 orange
finely grated rind and juice of 1 lemon
finely grated rind and juice of 1 lime
45 ml (3 tbsp) Grand Marnier
150 ml (¼ pint) medium sherry

1 Snip the apricots into small pieces and place in a bowl with the roughly chopped raisins, almonds and sultanas. Stir in the carrot with the suet, sugar and ground spices.

2 Split the cardamoms and remove the seeds. Crush the seeds, using a pestle and mortar or in a strong bowl with the end of a rolling pin. Add to the fruit with the orange, lemon and lime rinds and 90 ml (6 tbsp) strained juices.

3 Pour in the Grand Marnier and sherry and stir well to mix. Leave to stand for about 1 hour, then pack tightly into sterile jars. Cover with a waxed disc and a cellophane round, and secure with a rubber band. Store in a cool place for at least 2 weeks to mature before using to make mince pies and tarts with sweet Shortcrust Pastry (page 69).

MAKES ABOUT 1.1 KG (2½ LB)

— SEVENTEEN —

ESSERTS

Given the option, most people can manage something sweet at the end of a meal, whether it is something simple, like a piece of fruit or a bowl of yogurt flavoured with honey or fruit purée, or something outrageously sweet and rich. Here you will find a range to suit all occasions, palates and waistlines!

If you want something really wholesome, poach a mixture of dried fruits, such as apricots, prunes, pears and apples, in fruit juice, spices and a splash of port or sherry, or stuff apples with mincemeat (see page 206) or marzipan, prick the skins and cook in the oven or microwave until soft.

If the dessert is to follow a light, perhaps low-protein, main course, consider serving a protein-packed cheesecake, home-made real dairy ice cream or Fudge Nut Tranche (see page 211). To accompany the desserts, try our non-dairy Almond Cream or home-made yogurt (see page 216), or sweet white sauce (see page 182), or make your own custard with custard powder if you must, but the real thing is far superior (and incidentally, provides yet more protein). Put 300 ml (½ pint) milk and a vanilla pod in a small heavy-based (preferably non-stick) saucepan. Bring slowly to the boil, then remove from the heat and leave to infuse for at least 10 minutes. Pour the milk on to 2 beaten eggs with 15 ml (1 tbsp) sugar. Strain back into the pan and cook very gently, stirring all the time until the custard just coats the back of a spoon. Do not boil. Remove the vanilla pod before serving. If you're worried about overcooking the custard, cook it in a double saucepan or in a large bowl placed over a pan of simmering water. Made this way it will take much longer to thicken.

FRESH FIG TART

This quick, easy 'crunch dough' is a revelation to anyone who's nervous of pastry making. The edges of this tart aren't even trimmed – they're simply folded over the filling.

175 g (6 oz) unsalted butter, diced	30 ml (2 tbsp) lemon juice
275 g (10 oz) plain flour	30 ml (2 level tbsp) demerara sugar
2.5 ml (½ level tsp) salt	1 free-range egg yolk
5 ml (1 level tsp) caster sugar plus extra for sprinkling	10 ml (2 tsp) milk
8 small ripe figs	honey
550 g (1¼ lb) eating apples	

1 Stir the butter into the flour with the salt and sugar. Stir in 100 ml (4 fl oz) cold water and bind to a rough dough. Do not overmix. Wrap in greaseproof paper and chill for about 10 minutes. Meanwhile, slice the figs. Peel, quarter, core and slice the apples. Mix with the lemon juice and demerara sugar.
2 Thinly roll out the pastry on a lightly floured surface to a round about 35.5 cm (14 inches) in diameter and place in a 22.5 cm (9 inch) loose-bottomed flan tin. Press the dough over the base and into the sides, but do not trim away the edges.
3 Spoon the apple mixture into the tin and arrange the figs on top. Fold the excess pastry up and over the figs, glaze with the egg yolk beaten with the milk and sprinkle generously with caster sugar.
4 Bake at 200°C (400°F) mark 6 for about 20 minutes or until well browned. Cool slightly, then brush with a little honey.
SERVES 8

SUMMER PUDDING

You do not have to wait until summer to enjoy summer pudding; it can be made very successfully with frozen fruits.

175 g (6 oz) redcurrants, stalks removed	*225 g (8 oz) raspberries, hulled*
350 g (12 oz) blackcurrants, stalks removed	*225 g (8 oz) loganberries, hulled*
125–175 g (4–6 oz) granulated sugar	*12 thick slices of white bread, about 2 days old, crusts removed*
thinly pared rind of 1 large orange	

1 Place the currants, sugar and orange rind in a large saucepan. Cover and cook gently until the juices flow and the sugar has dissolved. Add the raspberries and loganberries, and continue cooking for about 5 minutes until they are softened. Leave to cool.
2 Cut a round from one of the slices of bread, large enough to fit in the base of a 1.7 litre (3 pint) pudding basin. Place the round in the basin, then line the sides of the basin with slightly overlapping slices of bread, reserving the rest for the centre and top.
3 Remove the orange rind from the fruit.

Spoon half of the fruit and juice into the lined basin, then place a layer of bread on top. Add the remaining fruit and juice, then cover completely with the remaining bread.
4 Put a small, flat plate on the top of the basin. Stand it on a plate to catch any juices that overflow. Place some heavy weights on top of the plate. Chill overnight.
5 To serve, gently loosen the pudding from the sides of the basin with a palette knife, then turn out on to a flat plate. Serve with cream, yogurt, fromage frais or ice cream.
SERVES 8

FRUIT CRUMBLE

Everybody has their favourite recipe for crumble. Purists use a simple mixture of flour, sugar and butter. We prefer a nutty mixture of oats, spices and chopped nuts. For the fruit, a mixture of either apples or pears, with a soft fruit such as raspberries, blackcurrants or blackberries was favoured by our tasters.

125 g (4 oz) butter or vegetable margarine	*50 g (2 oz) light muscovado or caster sugar*
175 g (6 oz) plain flour	*5 ml (1 level tsp) ground cinnamon*
50 g (2 oz) rolled oats	*5 ml (1 level tsp) ground mixed spice*
25 g (1 oz) sunflower seeds	*about 900 g (2 lb) prepared mixed fruit*
50 g (2 oz) chopped mixed nuts	

1 Rub the fat into the flour. Mix in all the remaining ingredients, except the fruit.
2 Put the fruit into a large, deep baking dish. Spoon the crumble mixture over the top and press down lightly, particularly around the

edge of the dish, to seal the fruit in. Bake in the oven at 180°C (350°F) mark 4 for about 45 minutes or until the crumble is golden brown and the fruit is just bubbling through.
SERVES 6

$\mathcal{R}$HUBARB AND ORANGE CRUMBLE CAKE

A light orange-flavoured sponge, topped with rhubarb and a crunchy crumble topping. Add a few chopped nuts, sunflower seeds or desiccated coconut to the topping or use other poached or canned fruit, as the fancy takes you.

175 g (6 oz) vegetable margarine or butter	*2 × 540 g (1¼ lb) cans rhubarb, well drained*
125 g (4 oz) caster sugar	*125 g (4 oz) plain flour*
125 g (4 oz) self-raising flour	*30 ml (2 level tbsp) granulated sugar*
2 free-range eggs, beaten	*2.5 ml (½ level tsp) ground cinnamon*
finely grated rind of 1 orange	*icing sugar*

1 Grease a 23 cm (9 inch) spring-release cake tin and line the base with greaseproof paper. To make the cake, beat 125 g (4 oz) of the fat, the caster sugar, self-raising flour, eggs and orange rind together until smooth and well mixed. Spoon into the tin.
2 Spoon the rhubarb over the cake mixture. To make the crumble mixture, rub the remaining fat into the plain flour, then stir in the granulated sugar and the cinnamon. Sprinkle the mixture over the rhubarb. Bake in the oven at 200°C (400°F) mark 6 for 45 minutes–1 hour or until firm to the touch and golden brown. Serve warm, dredged with icing sugar.
SERVES 8

Rhubarb and Orange Crumble Cake

EMON CARAMEL RICE

This variation on the nursery favourite has a light, creamy texture with a delicious caramelised lemon topping. Semi-skimmed milk works equally well.

butter or vegetable margarine	grated rind of 2 lemons
50 g (2 oz) ground rice	2 free-range eggs, separated
568 ml (1 pint) milk	30 ml (2 level tbsp) lemon curd
50 g (2 oz) caster sugar	icing sugar

1 Lightly grease a 1.4 litre (2½ pint) soufflé dish.
2 Place the ground rice, milk, caster sugar and lemon rind in a medium saucepan and simmer for about 10 minutes, stirring all the time until thickened.
3 Off the heat, beat in the egg yolks and then cool slightly. Whisk the egg whites until stiff but not dry and gently fold into the rice mixture. Spoon into the prepared dish. Bake at 170°C (325°F) mark 3 for about 50 minutes–1 hour or until golden and firm.
4 Mix the lemon curd to a pouring consistency with 15 ml (1 tbsp) water. Drizzle over the cooked pudding. Sieve a little icing sugar over the whole surface and brown under a hot grill until caramelised. Serve.
SERVES 4

UDGE NUT TRANCHE

This tranche is wickedly rich but quite delicious too! Serve it after a light, healthy main course to ease the conscience and the waistline.

250 g (8 oz) butter or vegetable margarine	125 g (4 oz) pecan nuts, toasted and chopped
175 g (6 oz) plain flour	1 lemon
25 g (1 oz) caster sugar	1 free-range egg, beaten
75 g (3 oz) soft light brown sugar	175 g (6 oz) mixed whole nuts, such as brazils,
150 ml (5 fl oz) double cream	walnuts or hazelnuts
125 g (4 oz) skinned hazelnuts, toasted and chopped	30 ml (2 level tbsp) warm apricot jam, to glaze

1 Rub half of the butter or margarine into the flour until the mixture resembles fine breadcrumbs. Stir in the caster sugar and bind to a dough with 30–45 ml (2–3 tbsp) water. Roll out and use to line a 34 × 11 cm (13½ × 4½ inch) loose-based fluted tranche tin or a 23 cm (9 inch) fluted flan tin. Bake blind at 200°C (400°F) mark 6 for 10–15 minutes or until golden and well dried out.
2 Meanwhile, warm the remaining fat with the brown sugar and the cream until the fat has melted and the sugar has dissolved.
3 Cool slightly, then stir in the chopped nuts, finely grated lemon rind, 30 ml (2 tbsp) lemon juice and the beaten egg. Mix well.
4 Pour into the flan case. Arrange the whole nuts over the top. Bake at 180°C (350°F) mark 4 for 25–30 minutes, or until lightly set.
5 Brush the flan evenly with the warm apricot jam; serve warm.
SERVES 8

ANADE

Using sweet eating apples and pears means that there's no need to add sugar to the filling of this tart, based on one of the specialities of the boulangeries of Provence.

175 g (6 oz) butter or vegetable margarine	*700 g (1½ lb) ripe pears*
225 g (8 oz) plain flour	*grated rind and juice of 1 large orange*
a large pinch of ground cinnamon	*beaten free-range egg and caster sugar, for glazing*
700 g (1½ lb) sweet eating apples	

1 Rub 125 g (4 oz) butter or margarine into the flour and cinnamon until the mixture resembles breadcrumbs. Add about 90 ml (6 tbsp) chilled water, to bind to a soft paste.

2 Roll the dough out thinly and line a 24 cm (9½ inch) loose-bottomed fluted flan tin. Re-roll the excess pastry and cut into 1 cm (½ inch) wide strips. Cover and refrigerate until required. Bake the flan blind in the oven at 200°C (400°F) mark 6 for about 20 minutes.

3 Meanwhile, melt the remaining butter in a large non-stick frying pan. Stir in the peeled, cored and grated apples and pears, the orange rind and 45 ml (3 tbsp) orange juice.

4 Cook over a high heat, stirring constantly, until all excess moisture has evaporated and the mixture is dry. Spoon into the flan case.

5 Quickly lattice the pastry strips over the fruit mixture. Brush with beaten egg and dust with caster sugar. Bake at 200°C (400°F) mark 6 for about 20 minutes, or until golden. SERVES 6–8

RANGE SEMOLINA SOUFFLÉS

These individual soufflés, baked in orange shells, are good served with thinly sliced oranges sprinkled with a little orange-flavoured liqueur or orange flower water.

5 large juicy oranges	*3 free-range eggs, separated*
25 g (1 oz) granulated sugar	*icing sugar, for dusting*
25 g (1 oz) semolina	

1 Finely grate the rind and squeeze the juice from 2 of the oranges. You will need 300 ml (½ pint) juice. Make up with juice from one of the remaining oranges if necessary.

2 Halve the remaining oranges. Scoop out any loose flesh still attached to the skins and eat separately or use in another recipe. You need six clean orange halves. Cut a thin slice from each so that they stand flat.

3 Place the orange juice and rind, sugar and semolina in a pan and simmer until thickened, stirring all the time.

4 Cool slightly, then stir in the egg yolks. Whisk the egg whites until stiff and fold into the mixture. Spoon into the reserved orange shells and stand on a baking sheet.

5 Bake in the oven at 200°C (400°F) mark 6 for 15–20 minutes or until risen and golden brown. Dust with icing sugar and serve. SERVES 6

PINEAPPLE TARTE TATIN

Ginger cream makes a delicious accompaniment to this pudding inspired by the classic Tarte Tatin. Simply stir together equal quantities of whipped cream and Greek-style natural yogurt. Gently fold in a few pieces of finely chopped stem ginger and sugar to taste.

50 g (2 oz) caster sugar	*60 ml (4 level tbsp) double cream*
175 g (6 oz) butter or vegetable margarine	*900 g (2 lb) fresh pineapple*
2 free-range egg yolks	*Kirsch (optional)*
125 g (4 oz) self-raising flour	*fresh mint sprigs, to decorate*
125 g (4 oz) granulated sugar	

1 In a medium bowl, beat together the caster sugar and 50 g (2 oz) of the butter or margarine until pale and light. Beat in the egg yolks then fold in the flour and knead lightly together to form a smooth dough. Wrap and chill for 30 minutes.

2 In a small saucepan, slowly heat the remaining butter or margarine with the granulated sugar until both have melted. Bring to the boil, then simmer for 3–4 minutes, beating continuously until the mixture is smooth, dark and fudge-like. (It will probably separate at this stage, but don't worry as it will come back together again.) Take off the heat, cool for 1 minute and stir in the cream, beating until smooth. If necessary, warm gently, stirring, until completely smooth. Spoon into a shallow 21.5 cm (8½ inch) round

non-stick sandwich tin.

3 Peel, core and thinly slice the pineapple. Arrange neatly in overlapping circles on the fudge mixture. Drizzle over 15 ml (1 tbsp) Kirsch if wished.

4 Roll out the prepared pastry to a 25.5 cm (10 inch) round. Place over the pineapple, tucking and pushing the edges down the side of the tin. Trim off any excess pastry. Stand the tin on a baking sheet.

5 Bake at 200°C (400°F) mark 6 for about 20 minutes or until the pastry is a deep golden brown. Run the blade of a knife around the edge of the tin to loosen the pastry. Leave to cool for 2–3 minutes, then invert on to a heatproof serving dish. Cook under a hot grill for 2–3 minutes to caramelise the top.
SERVES 6

STICKY PEAR UPSIDE DOWN PUDDING

A hearty pudding that is quickly put together from storecupboard ingredients, yet is hard to resist. Ideal to serve at short notice.

175 g (6 oz) butter or vegetable margarine	*2.5 ml (½ level tsp) grated nutmeg*
275 g (10 oz) light brown soft sugar	*15 ml (1 level tbsp) ground cinnamon*
two 415 g (14½ oz) cans pear halves in natural juice	*finely grated rind and juice of 1 large lemon*
225 g (8 oz) plain flour	*175 g (6 oz) black treacle*
5 ml (1 level tsp) bicarbonate of soda	*200 ml (7 fl oz) milk*
a pinch of salt	*2 free-range eggs, beaten*
10 ml (2 level tsp) ground ginger	

1 To make the pear layer, warm half of the butter and 125 g (4 oz) of the sugar together until the fat melts. Spoon into a 2.3–2.6 litre (4–4½ pint) shallow ovenproof dish. Drain the pears and arrange cut side down around the base of the dish.

2 To make the sponge, mix the flour, remaining sugar, bicarbonate of soda, salt and spices together in a bowl. Add the lemon rind, then make a well in the centre of the dry ingredients.

3 Warm the treacle and remaining butter together. When the fat has melted pour into the well with the milk and 45 ml (3 tbsp)

lemon juice. Add the eggs and beat well.

4 Spoon the sponge over the pears. Stand the dish on an edged baking sheet.

5 Bake in the oven at 200°C (400°F) mark 6 for about 25 minutes. Reduce the oven temperature to 190°C (375°F) mark 5 and continue to cook for about a further 50 minutes, covering lightly if necessary. The pudding should be firm to the touch.

6 Leave the pudding to stand for about 5 minutes. Run a blunt-edged knife around the edge of the pudding. Invert on to an edged platter. Serve warm.
SERVES 6–8

CHRISTMAS PUDDING

Around November we are inundated with letters and telephone calls asking for our Christmas Pudding recipe. Here's our vegetarian version. Serve it with lashings of custard, cream or brandy butter.

125 g (4 oz) prunes, stoned and chopped	2.5 ml (½ level tsp) salt
175 g (6 oz) currants	75 g (3 oz) fresh breadcrumbs
175 g (6 oz) raisins	125 g (4 oz) shredded vegetarian suet
175 g (6 oz) sultanas	125 g (4 oz) soft dark brown sugar
25 g (1 oz) blanched almonds, chopped	2 free-range eggs, beaten
finely grated rind and juice of 1 lemon	30 ml (2 tbsp) black treacle
125 g (4 oz) plain flour	150 ml (¼ pint) brown ale
2.5 ml (½ level tsp) grated nutmeg	150 ml (¼ pint) brandy, rum or sherry
2.5 ml (½ level tsp) ground cinnamon	about 75 ml (5 tbsp) brandy, to flame

1 Grease a 1.7 litre (3 pint) pudding basin.

2 Place the dried fruits, nuts, lemon rind and juice in a large bowl. Mix well.

3 In a separate bowl, sift the flour, nutmeg, cinnamon and salt together. Add the breadcrumbs, suet and sugar and mix.

4 Pour in the beaten egg, black treacle and brown ale, and beat well. Stir in the dried fruit until evenly incorporated. Cover and leave in a cool place for 24 hours.

5 The next day, add the brandy, stirring well. Pack the mixture into the pudding basin.

6 Cover with pleated greaseproof paper and

foil. Secure with string. Steam for 4–5 hours.

7 Remove the pudding from the pan and leave to cool completely for 1–2 hours. Unwrap the pudding, then rewrap in fresh greaseproof paper and foil.

8 Store in a cool, dry place for at least 1 month (or up to 1 year) before serving.

9 To serve, steam for 2–3 hours. Turn out on to a warmed serving dish.

10 To flame the pudding, warm the brandy gently in a small saucepan, pour over the pudding and light carefully with a match.
SERVES 8

OGURT

The consistency of the finished yogurt depends on the milk used. Rich, creamy Channel Islands milk or condensed milk give the thickest results. Semi-skimmed milk makes a less creamy yogurt but one that is lower in calories. The addition of skimmed milk powder makes it even thicker. Goats', ewes' or soya milk can be used to make yogurt.

---

600 ml (1 pint) pasteurised or UHT milk of your choice (see above)

15 ml (1 tbsp) 'live' natural yogurt, beaten

30 ml (2 level tbsp) skimmed milk powder (optional)

---

1 Bring the milk and skimmed milk powder, if using, to the boil in a large, heavy-based saucepan. Remove from the heat and leave to cool to 43°C (110°F) on a thermometer. If using UHT milk it does not have to be boiled; just heated to the correct temperature.
2 Meanwhile, rinse a clean wide-necked vacuum flask or a 900 ml (1½ pint) container (with a lid) with boiling water.
3 When the milk is the correct temperature, gradually blend it into the yogurt. Pour into the warmed vacuum flask or container. Replace the lid and leave in a warm place for 6–8 hours, undisturbed, until just set. (Once you've made it a few times you will get to know how long it takes.)
4 As soon as it is set, transfer to the refrigerator to chill. Once set, yogurt is best used within 4 days. Save some of the yogurt for making your next batch.

NOTES
If making Vegan yogurt using soya milk, the first batch will not be totally vegan because of the yogurt – but use a spoonful of this to make a second batch and that will be.

If the yogurt does not set it could be because the milk was not brought up to boiling point, the milk was stale to start with, the starter yogurt was not mixed in properly, the starter was not 'live', the temperature was not correct – too high when the starter was added or not warm enough when the yogurt was left. Too much starter makes sour, grainy yogurt.

To make thick, Greek-style yogurt, line a colander with a double thickness of muslin, spoon in the yogurt and leave to drain. Transfer to a clean bowl, cover and refrigerate.
MAKES ABOUT 600 ML (1 PINT)

LMOND 'CREAM'

This makes a useful sauce to serve in place of dairy products like cream, ice cream and fromage frais. It's based on tofu. If you don't like tofu, don't be put off – you'll never know that it's there. Increase or decrease the quantity of water to achieve the desired consistency.

---

125 g (4 oz) tofu

75 g (3 oz) very fresh ground almonds

30 ml (2 level tbsp) vanilla sugar, or to taste

ground cinnamon, to decorate

Put everything in a blender or food processor with 45 ml (3 tbsp) water and process until well blended. Add a few more tablespoons of water to achieve the desired consistency. Serve sprinkled with a little ground cinnamon.
SERVES 4

CREAMY CHEESECAKE

A simple, delicately flavoured cheesecake baked in a pastry shell.

125 g (4 oz) butter or margarine	*2.5 ml (½ tsp) vanilla essence*
225 g (8 oz) plain flour	*200 ml (7 fl oz) double cream*
50 g (2 oz) plus 45 ml (3 tbsp) caster sugar	*150 ml (5 fl oz) soured cream*
400 g (14 oz) full fat soft cheese	*icing sugar, for dusting*
2 free-range eggs, separated	

1 Rub the butter into the flour with the 45 ml (3 tbsp) caster sugar. Bind to a dough with about 60 ml (4 tbsp) water. Roll out on a lightly floured surface and use to line a 21.5 cm (8½ inch) deep, fluted loose-bottomed flan tin. Chill for 15 minutes, then bake blind at 200°C (400°F) mark 6 for 20–25 minutes or until pale golden brown and cooked through.
2 Beat together the soft cheese, egg yolks and vanilla essence. Gradually beat in the creams.
3 Whisk the egg whites until they just hold

their shape. Fold in half the remaining sugar and whisk until stiff. Whisk in the remaining sugar. Fold into the cheese mixture.
4 Spoon into the flan case. Stand the tin on a baking sheet and bake at 220°C (425°F) mark 7 for 20 minutes. Reduce the oven temperature to 180°C (350°F) mark 4 for a further 35–40 minutes or until the cheesecake is golden brown and just set. Cool in the tin.
5 Serve warm dusted with icing sugar.
SERVES 6

COCONUT ICE CREAM

We felt this was best made with canned coconut milk which is sold in Indian and oriental grocers. However, it works almost as well if made with creamed coconut or dried coconut milk (sold in sachets). If using creamed coconut, use four 225 g (8 oz) packets each made up with 450 ml (¾ pint) water. If using instant coconut milk powder, you will also need four 100 g (3.5 oz) packets, each made up with 450 ml (¾ pint) water.

275 g (10 oz) granulated sugar	*four 450 ml (¾ pint) cans coconut milk*
600 ml (1 pint) water	

1 To make the syrup, place the sugar and water in a medium saucepan. Heat gently until the sugar dissolves, then boil gently for 10 minutes without stirring. Leave to cool.
2 Mix the cold syrup with the coconut milk and pour into a shallow freezer container. Cover and freeze on fast freeze for about 3 hours or until just frozen all over. The mixture will have a mushy consistency.
3 Spoon into a bowl and mash with a fork to

break down the ice crystals. Work quickly so that the ice cream does not melt completely.
4 Return the mixture to the container and freeze for about 2 hours, or until mushy. Mash as step 4. Return to the freezer and freeze for about 3 hours or until firm.
5 Remove from the freezer and leave at room temperature for 20–30 minutes to soften before serving.
SERVES 8

$\mathcal{M}$ARINATED FRUITS

Store the fruits for at least 2 hours to give them lots of time to absorb the wine before serving.

900 g (2 lb) fresh raspberries or a mixture of summer fruits, such as strawberries, blackberries and currants

75 g (3 oz) caster sugar
about 300 ml (½ pint) red wine

1 Pick over the fruit, brushing off any dirt and discarding any damaged fruit. Halve the strawberries, if using.
2 Layer the fruit and sugar in a bowl. Pour over the wine so the fruit is covered.
3 Cover tightly and store in the refrigerator for up to 24 hours.
SERVES 6–8

RASPBERRY ROSE ICE CREAM

This makes a relatively low calorie, egg free ice cream based on custard.

15 ml (1 level tbsp) custard powder	*450 g (1 lb) raspberries*
15 ml (1 level tbsp) caster sugar	*15 ml (1 tbsp) rose water (optional)*
300 ml (½ pint) milk	*300 ml (½ pint) double cream*

1 Blend the custard powder and sugar to a paste with 15–30 ml (1–2 tbsp) milk.

2 Heat the remaining milk until boiling, then pour on to the blended mixture, stirring.

3 Return the mixture to the pan and bring to the boil, stirring continuously. Cook for 1–2 minutes after the mixture has thickened to make a smooth, glossy sauce. Leave to cool. Cover the surface of the custard with a piece of damp greaseproof paper.

4 While the custard is cooling, mash the raspberries then push through a nylon sieve to make a purée. Stir in the rosewater, if using.

5 Whisk the cream into the cold custard mixture, then stir in the raspberry purée. Pour into a shallow non-metallic, freezer container. Cover and freeze for about 3 hours.

6 Spoon into a bowl and mash with a fork to break down the ice crystals. Work quickly.

7 Return the mixture to the container and freeze again for about 2 hours until mushy.

8 Mash again as step 4, then return to the freezer for a further 3 hours or until firm.

9 Remove from the freezer and leave at room temperature for 20–30 minutes to soften.
SERVES 6

FRAGRANT FRUIT SALAD

Exotic fresh lychees are available most of the year round now in greengrocers and supermarkets. They lend a unique texture, flavour and fragrance to this special fruit salad.

50 g (2 oz) caster sugar	*700 g (1½ lb) lychees*
grated rind and juice of 1 lemon	*3 ripe mangoes, peeled*
2 pieces of stem ginger (from a jar of ginger in syrup), finely chopped	*450 g (1 lb) fresh or canned pineapple in natural juice*
	4 ripe kiwi fruit, peeled
60 ml (4 tbsp) ginger wine	*50 g (2 oz) Cape gooseberries, to decorate (optional)*

1 Put the sugar in a pan with 150 ml (¼ pint) water and the lemon rind and juice. Heat gently until the sugar dissolves. Bring to the boil and simmer for 1 minute. Remove from the heat and stir in the chopped ginger and wine. Leave to cool.

2 Peel the lychees, cut in half and remove the shiny stones. Cut the mango flesh away from the stones. Cut the flesh into cubes.

3 If using fresh pineapple, peel, slice and remove the tough centre from each slice. Cut the pineapple slices into cubes. Thinly slice the kiwi fruit and halve the slices.

4 Mix together the fruit and syrup. Cover and refrigerate for several hours to allow the flavours to develop. If using Cape gooseberries, peel back each calyx to form a 'flower'. Clean the orange berries by wiping with a damp cloth. Arrange on top of the fruit.
SERVES 8

CARAMELISED CLEMENTINES

We used whole clementines for this. Segments of larger citrus fruit could also be used.

275 g (10 oz) granulated sugar	*vegetable oil*
18 small clementines	*50–75 g (2–3 oz) caster sugar*

1 First prepare the caramel sauce. Put the granulated sugar in a medium, heavy-based saucepan with 125 ml (4 fl oz) water. Heat gently until all the sugar dissolves, then bring the mixture to a rapid boil. Have ready 125 ml (4 fl oz) warm water. Bubble down the sugar mixture, gently shaking the pan occasionally, until it turns a rich dark caramel. Immediately take off the heat. Cover your hand – the mixture may splutter – and pour in the warm water in one fast stream. Stir until evenly mixed, returning to a low heat if necessary, until the mixture is smooth. Pour into a heatproof jug and leave to cool.
2 Peel the clementines, removing all pith but keeping them whole. Place in a bowl. Pour the syrup over the fruit and gently stir. Cover and chill until required.
3 Line a small baking sheet with foil and brush generously with oil. Sprinkle the caster sugar evenly over the foil. Cook under a hot grill until melted and golden. Don't take your eyes off it for a second as it can suddenly catch and burn! The sugar will have run into uneven pools of caramel. Remove from the grill immediately and allow to cool slightly before peeling off the foil and breaking into pieces. Store in an airtight container.
4 To serve the fruit, transfer to a glass serving dish and scatter with the caramel pieces. (Add them just before serving or they will dissolve.)
SERVES 6–8

MULLED PEARS

Mulled Pears are best served cold but not chilled, with Almond Cream (see page 216).

8 small pears, firm but ripe	*a few strips of orange peel*
about 300 ml (½ pint) medium dry red wine	*4 cloves*
150 ml (¼ pint) orange juice	*1 mulled wine spice sachet*
3 cinnamon sticks	*60 ml (4 level tbsp) soft dark brown sugar, or to taste*

1 Peel the pears, leaving the stalks attached. Put them in a heavy-based saucepan with the remaining ingredients, cover and simmer very gently for 35–40 minutes or until tender. While the pears are cooking, baste them with the liquid from time to time, and move them about in the saucepan so that they all get evenly cooked and coloured red. Some may cook quicker than others so test them.
2 Remove the cooked pears from the saucepan using a slotted spoon and arrange in a heatproof serving dish. Bring the cooking liquid to the boil and boil rapidly for 5–10 minutes or until reduced by half. Pour over the pears and leave to cool. Serve cold.
SERVES 4–6

Caramelised Clementines

INDEX